Fred Macnicol

Hungarian Cookery

Allen Lane

Illustrated by Daria Gan

ALLEN LANE
Penguin Books Ltd,
17 Grosvenor Gardens, London SW1W 0BD

First published 1978
Published simultaneously by Penguin Books

ISBN 0 7139 1102 6

Set in Monotype Times

Printed in Great Britain by Billing and Sons Ltd.,
Guildford, London and Worcester.

Árpádnak, Dezsőnek szeretettel

Contents

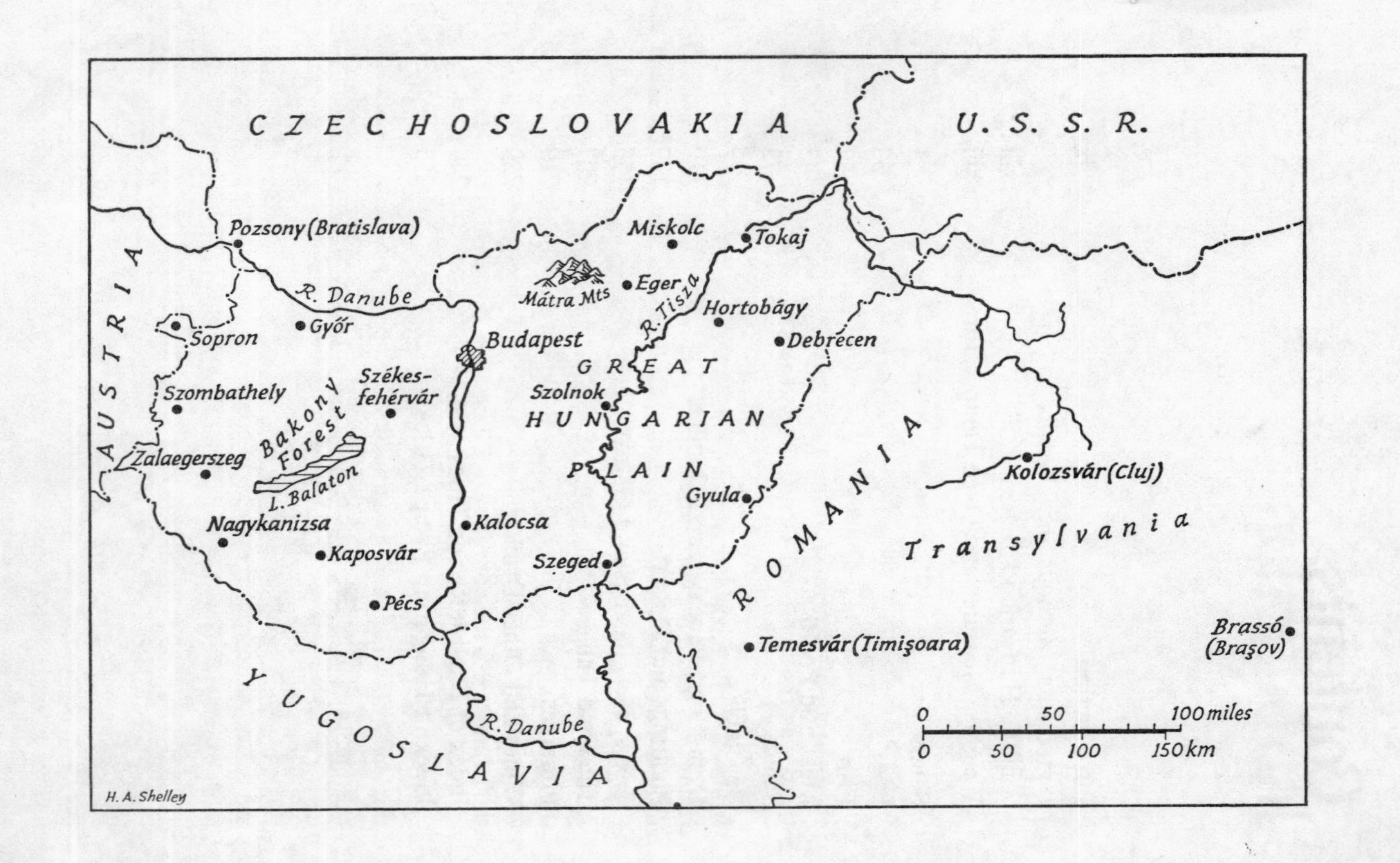
CZECHOSLOVAKIA
U.S.S.R.
AUSTRIA
Pozsony (Bratislava)
Miskolc
Tokaj
R. Danube
Mátra Mts
Eger
R. Tisza
Hortobágy
Győr
Sopron
Budapest
Debrecen
GREAT
HUNGARIAN
PLAIN
Székes-
fehérvár
Szolnok
Szombathely
Bakony
Forest
Zalaegerszeg
L. Balaton
ROMANIA
Kolozsvár (Cluj)
Gyula
Transylvania
Kalocsa
Nagykanizsa
Kaposvár
Szeged
Pécs
Temesvár (Timişoara)
Brassó
(Braşov)
YUGOSLAVIA
R. Danube
0
50
100 miles
0
50
100
150 km
H. A. Shelley

Introduction

When, at the beginning of 1969, I was awarded scholarships to go to Hungary to study music, it did not occur to me that one of the most tangible results would be a cookery book. The five and a half years which I spent in Budapest, first of all studying and later working, gave me an exceptional opportunity to learn the notoriously difficult Hungarian language and to enter in some depth into the aspects of Hungarian life which interested me most. One of these was the fine food I encountered from my very first day in Hungary, in an unassuming basement restaurant round the corner from where I lived; wherever you live in Budapest there is *always* a restaurant round the corner or even nearer and it is virtually certain to be a good one.

Later, the many friends I made through my studies at the Academy of Music took great delight in introducing me to traditional Hungarian dishes which were still new to me. It was a couple of these student friends who first invited me to stay with their families in the country and these little expeditions always led to a few more culinary discoveries.

However, the casual tourist in Budapest, or indeed in any of the three or four other large towns in Hungary, might well find himself eating more or less the same dishes, cooked in more or less the same way, as he had just eaten in Paris, Munich or Vienna earlier in his travels. The big 'international' restaurants and hotels in Hungary are the best advertised, they are situated in places where the tourist is in any case likely to find himself, they print their menus in German and sometimes in English and so it is not difficult for them to attract foot-weary visitors who are relieved to stumble upon a restaurant with a name they have seen proclaimed in brochures and with food they can recognize.

This book is not about the food served in such establishments.

It takes more courage for the foreigner to venture into one of the multitude of small, modest restaurants and to try with pointing fingers to make sense of the menu and the waiter and to wait for what he has hesitatingly ordered, more than a little apprehensive that what will arrive may be entirely inedible. His courage will, however, be amply rewarded – particularly if he previously arms himself with a bare minimum of information about what he should try out and how to look for it under its Hungarian name. The food in these little restaurants is much closer to what Hungarian home cooking is all about and I hope that anyone who browses in the pages of this book will emerge well equipped to get the culinary best out of a visit to Hungary.

But this is a cookery book and not merely a few summary hints for travellers. And so – to the food.

Hungarians have always had a celebratory approach to food which has made any and every special occasion a good excuse for a feast. When between 892 and 896 the early nomadic Magyars first wandered into the area now known as Hungary and settled there, they straight away offered sacrifices to the gods and held a four-day feast. The area was rich in game, fish and edible plants and this meant it was never difficult to find food: nor was it difficult to provide a feast to celebrate the success of the subsequent marauding expeditions which seem to have made up Hungarian history for some time after the initial settlement. Such feasts would often include some new dish discovered among the peoples they had gone out to conquer.

Since these early days Hungary has never been short of visitors, but only some of them were actually invited, such as the Walloon and Italian wine producers King Béla IV asked to settle in the Tokaj area after the quite uninvited and calamitous invasion by the Tartars in 1241. All the records suggest a time of great abundance in the late fifteenth century during the reign of King Mátyás, whose Italian wife Beatrix brought a great deal of Italian influence to bear on the culinary habits of Hungary. She had no desire to stop eating the dishes she was used to and since Mátyás was very willing to try out new things, Beatrix was permitted to introduce onions, garlic, dill, cheeses and chestnuts from Italy. There are records of meat roasted on open spits as well as the strongly spiced stews in large cauldrons which are known to be the most ancient dishes of the Magyars. The juices of these early stews were often thickened with bread – a method used in the ancient Roman kitchen as well as in Transylvanian cooking, and Hungarians still continued the practice well into the nineteenth century. At King Mátyás's table the most favoured fowl was the peacock but in 1490 he had the turkey introduced from Milan.

In 1526 the Hungarian army was routed at the disastrous Battle of Mohács by the conquering Turkish forces. There followed more than a century and a half under the Ottoman empire, which period is regarded by Hungarians as one of the least productive of their whole history. They must have felt as if they would never be their own masters again but in 1683 the Turks, in an effort to make even further conquests, were defeated at Vienna – which had two attractive culinary results in Hungary. Viennese bakers, who in the course of their night work had uncovered a crucial Turkish plot and thus foiled an attack, began baking salted croissants, shaped like the Turkish half-moon, and called them *Kipfel* and I think this is the origin of the Hungarian word '*kifli*'. The '*császárzsemle*' (emperor's roll) also dates from this event: to mark the victory of Christendom over the Turks, Viennese bakers made a roll with a deep cross marked on the top. Both salted *kiflis* and emperor's rolls are still popular today in Hungary. It is from this period that coffee, too, has been part of Hungarian life. And it is claimed that it was the Turks who first brought the pepper plant to Hungary – at that time, however, Hungarians despised paprika as a flavouring used only by peasants. Once they came to enjoy both the raw vegetable itself and then its use as a flavouring, many of the then traditional spices were pushed into the background and some, such as ginger and saffron, disappeared completely.

The liberation from Turkish domination was followed by an intolerable period of Habsburg oppression. But the Hungarians bent their backs and got on with building up their agriculture again.

At the Viennese court of Maria Theresa and Joseph II the cuisine was virtually entirely French – which had considerable influence on the Hungarian, Polish and Czech aristocracy at the court. In Hungarian cookery books of the time there is much talk of *consommé*, *braise*, *fricassée* and *ragoût*. This French influence reached a climax in the second half of the nineteenth century, when restaurants began to be of importance in Hungary; many French chefs were employed.

Although the development of cooking and eating in Hungary is directly related to its political history, the largest contribution to its modern cuisine has undoubtedly been made by the Hungarians themselves. Apart from all the solicited and unsolicited contact with the food of other countries, Hungarian cooking is more than anything else a combination of the elements which the various parts of Hungary contribute naturally. Foreign influences on Hungarian cooking have never been followed for long merely as fashions: Hungarians have always based their culinary art on good experiences – if they like something they adopt it, changing it, adding to it, refining it until it assumes a character which satisfies them completely.

Today Hungarian cooking is rich with sour cream, eggs, butter, wine, pure pork fat; it is simple but ingenious – you will find the same plain dough cropping up in countless variations; it is moderate and subtle in its seasoning – the really fiery dishes are few and far between and count more as peculiar specialities. The quality of the raw materials available today to the Hungarian urban housewife would be the envy of most British cooks. And the modern emphasis on health and good eating habits tends to keep that quality high.

Many of us are inclined to approach the cuisine of a foreign country with strong and arbitrary preconceptions: Indian cooking is all curry powder, Italian all pasta – and Hungarian all fiery paprika. I think this book was probably born because I encountered so many wonderful dishes in Hungary which are not generally known outside its boundaries: I hope it will pass on some of the great warmth of those who introduced me to the recipes, particularly Marika Kostyál and Edith Raskó, and that it will win many new friends for the best in traditional Hungarian cooking.

Ingredients, Methods and Utensils in the Hungarian Kitchen

One encouragement for anyone approaching Hungarian cooking for the first time is that there are no mysterious ingredients which are not generally available in Britain, and indeed anywhere in Europe. There is only one single detail which it is important not to lose sight of: the sheer quality of, for example, Hungarian pork or Hungarian paprika powder is not easily equalled. Other differences in emphasis will become clear in what follows.

Paprika

This Hungarian word is used to cover all the varieties of sweet and strong vegetable peppers and also the different dry powders prepared from them. I have described some of the ways in which the fresh peppers themselves are cooked in the section on vegetables. As far as paprika powders are concerned, several kinds are produced. All are basically a mixture of the fleshy part of the vegetable and a proportion of the seeds, which are first washed to remove at least part of their strength.

Különleges (special) *paprika* is the finest in quality and it is also the most finely ground.

Its bright red colour is full of light, its pleasantly spicy aroma is warm but not pungent, and it has virtually no sharpness to it at all. In the preparation of this powder the proportions are 100 kg of paprika flesh combined with 40 kg of the washed seeds.

Csípősségmentes paprika ('paprika which is free of all sharpness') is a bright yellowish red and it is not so finely ground as the *különleges paprika.*

Csemegepaprika is, too, a bright yellowish red, and although it is still among the milder paprika powders it does contain a slightly larger proportion of seeds: 45 kg to 100 kg of paprika flesh.

Édesnemes paprika (Sweet-noble paprika) is a darker powder which begins to be just very slightly nippy. It is not particularly finely ground and is made from 75 kg seeds to every 100 kg of peppers.

Félédes paprika (Half-sweet paprika) has a lighter, but duller colour. This is a pleasantly sharp powder, but it is particularly useful in that you can use enough of it to give good colour to a dish without making it unbearably hot.

Rózsapaprika (Rose paprika) This paprika is decidedly sharp in flavour and is medium ground.

Erős paprika (Strong paprika) has a colour which varies from brownish red to yellow. This is a fiercely sharp powder, ground roughly, and must be used sparingly until you have acquired a taste for it.

Although the sweeter powders are now the most characteristic spices used in the Hungarian kitchen, they have only been used in cooking since the nineteenth century. They have become so important that in the interests of maintaining the quality of all the paprika powders produced in Hungary, the Szeged and Kalócsa districts, which are the main centres of production, have been declared protected paprika areas.

Many Hungarian dishes are begun by lightly frying an onion and sprinkling some paprika powder over it. If paprika is used in this way it is necessary to proceed with caution: the powder burns very easily and so you have to move it about a lot while it is frying.

Vanilla

Almost every household in Hungary has a large jar of sugar with a vanilla pod in it. Within hours of inserting the vanilla, the whole jarful of sugar takes on a strong vanilla flavour and this is what Hungarians like to use in baking and in the preparation of sweets and creams. Vanilla sugar is on sale in small sachets but it is, of course, cheaper, and better, to make your own.

Parsley Root

You will find that many of the recipes call for a whole or a piece of parsley root. Some varieties of parsley are grown for their edible root, which is whitish in colour, has a delicate, mild flavour and looks rather like a small parsnip which in fact I somewhat regretfully use as a substitute in Britain. Although I have never seen edible parsley root in the London markets, you can grow your own from seed which is available from the larger seed companies such as Thompson & Morgan of Ipswich.

Black Pepper

Although the point has already been made so often, it had better be restated that black pepper must be freshly ground to be of any value. In Hungary black pepper is not among the most frequently used spices: our British salt and pepper sets are replaced on the Hungarian dining-table by salt and paprika. When pepper is used, however, it is always fresh from the pepper mill.

Dill

Fresh dill is greatly favoured by Hungarian cooks. The feathery green leaves form the basis of sauces; it is widely used as a garnish and its light fresh flavour makes it a helpful and surprising ingredient in curd pies.

The seeds are included in several preserves.

Caraway Seeds

The flavour of caraway seeds is an integral part of any *gulyás*. Hungarians tend to put these seeds into savoury rather than sweet dishes.

No other flavourings or spices used in Hungarian cooking would be unfamiliar to cooks in this country, although it may be important to point out that spices such as ginger and cinnamon are seldom sold in ground form: once you have experienced these spices freshly ground you will never want to return to the pale shadows of the real thing which are generally on sale. Ceylon cinnamon in whole pieces is the best – it is more valuable in taste and texture than the varieties from China and Indonesia. Boots Chemists usually stock root ginger in most of their branches.

Flour

For anyone travelling across the Great Plain in Hungary it would not be difficult to believe that Hungary is a great wheat-growing country. As far as the eye can see there is the golden glow of ripening wheat and this, together with the flatness, makes the Plain seem endless.

To arrive at some understanding of why Hungarian flour is so different from the ordinary white flours sold in British shops, we have to look at the wheat plant itself. It grows best in a deep loamy soil and it likes a moderate amount of rain, snowy severe winters and dry hot summers: Hungary, parts of Russia and North America all provide ideal conditions. There are two basic types of wheat – winter and spring. It is the former which is grown in England, with its milder and shorter winters, whereas Hungary grows spring wheat. The longer growing period of a winter wheat tends to give a 'soft' flour with a good flavour but low in protein. The shorter growing period of the spring wheats gives a 'strong' flour with a much higher protein and gluten content. Because of such differences, several types of wheat are often blended in this country to produce a more generally useful flour, but this blending is minimal in Hungary. When I use Hungarian recipes in this country I sometimes find the various bread flours or 'strong' flours more successful, not only for breads but for cakes as well.

Brown or wholemeal flours and brown bread are not popular in Hungary today: only two non-white breads are sold in the shops, one of which is a very substantial and tasty medium-brown rye bread.

Tejföl – Sour Cream

Sour cream is another ingredient which is used more frequently in Hungarian cooking than in western Europe. *Tejföl* is the product of a culture and is sold in small cartons much as yoghurt is in Britain. Some British dairies now market sour cream through delicatessens. It has, to my taste, distinct advantages over fresh cream. Its texture is lighter and its flavour has the benefit of a slight tartness which adds a great deal more subtlety to a soup or a sauce, for example, than fresh cream does.

Aludt tej – Sour milk

I feel it is a little unfortunate that the word 'sour' has off-putting connotations for the native English speaker. The spread of the 'sweet and sour' concept may have helped in a small way but it would still take a fair amount of courage for an Englishman to drink a glass of 'sour' milk. *Aludt tej* literally means 'slept milk' and it was this opportunity to get away from the word 'sour' which enabled me to view the substance with greater impartiality. Provided you have excellent milk to start with, this proves a deliciously refreshing drink. Hungarians will often accompany it with a piece of plain bread.

Túró – Curds

Crumbly fresh curds are a constantly recurring theme throughout Hungarian cooking. They act as the main ingredient in savoury and in sweet dishes. A number of curd cheeses are currently marketed in this country; you will, however, be amply rewarded, if you choose to take the trouble to make your own from a couple of pints of good milk.

To make the curds, leave one litre (two pints) of good milk at room temperature until it sours – between 24 and 36 hours in most kitchens. Put the milk in the pan and heat it to boiling point very slowly. The curds will then separate from the whey and float on top. Remove the pan from the heat and let it stand for 5–10 minutes. Pour the contents of the pan into a sieve. Give the curds, which are retained in the sieve, about half an hour to dry a little: then they are ready to use.

The curd cheeses which are commercially available are a perfectly adequate substitute, but you have to be careful to find out how salty they are before using the seasoning quantities given in the recipes in this book.

Vaj – Butter

Hungarian butter manages to retain a fresh 'country butter' flavour and texture which make it a delight to eat and to use in baking. It is always sold unsalted and if Hungarians take some simple bread-and-butter (which they very rarely do), they sprinkle salt over it before eating it.

Nuts

Nuts are a very popular traditional ingredient in Hungarian baking. Almonds and walnuts are widely used, but much more use is also made of the hazelnut than I am aware of in this country. The creams and cakes which include roasted hazelnuts are among the most attractive recipes I have found in Hungary.

Oil

Pure pork fat is what traditional Hungarian cooking demands, but oils are gradually becoming more popular in Hungary for cooking purposes. The main vegetable oils are produced from sunflower seeds, rape and gourd seeds.

Szalonna – Bacon

Bacon is not cut in the same way as in this country and the cuts which result have a much larger proportion of fat. Most bacon is sold salted, marinaded and smoked, and eaten without cooking.

A note on freshness

In markets poultry is available live, and when you choose a fish you want to buy, you must point to the one you want as it swims about in the enormous tanks in which the fishmongers keep their stock. Some people will even go so far as to take a polythene bag to the fishmonger, take home the fish in that, and then leave it swimming around in the bath until the moment arrives when it is to be prepared for cooking. Chickens are left in a similar way to run around in the cellar until the last minute! I get the impression that younger people now regard such practices as unnecessary, but this attitude is as yet by no means general.

Galuska

This word crops up in so many contexts throughout the book that it may be confusing to readers: *galuskas* are simply small pieces cut off some larger piece of dough or other mixture.

Plain flour and water *galuskas* are added to some soups, or replace potatoes to accompany *pörkölt*, one of the main meat dishes in Hungary (see page 46). At the other end of the scale there are recipes for *galuskas* made from stiffly beaten white of egg served chilled with a thick vanilla sauce. So when you see the word *galuska*, just think of 'little bits'.

Thickening

Two methods are used. One is called *rántás*, which is a *roux* made for soups and vegetable dishes. This is distinguished from *habaràs*, where flour is mixed with sour cream and the mixture is added to the main ingredients.

Rántott or *Kirántott*

Literally 'covered' or 'coated'. The term is used for a particular kind of 'coating' for meat slices, fish and vegetables such as mushrooms or sprigs of cauliflower. The food to be coated is dipped first in flour, then in slightly salted beaten egg (possibly with a little milk added) and finally in breadcrumbs. Food coated in this way is fried in hot fat.

Párolás

This means tenderizing meat, vegetables or fruit with the barest minimum of water so that the food softens in the steam. Vegetables are usually given a quick fry in a little hot fat and then steamed in their own juices, or with the addition of water as necessary – as little as one tablespoon at a time.

Palack

A *palack* is a bottle for wine or brandy. Apart from the Rhine and Bordeaux types of bottle there are two others which are used in Hungary. The *füredi palack* is a green, short necked bottle holding either one litre or half a litre and it is used for the cheaper table wines. The Tokaj wines are put on the market only in *Tokaj* bottles, which are clear long necked bottles holding half a litre.

Szüröanál

A large spoon, usually in enamel, with holes in it, used for draining cooked *tészta*, *galuskas* or pasta etc. – a mini-colander.

Galuskadeszka

This is a small flat piece of wood with a sloping edge and it is used for chopping off *galuskas* into a pan of boiling water from the lump of dough.

Terítés – Setting the Table

Although up to the eighteenth century Hungarian gentlemen and ladies carried their own cutlery with them in a bag on their belt if they were invited to dine, present-day table setting in Hungary does not differ much from the rest of Europe. As I have mentioned elsewhere, paprika replaces pepper in condiment sets, and it is considered 'untidy' to serve food already on plates. Soup is therefore always served in a tureen.

Weights, Measures and Oven Temperatures

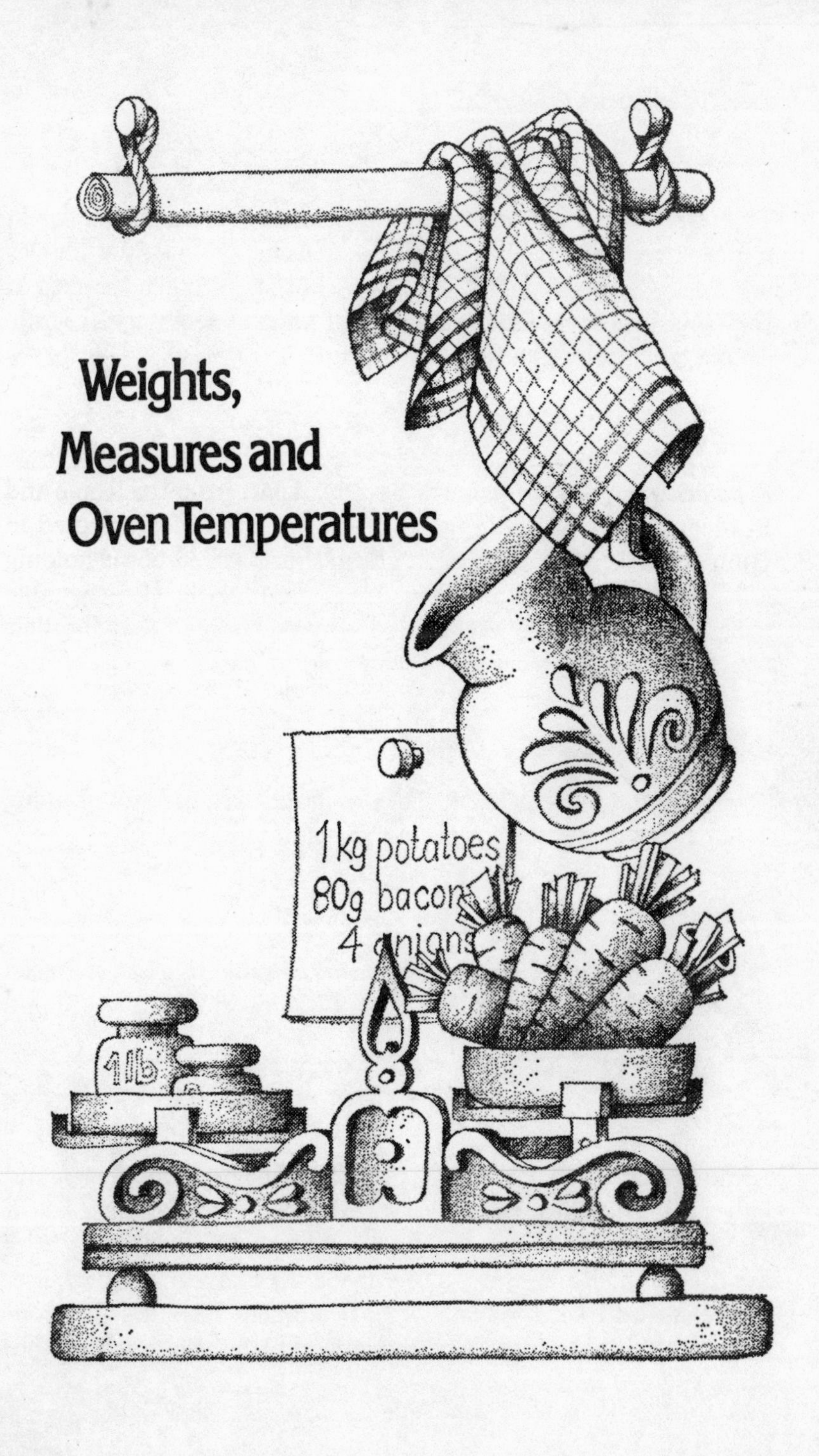

Measures

It is virtually impossible to convert the ingredient quantities which are convenient in one system into equally convenient measures in another system. Where necessary I have endeavoured to be as precise as possible, but there are occasions when this is not essential – for example, in showing how much sour cream one needs to serve with a soup, it does not really matter whether one uses the almost exact ⅜ gill prescribed by the *1 dl* of the Hungarian recipe or whether one makes it into a more recognizable ¼ pint.

Or you may notice that I have converted the metric 100 grams sometimes into 3½ ounces, sometimes into 4 ounces and occasionally into 3 ounces. The inconsistency is only apparent: the proportion of one ingredient to the others is what matters. Sometimes it must be very exact as in many of the baking recipes, but sometimes a little more or less will make no great difference. The main point is that you should stick to one system or the other: if you measure one ingredient by the metric system then measure all the other ingredients metrically, but if you prefer to use the imperial measures then use them for all the ingredients. *N.B.* The quantities I have given in each recipe are for four people, unless otherwise stated.

Oven temperatures

No ovens in Hungary except the newest, and certainly no traditional cooks, have any regard for temperature control. The most one can expect is low-medium-high. Since, however, there are no special baking methods which would be new to British cooks, this is not so much of a problem as it sounds: you will already be perfectly aware how your own oven behaves and how long you can expect, for example, a sponge mixture to take at a moderate temperature in that oven.

Liquid Measures

British

1 quart	=	2 pints	=	40 fl oz.
1 pint	=	4 gills	=	20 fl oz.
½ pint	=	2 gills or 1 cup	=	10 fl oz.
¼ pint	=	8 tablespoons	=	5 fl oz.
		1 tablespoon	=	just over ½ fl oz.
		1 dessertspoon	=	⅓ fl oz.
		1 teaspoon	=	⅙ fl oz.

Metric

1 litre	=	10 decilitres (dl)
	=	100 centilitres (cl)
	=	1000 millilitres (ml)

Approximate equivalents:

British	*Metric*
1 quart	1·1 litre
1 pint	6 dl
½ pint	3 dl
¼ pint (1 gill)	1·5 dl
1 tablespoon	15 ml
1 dessertspoon	10 ml
1 teaspoon	5 ml
35 fl oz.	1 litre
18 fl oz.	½ litre (5 dl)
9 fl oz.	¼ litre (2·5 dl)
4 fl oz.	1 dl

American

1 quart	=	2 pints	=	32 fl oz.
1 pint	=	2 cups	=	16 fl oz.
		1 cup	=	8 fl oz.
		1 tablespoon	=	$\frac{1}{3}$ fl oz.
		1 teaspoon	=	$\frac{1}{6}$ fl oz.

Approximate equivalents:

British	***American***
1 quart	$2\frac{1}{2}$ pints
1 pint	$1\frac{1}{4}$ pints
$\frac{1}{2}$ pint	10 fl oz. ($1\frac{1}{4}$ cups)
$\frac{1}{4}$ pint (1 gill)	5 fl oz.
1 tablespoon	$1\frac{1}{2}$ tablespoons
1 dessertspoon	1 tablespoon
1 teaspoon	$\frac{1}{6}$ fl oz.
$1\frac{1}{2}$ pints + 3 tbs. (32 fl oz.)	1 quart
$\frac{3}{4}$ pint + 2 tbs. (16 fl oz.)	1 pint
$\frac{1}{2}$ pint − 3 tbs. (8 fl oz.)	1 cup

Solid Measures

British			***Metric***
16 oz.	=	1 lb.	1000 grammes (g) = 1 kilogramme (kg)

Approximate equivalents:

British	***Metric***
1 lb. (16 oz.)	450g
½ lb. (8 oz.)	225g
¼ lb. (4 oz.)	100g
1 oz.	25g

British	***Metric***
2 lb. 3 oz.	1 kg (1000g)
1 lb. 2 oz.	½ kg (500g)
9 oz.	¼ kg (250g)
4 oz.	100g

Temperature Equivalents for Oven Thermostat Markings

Fahrenheit	*Gas Mark*	*Centigrade*	*Heat of Oven*
225°F	¼	110°C	Very cool
250°F	½	130°C	Very cool
275°F	1	140°C	Cool
300°F	2	150°C	Cool
325°F	3	170°C	Moderate
350°F	4	180°C	Moderate
375°F	5	190°C	Fairly hot
400°F	6	200°C	Fairly hot
425°F	7	220°C	Hot
450°F	8	230°C	Very hot
475°F	9	240°C	Very hot

Soups

No Magyar is to be done out of his soup. Weather scarcely enters the matter at all – even in the summer heat, any meal which is not to be considered a makeshift must begin with a soup. The repertoire of Hungarian soups is so wide that it is often difficult to decide whether to repeat one delight already experienced, or to try out something which promises to be equally pleasing from the extensive range of recipes. There are light easy soups if the atmosphere is lazy, and there are lavish sustaining brews just pleading to be presented in traditionally shaped cauldrons to a ravenous dinner party.

In Hungary even the most complicated soups have a simple advantage: they quite adequately replace a main course – representing in fact the kind of cooking which Hungarians regard as having come down to them from their most distant ancestors. These well spiced, rich soups have always been the principal source of nourishment to keep the strenuous physical work going – farming, hunting and fishing may have a different face on them in Hungary now, but earlier they were very much the heart of the matter. Ancient chroniclers give vivid descriptions of the Magyars sallying forth on military expeditions – but before they set off they prepared great pots of fatty, spiced soup containing lumps of meat. They simmered the soup until all the liquid dried away and put the meat out in the sun to dry until it became hard. Then they tied it in bags which they strung on their saddles. Later it was easy to make this boot-leather preserve into a soup again between one skirmish and the next. Today we may prefer to tenderize our steak by other means than jolting up and down on it while we guide our nags to battle, but do try some of the descendants of these ancient convenience foods, one-dish meals such as the Palóc or fish soups described below – most people's favourite is the deservedly renowned, but undeservedly misrepresented, *bográcsgulyás*, or 'goulash'.

And what do you say to a fruit soup? To British ears this may sound like putting something of a cart where there ought to be a horse. On a sultry day when people are often too listless to enjoy the thought of dining there is nothing more guaranteed to coax the appetite into consciousness than a chilled sour-cherry soup.

First of all, however, here is a recipe which produces the kind of deliciously simple surprise which crops up so often in Hungarian cooking.

Meat and Vegetable Soups

Kelvirágleves – Cauliflower Soup

1 small onion
60g dripping from smoked streaky bacon (2 oz.)
1 medium or large cauliflower
1 egg yolk
1 large carrot
1 tbs. flour
4–5 tbs. sour cream
salt, freshly ground black pepper, parsley

Remove the green leaves from the cauliflower, separate the white part into its individual flowers, and wash them in a colander under running water. Parboil gently in a covered saucepan with enough lightly salted water to let the cauliflower move freely.

Meanwhile melt the fat in another pan and gently fry the chopped onion in it until it is just transparent. Add the diced carrot and, with the lid on the pan, let it cook gently for 5–7 minutes, stirring occasionally. Sprinkle with flour and continue cooking for 5 minutes, stirring constantly. Season with salt and freshly ground black pepper.

Add the almost cooked cauliflower, mixing it in carefully for a few minutes. Then, taking the pan off the heat, gradually add the water the cauliflower was boiled in and then add enough cold water to make up a scant 1½ litres (2–2½ pints) altogether. Return to the heat and bring to the boil, stirring all the time. Simmer until the cauliflower has softened.

A few *galuskas* (*see* below) should be added to this soup 5–10 minutes before serving.

Mix the egg yolk with the sour cream and either add to the soup once it has been removed from the heat and put into a serving tureen, or place a good tablespoon of the mixture in each person's plate, serve the hot soup onto this and mix in immediately. Garnish with just a little fresh chopped parsley.

Csipetke – Little Dumplings

When the soup recipes call for no more than *a few galuskas* these are not intended to play any main role and take their place more or less anonymously among the vegetables in the soup. This simplest soup addition is called *csipetke* – *galuska* itself is a wider term which includes a great variety of preparations (*see* pp. 127–9), and for four people you need about 50g (2 oz.) flour, salt as seasoning and just enough water to make a really firm dough. Chop off small pieces about the size of a penny into the soup 5–10 minutes before serving.

You will not violate the *csipetke* concept, or the sense of simplicity, if you add a little richness: combine the flour first with half a beaten egg and then mix to a firm dough with a minimum of water. This is particularly valuable if you do not have strong flour at your disposal.

Bableves – Bean Soup

In Hungary full use is made of the many varieties of dried beans available – white, mottled, red, large and small – but for Hungarian bean soup choose preferably beans of a mottled or dark variety, keeping the smaller white ones for *sólet*. It makes excellent sense to follow the Hungarian tradition of including the largest smoked knuckle bone you can find to make this nourishing soup even more substantial, and then follow it with one of the noodle recipes given later.

250g dried beans (8 oz.)
1–1½ tbs. flour
1 parsley root or small parsnip
¼ tsp. paprika powder
3–4 tbs. sour cream
60g bacon dripping (2 oz.)
1 carrot
1 small onion
1 clove garlic
parsley, salt

Soak the beans for a few hours in abundant water. Then bring them to the boil very slowly in 2 litres (3 pints) water. Add the sliced carrot and parsley root and simmer until the beans soften – two hours or more.

Prepare a *roux* from the fat and the flour and add the finely chopped onion, garlic, parsley, salt and paprika. Remove from the heat, gradually mix in a little cold water by tablespoons, and once it is perfectly smooth and even, add the *roux* to the soup, stirring all the time. Simmer gently for 10 minutes.

Take the soup off the heat and mix in the sour cream just before serving. If you decide to include the smoked knuckle, boil it gently, first in 2 litres (3 pints) of water until the meat on it is tender. Then use the liquid – making up the quantity again with water – to cook the beans. Before the soup is served, the meat is usually removed from the bone and eaten with the soup. If you don't use a knuckle bone, put in a few rashers of streaky bacon or even smoked rinds – they are far from being an adequate substitute for the knuckle but they do help.

A little wine vinegar, tarragon leaves or tarragon vinegar (always accompanied by a little sugar) sometimes replaces the sour cream to sharpen the taste of this wholesome soup. Vinegar, like the sour cream, should be added just before serving and once the pan has been removed from the heat.

Céklaleves – Beetroot Soup

Here is a soup which can be a real delight as an opener to a substantial meal, and does something to make people reconsider their over-familiarity with this vegetable. The preserved beetroot would, in Hungary, have a good pinch of caraway seeds for flavouring, so if you don't have that kind of beetroot preserve you should add some caraway directly to the soup.

300g beetroot preserved in vinegar (10 oz.)
1 level tbs. flour
salt and/or sugar
9 tbs. sour cream
1 egg yolk

Drain the vinegar thoroughly from the beetroot. Put half of the beetroot through a fine sieve and dice the other half into small cubes. Bring the sieved beetroot to the boil with about 1½ litres (2½ pints) of water. Mix the flour, a little sour cream and a glass of water in a bowl, and when it is completely smooth add the mixture to the hot beetroot. Now put in the diced beetroot and reheat to simmer for 10 minutes.

Mix the egg yolk with the remaining cream, place in a tureen and then pour the hot soup onto this, mixing it in gently. Season to taste with salt or sugar. Serve with toast or *croûtons.*

Gulyás erőleves – Hungarian Stew Consommé

Before we come to the real thing, *gulyás* itself, here is a sort of Hungarian *consommé* which treats you to the best of both worlds.

¾ kg lean beef (1½ lbs.)
1 large onion
½ tsp. caraway seeds
2 tomatoes
2 egg whites
celery leaves, parsley, marjoram
30g bacon dripping (1 oz.)
½ clove garlic
30g paprika powder (1 oz.)
1 sweet green pepper
1 sweet red pepper

Place ½ kg (1 lb.) of the beef, cubed and washed, in a pan with the spices and the finely chopped onion and garlic, mix well and with a little water bring to the boil. Turn down the heat and continue cooking at the lowest possible heat, with the lid on the pan, stirring from time to time. When the meat is about half cooked, pour on 2 litres (3 pints) of water, and add some chopped parsley and celery leaves. Reheat and continue to simmer until the meat is quite tender.

Now strain the soup and skim off the fat.

Mince the remaining beef finely; combine it well with the egg whites, one tomato and a little cold water. Add the liquid strained off the other mixture and bring to the boil slowly and with constant stirring. Then simmer for one hour. Remove from the heat and allow to rest for 10 minutes. Pour through muslin or cheesecloth and remove all fat from the strained liquid.

Place the meats, together with the finely chopped peppers and one tomato, in soup cups and pour the boiling *consommé* onto this.

Bográcsgulyás – Cauldron Gulyás

In Hungarian the word *gulyás* itself means, first of all, a herdsman, a cowboy, and it is not difficult to see the connection between that and its use to describe the stew he used to make in his watchful loneliness out on the *puszta.* With that sort of origin it is no surprise to find it is an all-in-one-pan affair and most of the Budapest restaurants lend an authentic touch by serving it in more refined replicas of the original open-air cauldron pots.

It was in Kunadacs, a little village in the Great Hungarian Plain, that my secure London-based feeling of knowing what 'goulash' was all about received its first severe knock.

The front of Old Man Dukay's whitewashed cottage was draped and festooned with cherry-paprikas (*cseresznye paprika*) hung up by the thousand to dry. These cherry-paprikas are one of the fiercely strong members of the paprika family but they are superior in every way to the ubiquitous chillis, particularly in texture and in taste. How many would actually end up in the midday pot? For a *halászlé* (fish soup) or *paprikás krumpli* (paprika potatoes) Old Man Dukay usually presented *one* cherry-paprika to his wife; that was considered quite enough for normal constitutions – for himself he stowed away another one which he added whole and raw to his own plate at the table, as he liked to have, he said, a bit of taste. But a mere half of a cherry-paprika was included in the Dukay *gulyás*, which was for seven people. And the head of the house added no more at table either.

I was soon to discover that *gulyás* is not in fact what I had been led by sundry international recipe books to believe. It seems sad that the very dish which has taken Hungary's name to the ends of the earth should be so misrepresented, and before I describe the dish, which is after all no great secret, proving itself as it does every day in every restaurant in Hungary, here is a brief corrective course for those foreign 'experts' who have perpetrated the main offences against it.

1. *Gulyás* and fiery chillis have very little to do with each other.

2. Most recipes I have read in Britain include hideous quantities of flour. Don't. The only flour necessary is to make a few *galuskas*, which is quite a different matter from thickening. Nor is any sour

cream included – no accident in a country which uses it so liberally.

3. These experts seem terrified of the caraway seed – or perhaps they feel its only place is in a good old seed cake. There is, however, no *gulyás* without caraway.

4. Rice? Never! The only accompaniment is bread door-steps.

¾ kg lean beef (1½ lbs.)
200g onion (7 oz.)
1 clove garlic
½ tsp. caraway seeds
pinch crushed cherry-paprika/ chilli powder
60g flour (2 oz.)
60g bacon dripping (2 oz.)
1 kg potatoes (2 lbs.)
1 tsp. paprika powder
20g salt (¾ oz.)
2 fresh sweet peppers
2 tomatoes
½ beaten egg

Cut the beef into cubes, wash it and leave it to drain in a colander.

Melt the fat and fry the finely chopped onion in it until it is transparent. Sprinkle with the paprika and the chilli powder, lower the heat, and continue to fry, stirring all the time. Add the meat then and mix well. Season with salt and put in the crushed garlic and the caraway seeds.

Add one or two tablespoons of water, cover and simmer very gently, stirring frequently. As the liquid evaporates, add another tablespoon of water.

When the meat begins to soften, add the sliced peppers, the tomatoes, and the cubed raw potatoes. Mix thoroughly and add enough water to cover well. Remember this is meant to be a soup with everything else included, rather than a stew which has become somewhat wet. Simmer until the potatoes are cooked and the meat tender.

Prepare a firm dough from about half a beaten egg and the flour. Break off thimble-size *galuskas* into abundant boiling, salted water in a separate pan. When they rise to the surface of the water, drain them in a colander and add them to the *gulyás*. Serve hot with thick chunks of bread.

That, then, is *the gulyás*, but not the end of the story. The regional variations of, for example, the Székely people of Transylvania – the most Hungarian part of Hungary, now in Romania – and the Csángós of Moldavia have an entirely different character: they are less soup-like and so I have included them in the vegetable section along with other cabbage dishes. But after the original basic *gulyás* you may enjoy this variation which always intrigues those eating it, although it is as simple to prepare as the everyday *gulyás*.

Sörgulyás – Beer Gulyás

800g lean beef (1¾ lbs.)
200g chopped onion (7 oz.)
20g paprika powder (½ oz.)
1 kg potatoes (2 lbs.)
150g tomatoes (5 oz.)
salt
100g dripping from smoked streaky bacon (3½ oz.)
1 clove garlic
good pinch caraway seeds
150g sweet peppers (5 oz.)
6 dl mild beer (1 pint)

Prepare this *gulyás* exactly as for *bogracsgulyás*, but when it comes to adding the water, put in the beer instead and make up with water to give the proper soup consistency.

Kaporleves – Dill Soup

Hungarians use dill much as we use parsley, although its sphere extends far beyond the garnishing limits – with lemon juice and a touch of vanilla it gets into a fine curd pie, the seeds are widely used in preserving, and if you want to put its taste to the test without supporting accompaniments, try this simple dill soup.

1 heaped tbs. chopped fresh dill leaves
1½ dl milk (¼ pint)
6 tbs. sour cream
salt
20g bacon dripping (¾ oz.)
20g flour (¾ oz.)
1 egg yolk

Prepare a light *roux* from the dripping and the flour. Remove it from the heat, mix in the dill and then gradually add about 4 dl (¾ pint) cold water, stirring constantly.

Return to the heat, bring to the boil and simmer gently for 10 minutes. Add 1½–2 dl (a good ¼ pint) hot milk.

Mix the sour cream and the egg yolk, place a spoonful of this mixture in each plate and serve the soup onto it, mixing it in straight away.

Croûtons are served with this soup.

Tojásleves – Egg Soup

30g dripping from smoked streaky bacon (1 oz.)
1 small onion
4 tbs. sour cream
salt
sugar
1 level tbs. flour
paprika powder
1 dessertspoonful vinegar
4 eggs

Prepare a dark *roux* from the flour and the dripping and add the finely chopped onion, sprinkle with paprika and add a good pinch of sugar. Cook this gently for 10 minutes. Thin by adding cold water very gradually, the quantity depending on whether you prefer a thick or a thin soup.

Beat the eggs with 1 teaspoon flour and a little water. Pour this mixture into the soup in a thin stream, whisking the soup all the time. The eggs will break up into tiny fragments. Then flavour with a little vinegar and remove immediately from the heat or the soup will curdle.

Serve onto 1 tablespoon sour cream in each plate.

It is also customary to include a bay leaf in this soup, and it is well worth experimenting with various combinations of bay leaf, sour cream and vinegar to see how you like it best. Some people, however, omit these tart ingredients, the bay leaf and the vinegar, and replace them with a handful of chopped parsley.

Palócleves – Palóc Soup

I am certain the villages of the Palóc people in the Cserhát Hills were never really built: they just grew out of this rolling, well-tempered countryside in northern Hungary. Their traditional embroidered patterns and forms of dress, their customs, children's games, folksongs and carved work preserve a truly ancestral character, but on high and holy days any village there is particularly like the gayest operatic scene in riots of flame red and black with yellow, blues and greens . . . The man's finest garment, for example, was traditionally the *szűr* – a long embroidered cloak. Once a young man had gathered enough together to provide himself with a splendid *szűr*, he could visit his girlfriend's house, and after taking his leave at midnight he could 'forget' to take his *szűr* with him. Much excitement until dawn: then he stole back to see the result. If there was no sign of the *szűr* it signified that his courting and intent to marry were accepted, but if the cloak was put out onto the veranda – irrevocable rejection.

And even today it is the bride's task to sew the ceremonial shirt for her groom, whom it graces only twice – on the day of his wedding, and when he dies.

Palóc people respect no king – but everyone else is in for a warm welcome. And, with the green beans and sour cream typical of their cooking, what better welcome than this Palóc soup?

700g shoulder of mutton (1½ lbs.)
100g smoked streaky bacon (4 oz.)
250g potatoes (8 oz.)
½ bay leaf
½ tsp. paprika powder
caraway seeds
½ tbs. flour
150g onion (5 oz.)
300g green beans (12 oz.)
3 dl sour cream (½ pint)
1 small clove garlic
salt, pepper
a good bunch of fresh dill leaves

Chop the bacon into small pieces and fry it on its own; it should therefore have plenty of fat on it. When the fat has begun to melt from the bacon, add the finely chopped onion to fry until it is transparent. Sprinkle the paprika over this and add the cubed and washed mutton. Season with salt, pepper, garlic and a good pinch of caraway seeds. Put in 2–3 tablespoons water and simmer very gently until the meat is tender, adding just enough water from time to time to prevent the ingredients from sticking to the pan.

Cut the potatoes into small pieces, and the beans evenly into three or four. Cook the potatoes and the beans separately in enough lightly salted water to cover.

When they are both ready, add them, with the water they were cooked in, to the meat. Put in the bay leaf and add more water if necessary to cover well. Bring to the boil.

Mix the flour and the sour cream together, pour the mixture into the soup, bring it to the boil once again and simmer for 5–10 minutes. Sprinkle liberally with freshly chopped dill and serve.

Lebbencsleves – Lebbencs Soup

Lebbencs is a dough rolled out very thin and cut into big irregular pieces, and this combination of potatoes and *lebbencs* makes a relatively cheap and very tasty soup.

To make the *lebbencs* use 100g (3–4 oz.) strong plain flour and work it together with about half a beaten egg. Roll out the dough, cut it up, or, rather, pull it into pieces – there is no 'regulation' size or pattern! – and leave it for a short time to dry before frying it, as described in the recipe.

150g *lebbencs* pieces (5 oz.)
½ kg potatoes (1 lb.)
paprika powder; parsley
100g smoked streaky bacon (4 oz.)
1 onion
salt

Dice the bacon and fry it in its own fat. Add the finely chopped onion – there should really be no more than a teaspoonful, but I like to have the whole onion – sprinkle with paprika and put in the *lebbencs*. Mix everything together well and continue frying for about 2 minutes. Pour in about 1 litre (2 pints) of water and then add the potatoes, peeled and sliced. Season with salt and simmer until both potatoes and *lebbencs* are cooked through – 10–15 minutes.

Köménymagleves – Caraway Seed Soup

This recipe shows the clear emphasis Hungarians lay on including caraway seeds in savoury rather than sweet dishes. Caraway seed soup has the same sort of fresh purity as dill soup. It is light, delicious – and Hungarians laugh at it and call it 'invalid soup'.

60g dripping from smoked streaky bacon (2 oz.)
1 onion
1½ rolls
salt
70g flour (2½ oz.)
1 level tsp., or less, caraway seeds
1 egg

Cut the rolls into cubes and toast them on a greased baking sheet in the oven.

With the dripping and the flour prepare a dark *roux*, add the caraway seeds and cook gently for 1–2 minutes. Very gradually add about $1\frac{1}{2}$ litres ($2\frac{1}{2}$ pints) cold water, stirring well. Simmer with one whole onion for 20–25 minutes. Strain before serving and then add one beaten egg.

Serve with the toasted bread cubes – and some chopped parsley if you like.

The four recipes which follow are the vegetable soups which are most popular in Hungary today: the vegetable itself is joined by the characteristic *roux* and sour cream to give simple soups full of flavour with just a hint of tartness.

Zellerkrémleves – Cream of Celery Soup

250g celery (8 oz.)
30g flour (1 oz.)
salt
60g bacon dripping (2 oz.)
2–3 tbs. sour cream or 2 dl milk ($\frac{3}{8}$ pint)

Cut the celery into thin flat slices, first rubbing it clean with a damp cloth. Braise it in hot dripping, with the lid on the pan and adding salt and, from time to time, a little water. Sprinkle with the flour, mix it about, and gradually add 1 litre ($1\frac{1}{2}$–2 pints) cold water. Let it come to the boil and then boil for 3–4 minutes. Pour the whole mixture into a fine sieve and force the celery through as well. Return it to the pan, thinning with milk if necessary.

Place the sour cream in a tureen, pour on the soup, and mix gently. Serve with dumplings of some kind or with squares of toast.

Zöldbableves – Green Bean Soup

Stock from $\frac{1}{4}$ kg veal (8 oz.) or pork bones and 12 dl ($2\frac{1}{4}$ pints) water, with a good bunch of parsley added
1 tbs. flour
$\frac{1}{4}$ tsp. paprika powder
vinegar
$\frac{1}{2}$ kg green beans (1 lb.)
4–5 tbs. sour cream
40–60g dripping ($1\frac{1}{2}$–2 oz.)
1 onion
salt, pepper
sugar

Clean the beans and, having cut them in two or four, put them into the strained stock. Bring to the boil again and then season with salt. Melt the fat and fry the sliced onion very gently until it is transparent, meanwhile sprinkling with the paprika, stirring constantly. Put in the flour and continue to stir for 2–3 minutes. Some parsley may also be included at this stage if desired. Taking the pan off the heat, mix in a cup of cold water very gradually.

When the beans are almost ready add the *roux*, mixing thoroughly. Bring to the boil once more and then simmer for 5 minutes.

Before serving, season with freshly ground black pepper and a good pinch of sugar. Hungarians like this to be a fairly tart soup: a good teaspoonful of wine vinegar is also used for flavour. Serve onto 1 tablespoon sour cream in each plate. *Galuskas* are usually included in this soup – use about 50g (2 oz.) flour and half a beaten egg to make the dough and that will give you more than enough.

Karalábéleves – Kohlrabi Soup

4 tender, young kohlrabi (400–500g – ¾–1 lb.)
sour cream
40g dripping (1½ oz.)
1 tbs. flour
parsley, salt

Slice the kohlrabi as thinly as possible, removing any stringy parts. Heat the dripping, put in the kohlrabi, season with salt, cover and fry gently until very soft: its flavour comes out fully only when it is as soft as butter.

Sprinkle with the flour and fry a few minutes longer, stirring all the time. Then gradually thin with water – about 2 pints – and simmer for 10–15 minutes.

Chop some fresh parsley and put it in the soup, or the individual plates, just before serving.

One tablespoon of sour cream may be mixed into the soup before it is served, but if you want a particularly rich soup, serve the soup onto 1 tablespoon sour cream in each person's plate. I prefer the lighter texture for this soup, and if you follow that method, add *daragaluskas*, *see* p. 28.

Spárgaleves – Asparagus Soup

½ kg veal or pork bones (1 lb.)
70g dripping (2½ oz.)
3–4 tbs. sour cream
1 parsley root, or very small parsnip
1 onion
parsley
paprika powder
½ kg asparagus (1 lb.)
2 tbs. flour
1 carrot
½ stick celery
a few black peppercorns
salt, sugar

Wash the bones and boil them for 1 hour in 2 litres (3½ pints) salted water. Add the carrot, parsley root, celery, onion, parsley leaves and peppercorns. Continue to simmer for another hour. Strain off the stock.

Clean the asparagus, cut in half lengthwise and then into pieces. Boil gently in the stock until tender.

Prepare a light *roux* from the flour and the dripping, add chopped parsley to taste and a good pinch of paprika, and then add this mixture to the asparagus soup, first thinning the *roux* with a little cold water or liquid from the soup.

Adjust the seasoning and stir in the sour cream, bringing the soup back to the boil before removing from the heat to serve.

Tárkonyos bárányleves – Tarragon Lamb Soup

Urban Hungary has today a strange disdain for lamb and mutton – chefs and cookery books complain of its 'odour' and are far from being keen to cook it: this is directly contrary to the long rural tradition, which still makes use of this fine meat in a variety of ways.

1 lamb's head
150g vegetables – carrot, parsley root, celery (5 oz.)
1 tbs. chopped tarragon leaves
1 egg yolk
vinegar
1 onion
250g lamb bones with some meat fragments on them (8 oz.)
1 tbs. flour
1 tbs. sour cream
salt

Remove the fatty parts from the head and bones and put the head in boiling water for a few minutes. Then scrape the white skin from the tongue and chin and cook them together with the bone meat.

If the lamb is really young put the vegetables and finely chopped tarragon in the water at the same time as the meat.

Once the vegetables are ready and the meat tender, remove the vegetables from the pan.

Mix the flour and the sour cream thoroughly and, first thinning it with a little liquid from the soup, add to the pan.

Remove it from the heat, flavour with about 1 tablespoon vinegar and pour the hot soup onto the egg yolk in a tureen.

Toasted squares should also be added just before serving. Dice the meat. The head should be served on a separate plate. The skull is then broken open and the brain eaten on bread with the soup.

Tejleves – Milk Soup

1 litre milk (2 pints)	1 tbs. flour
30g butter (1 oz.)	salt, sugar
rind of half a lemon	noodles

Put the milk in a pan and bring it to the boil, seasoning it lightly with sugar and a little salt.

Meanwhile roast the flour in a dry frying-pan (that is, without using any fat), stirring it about all the time. When it begins to become gently browned, add one or two tablespoons cold water, mixing it in smoothly. Then, pouring it through a sieve, add this to the boiling milk, stirring constantly. Bring to the boil again, adjust seasoning and add a little grated lemon rind.

Add noodles – just a few: 60g or 2 oz. is ample – and cook until they soften. Just before serving add the butter and serve very hot.

Sóskaleves – Sorrel Soup

Stock from 250g bones (8 oz.)	salt
1 carrot, 1 parsley root (small parsnip) cooked in 1½–2 litres (2½–3 pints) water for two hours	½ kg sorrel (1 lb.)
	60g dripping (2 oz.)
	4–5 tbs. sour cream
4 eggs	pinch sugar

Remove the stems and thicker veins from the sorrel and wash it thoroughly under running water.

Heat the dripping, fry the chopped onion in it, put in the sorrel, season with salt and the pinch of sugar, cover and braise until it becomes a pulp (about fifteen minutes). Combine the flour and the cream, gradually mix in the strained stock and then pour onto the sorrel. Bring to the boil and simmer for 5–6 minutes. Drop four eggs into the soup singly, and simmer for 4 or 5 minutes longer until the eggs set.

Spinach soup is made similarly and it is interesting and well worth the effort to try out the difference between the Hungarian variety and spinach soup as it is usually served in Britain.

Borleves – Wine Soup

In spite of wine becoming an increasingly standard part of our life, you may not yet have met it as a soup. I have been given two recipes for wine soup in Hungary, each with its advantages. The advantages of the first are none too subtle; if you want to attack your more demanding guests with a hard punch below the belt at the outset, try this:

12 dl good medium-dry white wine (2¼ pints)
a small piece of cinnamon
1 clove
5 egg yolks
150–200g sugar (5–6 oz.)
rind of 1 lemon

Put the wine and 4 dl (¾ pint) water to heat slowly with the sugar, cinnamon, lemon rind, in this case not grated, and clove. Before it becomes very warm take out half a cupful and beat the egg yolks with this liquid in the serving tureen. When the wine has come to the boil, allow it to simmer for 8–10 minutes and then whisk it into the egg yolk mixture. Fish out the cinnamon, lemon rind and clove, and serve.

That gives you enough for five people – or ten, depending on how you view the situation.

To return to a soup which is more like a soup, here is a modest wine soup which will hot guests up a bit but still leave them capable of dealing with whatever else you have prepared for them.

5 dl white wine (1 pint)
50g sugar (1½–2 oz.)
pinch of flour
1 lemon
3 dl water (½ pint)
1 egg
1 clove

Beat the egg lightly, sprinkle it with a little flour, and gradually add the water. Heat the wine separately, flavouring it with the clove and the grated rind of ½–1 lemon. Add this carefully to the egg mixture, also putting in the sugar. Put on the gentlest heat and whisk and beat it until it begins to thicken.

Strain the soup into cups and serve very hot. Serve with cubes of bread toasted in a dry frying-pan.

Halleves – Fish Soup

British cooks might not find Hungarian fish very exciting – unless they discover one or two of the really ingenious fish dishes which have much to offer even sea-surrounded Britain. Some of these dishes I have described later in a section of their own, but there is a sumptuous fish soup which must be included here.

½ kg fish – carp it would be in Hungary, or a marvellous fish called the European wels, which approximates to catfish or rock-salmon (1¼ lbs.)
1 level tbs. flour
1 dessertsp. sugar
60g chopped onion (2 oz.)
1 bay leaf
juice of half a lemon
2 dry rolls
parsley
150g roe or milt (5 oz.)
20g salt (¾ oz.)
100g vegetables – parsley root, carrot, celery, parsnip – whatever you want or whatever you have (4 oz.)
40 g dripping (1½ oz.)
freshly ground black pepper
1 tsp. paprika powder
6 tbs. white wine
5–6 tbs. sour cream

Clean the fish and the roe. Place them in 1½ litres (2½–3 pints) water and simmer until the fish flesh is tender. Remove the flesh from the bones.

Meanwhile slice the vegetables and, with the bay leaf, braise them in a little melted dripping until they are almost but not quite ready – they should still be firm. Let the liquid evaporate until only the fat remains. Sprinkle with half the paprika and the finely chopped parsley, stirring immediately. Add the fish stock, the wine and the salt, and then season with pepper and sugar. Simmer until the vegetables are ready.

With the remainder of the dripping and half the flour prepare a dark *roux*, adding the remainder of the paprika as well. Gradually add a little water to thin it. When it is thin and smooth add this mixture to the soup, stirring well. Adjust seasoning – possibly adding a pinch more sugar.

Mix the remainder of the flour with the sour cream and add to the soup. Bring it once more to the boil and then simmer for 5–10 minutes.

Place the fish flesh and the roe in a tureen, pour the boiling soup over them and add the lemon juice.

Dice the rolls, toast them in the oven and place some in each plate immediately before serving the soup.

Salátaleves – Lettuce Soup

This next recipe for lettuce soup provides a stimulating, acidy opener. It needs careful seasoning and although no Hungarians I know include pepper, I think it is worth experimenting with a very little.

2 firm lettuces	60g good dripping (2 oz.)
1 level tbs. flour	5–6 tbs. sour cream
2 cloves garlic	1 litre whey (2 pints)
fresh dill leaves	1 tsp.–1 tbs. wine vinegar
freshly ground black pepper	salt, sugar

Shred the lettuce. Melt the dripping and braise the lettuce in it gently, with the lid on the pan. When the lettuce is cooked, add the whey, the two crushed garlic cloves, 1 good teaspoon finely chopped dill, and salt and pepper to taste.

Combine the flour and the sour cream thoroughly and then gradually add a little water to make a thin sauce. Add this to the soup. Bring it to the boil again and let it simmer for 5 minutes. Then add a little vinegar and a good pinch of sugar.

Beat an egg in each person's plate and serve the soup onto this, mixing immediately. Many people also add small squares of bacon fat and rind fried very crisp.

Gombaleves – Mushroom Soup

I used to think it would be difficult to imagine anything new in the way of mushroom soup . . . and then I met it in Hungary. This soup should have a fine balance of just-sharp (a pinch of cherry paprika) and bland softness (*galuskas*) with sour cream in this instance no more than vaguely in the background.

250g mushrooms (8 oz.)
1 tsp. flour
1–1½ litres stock (2–2½ pints)
1 tbs. sour cream
salt
30g dripping (1 oz.)
1 onion
1–2 carrots, 1 parsley root (or very small parsnip)
paprika powder, and merest pinch cherry paprika or chilli powder
galuskas, parsley

Wash the mushrooms and cut them into fairly small pieces. Fry the finely chopped onion in the melted dripping, add the mushrooms and diced carrots and parsley root. Sprinkle very lightly with paprika powder and the pinch of chilli powder, cover and allow to cook gently for a few minutes.

Remove the lid. Once the liquid has been reduced to fat, sprinkle with a very little flour, mix it in well and let it cook for a few minutes longer. Then gradually add the cold stock, preferably made from 300g (10–12 oz.) veal bones, and season with salt to taste. Bring the soup to the boil and then simmer it gently until the carrots are quite cooked.

Before serving, garnish with parsley and mix in the sour cream.

The *galuskas* should be added to the simmering soup about 5–6 minutes before it is to be removed from the heat for serving: they are not to dominate, however, so use no more than 60g (2 oz.) flour and about half a beaten egg.

Erdélyi leves – Transylvanian Soup

1 litre beef stock (2 pints)
5–6 tbs. sour cream
fresh dill leaves, chives
2 rolls
40g butter (1½ oz.)
2 egg yolks
parsley, celery leaves

Prepare the stock in advance from 300g (10–12 oz.) good lean beef.

Fry the diced rolls golden in the butter.

Wash and cut up a bunch of parsley, chives, dill and celery leaves very finely.

Mix the cream and the egg yolks gently in a separate pan.

Strain the stock, removing all the fat. Bring it to the boil and pour it in a thin stream into the pan with the cream and egg yolks, meanwhile stirring and mixing with a whisk. Over moderate heat and stirring continuously, bring the soup to the boil and then immediately remove it from the heat.

Mix in the cut herbs, counting 1 heaped teaspoon for each person.

Serve with the fried bread cubes in a separate hot dish.

There are two other vegetable soups which cannot be omitted. Their titles are familiar: the recipes are less so.

Tomato soup with sugar? Before you shrug it away as Hungarians turning things upside down again, do try it. It is a delicious surprise.

As for the potato soup concept – I doubt whether anyone can make such good potato soup as my mother, with flank of real Scotch beef, and carrots, swedes, onion, potatoes all fresh from the garden, so I approached this dish and the recipe for it with all possible prejudices. It survived my initial scorn and thus refuses to be left out.

Paradicsomleves – Tomato Soup

Stock from 250g (8 oz.) veal or pork bones, 1 carrot, 1 onion, 2 celery leaves, all to be simmered in 1½ litres (2½–3 pints) salted water for 2 hours
salt
1 kg tomatoes (2 lbs.)
30g dripping (1 oz.)
1 level tbs. flour
1½ tsp. sugar
30–60g long-grain rice (1–2 oz.)
parsley (optional)

Strain the stock. Quarter the tomatoes, add them to the stock and bring to the boil. Once the skins have come away, put the tomatoes through a sieve and allow to cool.

Make a very light *roux* from the fat and the flour, remove it from the heat and gradually add the tomatoes and the stock. Season with a little salt, the sugar and a very little parsley if you like.

Wash the rice thoroughly in cold water, add to the soup and let it simmer as slowly as possible for 20 minutes.

In Hungary this soup is traditionally served with castor sugar on the table and this is then sprinkled liberally on to the soup by everyone according to taste.

Burgonyaleves – Potato Soup

250g veal or pork bones (8 oz.)
1 carrot
1 onion
1 tbs. flour
1–2 celery leaves
1 sweet green pepper and 1 tomato (optional)
½ kg potatoes (1 lb.)
1 parsley root (or very small parsnip)
80g bacon dripping (3 oz.)
½ tsp. paprika powder
parsley
4–5 tbs. sour cream
salt, pepper

Boil the bones in about 1 litre (2 pints) water with the sliced carrot and parsley root, until any bits of meat on the bones begin to peel off.

Fry the finely chopped onion in the fat until it is transparent, sprinkle on the flour and the paprika powder, and cook over medium heat for 5 minutes, stirring it about all the time.

Add the sliced potatoes, season with salt and pepper and cook gently until the potatoes appear glassy.

Strain off the stock liquid from the bones and gradually add it to the potatoes. If they are in season the sliced pepper and tomato are put in then. Sprinkle with the finely sliced celery leaves and a small bunch of parsley, and simmer for about 20 minutes.

When the soup is to be served put one good tablespoon of sour cream in each plate, serve the soup onto this and mix it in lightly.

Gyümölcslevesek — Fruit Soups

A magnificent speciality which appears in Hungary with the early cherries and lasts till the late plums and later medlars is the colourful range of fruit soups. There is nothing so light and cheerful as red-currant soup with foam *galuskas* floating on top, and making this kind of soup is one of the most enticing ways of using our unassuming and much neglected rhubarb. Apart from those in the recipes I have given below, black currants, white currants, cherries and gooseberries are the other main fruits home-grown in Hungary and treated in this way to great advantage. These soups are virtually always served cold, but made from preserved fruit and served hot in winter they are almost as successful.

Allow about three ounces of fruit per person. The fruit is brought to the boil and then simmered in water with sugar – it is important that the sugar should be put in at the start, because if it is only added later the fruit is inclined to remain more sour than is desirable. The other usual flavourings are cinnamon and lemon rind, but for special occasions 1–2 tablespoons of rum or white or red wine, depending on the colour of the fruit, are added to the water at the beginning.

Once the fruit has softened, thickening is added and this may take a variety of forms. It may simply be a mixture of flour and sour cream. A finer method is to roast the flour on its own, without any fat, in a heavy frying-pan until it just begins to change to a golden colour. Then mix this to a smooth mass by adding a tablespoon of cold water, more if necessary, but do it gradually. Put in the sour cream and mix so that the whole becomes thoroughly smooth. Add this to the fruit by pouring it through a sieve, stirring continuously. And then bring it to the boil. Yet a third method is to thicken with egg yolks alone, but most Hungarians compromise by using somewhat less flour with the cream and then serving the soup onto an egg yolk.

It improves the flavour, texture and colour of these fruit soups if you press at least half the fruit through a fine sieve when it has softened but is still hot – particularly important in the sour-cherry soup. If you have time to include this extra work, then use less of the flour and sour cream mixture as the sieved fruit itself has a thickening effect.

Once you have made the soup, allow it to cool. Then put it in the refrigerator to become really cold for serving.

Meggyleves – Sour-Cherry Soup

360g sour-cherries (morellos) (12 oz.)
6 tbs. sour cream
salt, cloves, cinnamon
120g sugar (4 oz.)
20g flour (½–¾ oz.)
lemon rind

Stone the cherries and bring them slowly to the boil in about 1 litre (2 pints) of water, using the sugar, a pinch of salt, a few cloves, ¼–½ teaspoon cinnamon, and the grated rind of half a lemon to flavour. When the fruit has become soft, press half of it through a fine sieve and thicken with sour cream and flour (*see* above). Bring to the boil again, then allow it to cool, and serve chilled.

Sour-cherry soup is greatly enhanced if you break down some of the cherry stones in a mortar or grinder and then simmer them very gently in just a little red wine. The liquid from this should then be added to the soup by pouring it through fine muslin. This is particularly helpful if you are forced to use ordinary cherries instead of sour cherries.

Almaleves – Apple Soup

600g dessert apples (1¼ lb.)
20g flour (½ oz.)
60g sugar (2 oz.)
2 dl sour cream (1½ gills)
½ tsp. cinnamon
1 egg yolk
rind of half a lemon
pinch of salt

Core the apples and slice them thinly. Stew them in about 1½–2 litres (3–3½ pints) water with the sugar, cinnamon, lemon rind and salt.

When the apples are soft add the flour and the sour cream mixed together. Bring to the boil again and simmer for 5 minutes. Pour the soup onto an egg yolk in a tureen and mix in straight away. If the flavour is not sufficiently tart and refreshing, add the juice of half the lemon as well.

I have often seen a few peeled and quartered fresh apricots being added to this apple soup, and many people in Hungary take a couple of peeled pears and grate them into the soup for extra flavour – it also helps the texture.

Ribizkeleves – Red Currant Soup

1 litre fresh currants (2 pints), preferably red, but white or black can be used in the same way
2 eggs
1 litre water (2 pints)
5 level tbs. sugar
6 tbs. sour cream
½ tbs. flour
salt

Clean the currants and cook them gently for 15 minutes with one cup of water. Put this mixture through a sieve, thin it with the rest of the water and return to the heat with 3 tablespoons sugar and a pinch of salt.

Combine the flour and the sour cream, add to the soup and bring to the boil again, simmering for 5 minutes longer.

Separate the eggs, placing the two yolks in a soup tureen and beating the whites until they are firm.

Add 2 tablespoons sugar to the whites and beat further until the mixture is quite smooth. Make *galuskas* from this foam by placing separate spoonfuls of it on to the simmering soup, turning them over once, and then lift them out very carefully.

Pour the hot soup onto the egg-yolks, mix well together and place the *galuskas* carefully on top.

Barackleves – Apricot Soup

450–500g fresh apricots (1 lb.)
2 tbs. breadcrumbs
1 egg
2 dl white wine (⅜ pint)
3–4 level tbs. sugar
6 tbs. sour cream

Peel and slice half the apricots and cook them gently in the wine.

Bring 1½ litres (2½–3 pints) water to the boil, add the breadcrumbs, soften the rest of the apricots in this and then press this whole mixture through a sieve. Pour this on to the first mixture of apricots and wine, add the sugar and bring to the boil.

Combine one egg thoroughly with the sour cream in a tureen and add the soup to this spoonful by spoonful, stirring it well in all the time.

Serve chilled, with cubes of toast if you wish.

Rebarbaraleves – Rhubarb Soup

½ kg rhubarb (1 lb.)	5 level tbs. sugar
6 tbs. sour cream	1 egg yolk
lemon rind	6 tbs. milk
50g flour (1½ oz.)	salt

Bring ¾–1 litre (1½–2 pints) water to the boil with the sugar, a pinch of salt and the grated rind of at least half a lemon.

Wash and clean the rhubarb, cut it into small pieces and add it to the boiling syrup.

Mix the flour with half the cream and enough milk to make a thin sauce and add this to the rhubarb when it is almost soft. Bring to the boil again and simmer for 5 minutes.

Combine the remainder of the cream with the egg yolk and in a thin stream pour this into the soup, stirring all the time.

Serve either hot or chilled.

Levesbevalók – Noodles, Dumplings and Galuskas for Soups

It is not, however, just a question of the soups in this chapter – there is, in addition to the *csipetke* described on page 5, a wealth of *levesbevalók* (literally 'for putting into soup') including all kinds of dumplings and fine concoctions, which are not to be taken as optional extras.

These start with a simple egg and flour dough cut into squares, strips, threads, stars, 'strawberry leaves' or the beautiful *csiga-tészta*, 'snail dough', curled on a special undulating mould into a sort of shell form with a reticular surface. Nowadays Hungarian housewives can buy a great variety of these forms in the shops so that they need only to be added to the soup, but it is difficult to see who actually buys them because all the family cooks I know show true Hungarian independence and outrage at the very idea of being deprived of that part of their art.

At the other end of the range are much more serious, substantial affairs, such as the liver dumplings and liver rice which make a particularly fine balance served in *consommé*. Here are the recipes for some of the more interesting 'lumps and bumps' you are likely to find in Hungarian soups.

Daragaluska (1) – Semolina Galuskas

50–60g semolina (2 oz.) 1 egg

Beat the egg white stiff. Fold the yolk in gently and as much semolina as will give a light, pliable dough, about 50–60g or 1½–2 oz. Cut off thumb-sized and thumb-shaped *galuskas* into the soup and let them simmer for 2–3 minutes. Then, taking the pan off the heat, leave for a few minutes to give the little dumplings time to swell.

Daragaluska (2) – Semolina Galuskas

Beat the egg yolk with 30g (1 oz.) butter or 20g (¾ oz.) dripping from smoked streaky bacon. Then fold in the stiffly beaten egg white, and finally the semolina.

Add a pinch of baking powder to either recipe for an even lighter texture. Serve carefully so that the *galuskas* do not break.

Májgombóc – Liver Dumplings

120g calves' or pigs' liver (4 oz.)
30g fat (1 oz.)
1 tbs. flour
salt, black pepper
1 roll
1 tbs. fine breadcrumbs
1 egg
1 tsp. chopped onion
marjoram, parsley
milk

Mince the liver and add the roll, which should previously be soaked in milk and then squeezed gently to expel surplus moisture.

Fry the onion in the fat and add a teaspoonful of chopped parsley. Then add the mixture to the liver. Season with salt, freshly ground black pepper, marjoram. Break in the egg and finally combine with the flour and the breadcrumbs. Mix thoroughly, form small dumplings and cook them gently in simmering *consommé* until they soften and swell.

Májrízs – Liver Rice

100g liver (3½ oz.)	50g flour (1½ oz.)
1 egg	salt, pepper

Combine the flour and the egg to make a dough. Mince the liver and add it to the dough. Season with salt and pepper. Press this mixture through a sieve with large holes or through a grater into the soup and allow to cook for 5 minutes.

Májpiskóta – Liver Cake

1 tbs. minced or grated liver	1 tbs. flour
1 egg	10g bacon dripping or butter (¼ oz.)

Mix all the ingredients together, using only the yolk of the egg at first, and season with salt and pepper. Then fold in the stiffly beaten egg white. Spread the mixture on a greased and floured baking sheet so that it is about half an inch thick, and bake it in a moderate oven. Then cut it into small squares, which should be simmered in the soup for a few minutes before serving.

Maceszgombóc – Matzo Dumplings

1 egg and 1 egg yolk	60–70g butter (2–2½ oz.)
100g matzos (4 oz.)	1 tsp. chopped onion
salt, pepper	parsley
pinch of ginger	

Lightly fry the chopped onion and a little parsley in half a teaspoonful of butter. Beat the remainder of the butter until it is frothy, then cream with the whole egg and the egg yolk. Let the onion and parsley cool and add them to the butter and eggs; season with salt, pepper and ginger. Adding a tablespoon of cold water, beat well with a whisk. Lastly mix in the crumbed *matzos* and leave to rest for half an hour.

With a knife dipped in water between each one, form golf-ball dumplings from the mixture and cook them for about half an hour in boiling water.

These dumplings may be cooked directly in the soup or separately in salted water, but in either case the cooking should be slow and with the lid on the pan. Particularly appropriate to goose or chicken soup.

Vajgaluska – Butter Galuskas

30g butter (1 oz.)	1 egg
100g flour (3–4 oz.)	salt

Beat the egg yolk with the butter to make a frothy cream. Beat the egg white stiff and fold it into the butter mixture. Sprinkle this with the flour, as much as it takes to make a fairly dry dough, season with salt, mix well but gently, and then slice off small *galuskas* – less than a teaspoon for each – into the soup, letting them simmer for 5–6 minutes before serving.

Burgonyagombóc – Potato Dumplings

Mix 250g (8 oz.) cooked and mashed potatoes with 2 tablespoons flour, 1 tablespoon semolina, 1 dessertspoon chopped onion fried in 30g (1 oz.) bacon dripping, some chopped parsley, salt and pepper seasoning and about half a beaten egg.

Form small dumplings from the mixture and cook for seven to ten minutes in the soup.

Palacsintametélt – Pancake Strips

Make a pancake dough by combining 1 egg and 60g (2 oz.) flour and then gradually adding 6 tablespoons milk or soda water. Fry some pancakes in the usual way from this mixture, cut these into thin strips and put them into the soup just before serving, or serve in a separate plate so that everyone can take as much as they feel like.

Tojáskocsonya – Egg Jelly

2 eggs	6 tbs. milk
salt	nutmeg

Beat the eggs, add the milk and season with salt and nutmeg. Pour into a buttered fireproof dish. Put cold water in a larger dish and place the egg dish in this *bain-marie*. Cover the eggs and steam gently in a moderate oven. The water round the egg dish should not be allowed to boil or the egg jelly will tend to have holes in it.

Once the eggs have become solid, remove them from the oven and place the dish in cold water for a few moments; then slip the eggs onto a chopping board and cut into small squares. Add some of these to each plate just before serving the soup. Count half an egg for each person.

Gyűszűtészta – Thimble Dumplings

Make a soft dough from 1 egg and about 100g (3 oz.) flour using a little water to bind if necessary.

Roll the dough out very thinly and then fold it over in two. Cut small rounds from the double layer with a thimble and fry them in deep fat, moving them about with a fork. When the tiny dumplings are being cut with the thimble the edges of the separate layers will stick together and the little rounds will puff up into balls during the frying.

Rántott borsó – Dough Peas

6 tbs. milk
1 egg
salt

60g flour (2 oz.)
70g dripping or fat ($2\frac{1}{2}$ oz.)

Work the flour together with the egg and then thin gradually with the milk. Add a good pinch of salt and mix until smooth.

Heat the fat until it just begins to smoke. Put a tablespoon of the dough into a holed draining spoon, allowing the mixture to drip into the hot fat. Get the little balls of dough golden all over – removing from the heat from time to time when it becomes too fierce. Take care not to drip too many drips into the pan at once or they will get together and the resulting congregation is not the desired objective. When they are nicely golden, drain the 'peas' thoroughly, place some in each plate and serve the soup onto them.

Eggs

Although there is no scarcity of eggs in Hungary or in Hungarian cooking – they get into many things by the half-dozen as you will notice later among the cakes, and they come in a variety of guises as fillings, etc. – there is no extravaganza of egg dishes. There are naturally the familiar simplicities – boiled, fried, poached, and scrambled eggs – but to get to the really interesting egg ideas in Hungary you have to go off into the country.

The Kalocsa style, for example, is to clean tomato-paprikas, the big round sweet red peppers, removing the seeds and inside veins, turn them about a bit in hot fat, place them in a fireproof dish and break an egg into each. If you use about ten for four people, it makes an excellent starter – bake the red cups in a moderate oven until the egg white sets.

In Szeged they have traditionally a more elaborate way of serving fried eggs. For this you will need:

300g cod roe (11 oz.)	250g mushrooms (8 oz.)
200g dripping (7 oz.)	10 eggs
150g chopped onion (5 oz.)	10 large rolls
salt, pepper and paprika powder	parsley

The crusts of the rolls need to be firm and if they are crisp, too, so much the better.

Braise the roe in a minimum of fat with the onion.

Slice off the top third of the rolls and cut out the insides carefully Fry these insides – they should each be in one piece – golden in the fat.

Chop up the mushrooms, fry them lightly and make a soft *purée* from them. Spread this on the fried crumb of the rolls.

Fill the roll shells with the braised roe and top each shell with a fried egg. Season with salt and pepper and then decorate with paprika and parsley. Serve the mushroom part alongside. The tops of the rolls are kept for making breadcrumbs.

But to be quietly Hungarian, eggs baked in sour cream is the perfectly peaceful opener.

Grease a shallow fireproof dish and pour ½–1 inch depth of sour cream into it. Break the eggs into this singly, counting one per person. Put salt on the whites and bake in a hot oven for 6–8 minutes.

Just before serving place a knob of butter on each egg and sprinkle with a little sweet paprika powder.

A more substantial variation is to bake the eggs in creamed potatoes. Before serving, but after baking, the eggs are dotted with butter and then a layer of grated cheese is sprinkled on top.

Fish

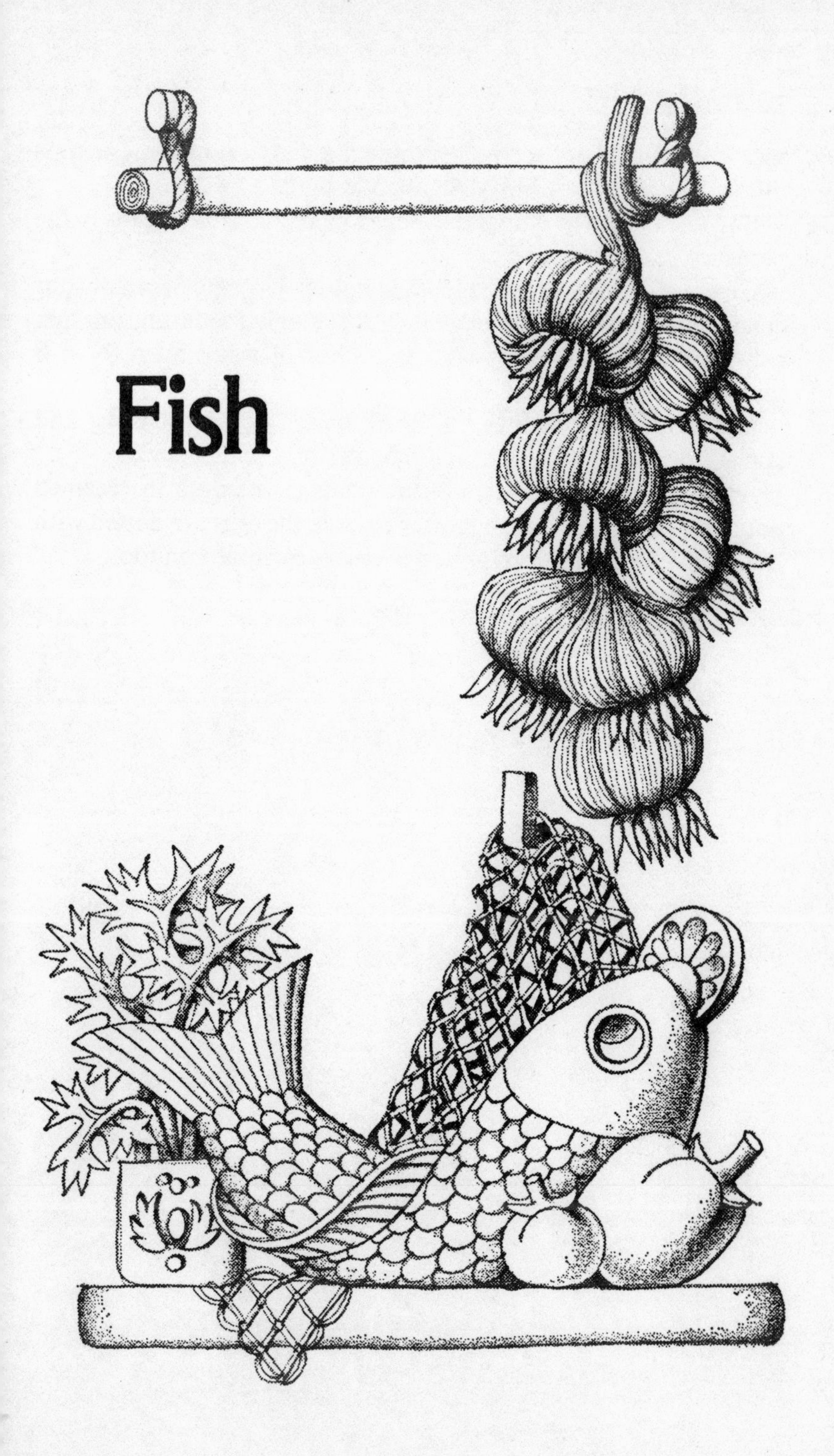

Since Hungary has today no sea coast of her own, most of the fish available is freshwater either from Lake Balaton or the Hungarian rivers, the largest of which are the Danube and the Tisza. Although increasing use is being made of interesting fish such as the razor fish and the barbel, most popular of all is still the carp. The pike-perch, sometimes known as the wall-eye, is also plentiful in all Hungarian waters and is greatly prized for its lean white flesh and lack of irritating small bones.

However lean and white the flesh of the gluttonous pike itself may be, Hungarians tend to find it rather dry and bony but they value it for its liver, from which an oil is prepared which enjoys something of the same reputation as cod liver oil does in Britain.

A special delicacy, particularly in the Balaton, is the freshwater sturgeon, or sterlet – *Acipenser ruthenus* – and the list of the fish more commonly eaten in Hungary is completed by the European wels, which is roughly similar to the catfish.

Any Hungarian fishmonger makes the freshness of fish an absolute certainty by keeping his stock, consisting mainly of carp, in enormous tanks from which the live fish is extracted only when the customer has indicated which specimen he or she wishes to buy. Indeed the recommended procedure goes even further – the customer will bring along a container, nowadays usually a large polythene bag. Into this he slips the fish until he gets it home, and the fish will then probably spend the final stages of its life swimming happily in the bath or a large tub.

I think it is well worth taking the trouble to look around for a carp rather than replacing it in these recipes with any of the fish which are more readily available at British fishmongers. Carp flesh is so juicy that you scarcely feel you are eating a solid flesh at all – the texture is more like that of braised mushrooms and, at its best, it is even more like a succulent jelly. Carp 'steaks' coated in bread-crumbs is a recipe which provides the perfect foil for this texture.

Rántott ponty – Carp Steaks in Breadcrumbs

1½ kg carp (3 lbs.)
salt
50g flour (1½ oz.)
2 eggs
150g fine breadcrumbs (5 oz.)
250g fat (or oil) (8 oz.)

If necessary, prepare the carp. Scale it, slit open the stomach and clean the fish. Cut off the head and slice the body in two lengthwise. From these lengths cut steaks and salt them well. Dip them first in flour, then in beaten egg and finally in fine breadcrumbs. Fry them fairly quickly in hot fat.

Serve with buttered potatoes and tartare sauce, and possibly a wedge of lemon.

Rácponty – Serbian Carp

Here is another strikingly simple recipe which presents the texture and delicate flavour of carp in a most subtle way. It is common in all parts of Hungary although it is originally from the southern part of the country.

1 large carp 1½–2 kg (3½–4 lbs.)
180g smoked streaky bacon (6 oz.)
salt
½ tbs. flour
½ litre sour cream (1 pint)
2 tomatoes
200g onion (7 oz.)
120g fat (4 oz.)
paprika powder
1 kg boiled potatoes (2 lbs.)
1 sweet pepper
melted butter

Clean and wash the carp and cut it into steaks. Make small slits in these pieces and lard with strips of bacon. Season with salt and sprinkle with paprika powder.

Smear an ovenproof dish with the fat and in the bottom place the potatoes cut into slices. Put the fish pieces on the potatoes and cover with rounds of onion, sweet pepper and tomato. Sprinkle with melted butter and cook in a moderate oven for 20 minutes.

Mix the sour cream with the flour, pour this over the fish and continue to bake for about 15 minutes more.

Halpaprikás – Fish with Paprika Cream Sauce

For the recipe which follows there is no need to restrict yourself to the particular fish which Hungarians would use. The method provides an excellent dish from fillets of any of the fleshier fish.

1 kg fleshy fish (2 lbs.)
2 dl sour cream ($\frac{3}{8}$ pint)
1 dessertsp. paprika powder
60g butter (2 oz.)
120g onion (4 oz.)
salt

Cut the cleaned fish into cubes, salt them and set them aside for half an hour.

Chop the onion very finely and fry it in the butter until it is transparent. Remove from the heat and sprinkle on the paprika. Mix in the sour cream, put in the fish pieces – and in season include 1 sweet pepper and 1 tomato. Cook very slowly for 25–30 minutes. Serve with light *galuskas*. To make these use the recipe given after *Marhapörkölt* (p. 46) but using 2 eggs and therefore a little less water. Instead of mixing the whole eggs with the water, use only the yolks, setting aside the whites. Then beat the whites until they are stiff, fold them into the dough and cook the *galuskas* as described in the recipe.

Halászlé – Fish Soup

This is a dish which any Hungarian feels to be as traditionally Magyar as *gulyás*. There are differences in emphasis from region to region, that from Szeged probably enjoying the highest reputation, but basically it is a fiery paprika fish soup.

Best results are obtained by using more than one kind of fish.

Traditionally carp is the mainstay of the *halászlé*, accompanied by catfish, sturgeon and perch. Sometimes only one kind of fish is used with the additional flavour and juice being provided by including a variety of smaller fish which are later removed.

For each person count 250g fish (8 oz.) and take 1 onion to $\frac{1}{2}$ kg (1 lb.) fish.

Cut the onion into rings and simmer gently for 15 minutes in water – about 4 dl ($\frac{3}{4}$ pint) per person – with a good tablespoon of paprika powder and 1 whole cherry paprika or chilli. If you use smaller fish for flavour, include them straight away at this stage and cover with water, simmering for 30 minutes.

Cut the fish proper into 100g (3–4 oz.) chunks, salt these and keep them in a cool place for an hour. Then strain the onion liquid onto the fish, add 1–2 sweet peppers and 1 tomato, and simmer very gently for 40–45 minutes. Do not stir it – shake it occasionally. No thickening is used in this fish soup – *halászlé* is a thin fiery red soup with whole chunks of fish in it and the juices from the fish and the paprika will be rich enough without any thickening.

Meat and Poultry

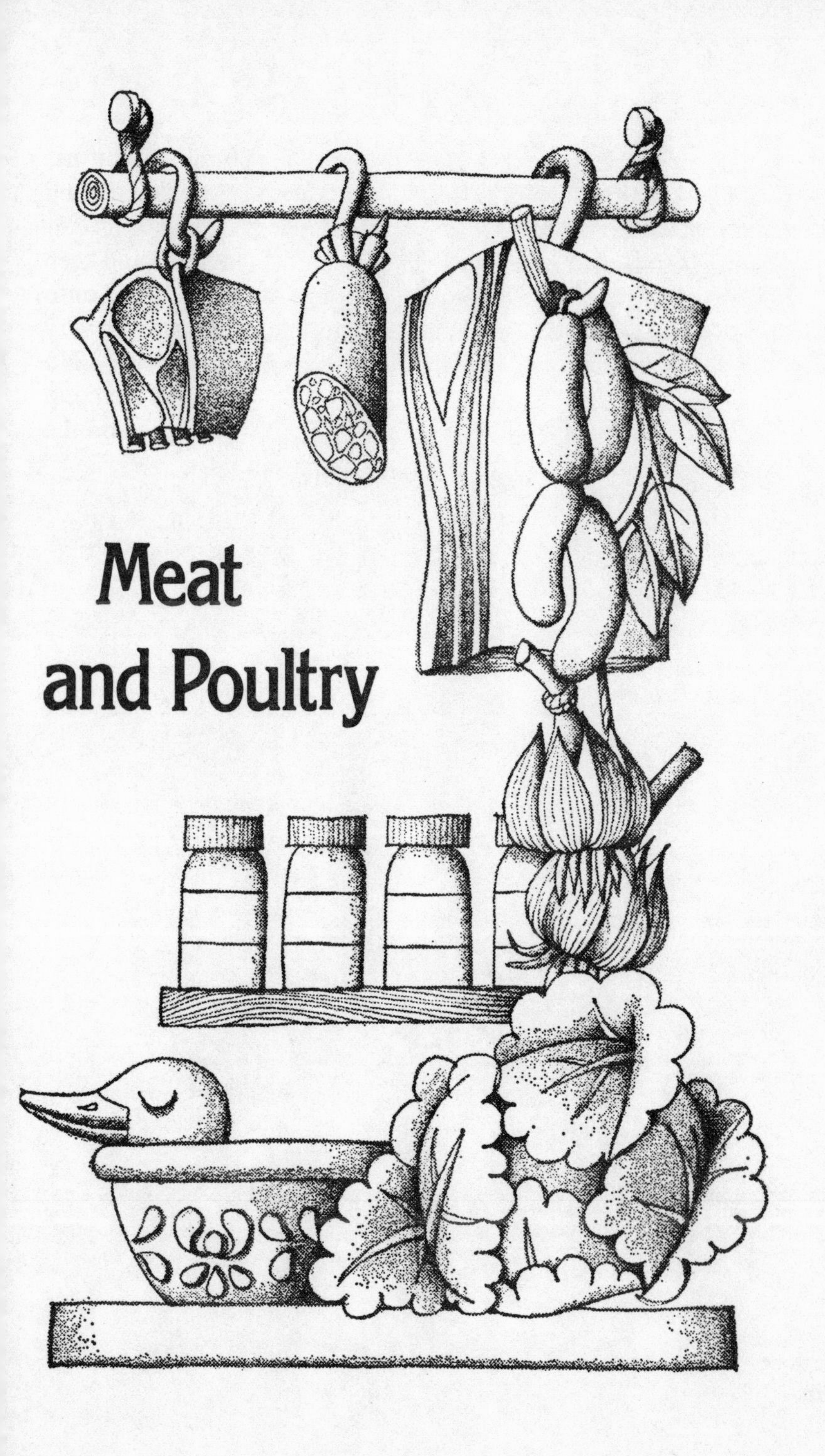

Hungary probably stands alone in that pork is the meat most frequently used. This has only come about during this century, and everyone in Hungary still considers beef to be better from the dietary point of view, and Hungarian chefs hold that beef can be cooked in a greater variety of ways and more tastily than pork. There is also a theory that beef demands much more care in cooking than pork. In practice, however, pork prevails and there are more pork than beef dishes to choose from. The range of available meats is completed by an occasional – in the country, much more than occasional – mutton recipe, a superfluity of chickens, many very fine geese, and excellent turkeys, the fate of many of which is to be exported to Britain for Christmas.

Hunting is now a very fashionable sport among those who can afford it in Hungary, but some of the booty from the game world does find its way to more everyday people at more everyday prices. The special treat in this area is wild boar, but there is no lack of things more delicate from which to choose – roedeer, quail, partridge, pigeon, pheasant, woodcock.

Stews

The meat recipes begin with the characteristic dishes using small cubes of meat. You will find the recipes for whole steaks, *escalopes*, and roasts in the second half of the chapter. Between these two main sections I have included a few interesting recipes which do not fit into either section – there is a traditional wedding dish, then some preparations connected with the killing of a pig and finally a recipe from the Hortobágy Plain in the east of Hungary for a meat-filled pancake.

The first and most truly characteristic Hungarian meat dish is a *pörkölt*, a simple braise of which, as they say in Hungarian, 'let the juice be short'. Beef *pörkölt*, I think, produces a richer result than pork and makes a fine dark contrast to the *galuskas* which are the traditional accompaniment.

Marhapörkölt – Beef Pörkölt

600g (1¼ lbs.) lean beef (chuck, shin, add a bit of heart or kidney if you like)
salt
50g fat (1½–2 oz.)
1 onion
½ tsp. paprika powder

Cube the meat.

Chop the onion finely and fry it gently in the fat, not allowing it to become brown. Sprinkle with the paprika and immediately add the meat. Mix gently for a few minutes so that the meat becomes sealed on all sides. Season well with salt – no pepper! – add enough water to almost cover the meat and, with the lid on the pan, braise slowly for about 2 hours.

If necessary, add water later, but always just a little at a time – the liquid with any *pörkölt* should indeed be 'short'; on the other hand, it should be thick only in the sense that it becomes full and rich from the meat juices.

The traditional accompaniment is *galuskas*, *see* below. Individual tastes lead to additions such as a little of the stronger paprika powders available in Hungary, even a good pinch of chilli powder, or a few caraway seeds, or a few spoonfuls of red wine.

Galuska pörkölthöz – Galuskas for Pörkölt

½ kg flour (1 lb.)
1 egg
40g fat (1½ oz.)
salt

Bring 3 pints salted water to the boil.

Mix the egg with about 3 dl (½ pint) of cold water and add a good teaspoon of salt. Mix in the flour and, when the salted water boils, break off thimble-sized twirls from the dough into it.

Keep boiling until the *galuskas* rise to the surface of the water. Drain them into a colander and rinse them quickly but thoroughly in cold running water.

Make the fat hot and toss the *galuskas* about in it to get them well covered. Season with salt, serving them in a well heated bowl.

Pusztai pörkölt – Pörkölt from the Puszta

A *Pusztai Pörkölt* has nothing in common with the pure traditional *pörkölt* except that there is very little liquid in the stew. The title is therefore misleading but the dish itself is very good.

800g lean braising beef (1 lb. 10 oz.)
1 clove garlic
4 sweet peppers
3 tomatoes
marjoram
120g dripping (4 oz.)
150g onion (5 oz.)
1 tsp. paprika powder
1 kg potatoes (2 lbs.)
3 dl white wine (about ½ pint)
salt and pepper

Wash the beef and cut it into big cubes.

Lightly fry the finely chopped onion and the crushed garlic in the fat, sprinkle some paprika over them and mix in the meat straight away.

Pour on half the wine and a little water, season with salt, freshly ground black pepper and a pinch of marjoram, cover and allow to braise gently.

Peel the potatoes and cut them into cubes. Clean the peppers, removing the seeds, and cut them lengthwise into six pieces. Cut the tomatoes into six, too, and add all these vegetables to the meat when it begins to become tender. Put in the rest of the wine, adding water if absolutely necessary to prevent sticking, cover again and put the *pörkölt* into a rather slow oven to finish. Stir occasionally and take care to keep the liquid to a rich minimum.

Pacalpörkölt – Tripe Pörkölt

Hungarian cooks have a very successful way of dealing with tripe. *Pacal* is the first and second stomachs of the cow and if you give it this *pörkölt* treatment you will find it removes any trace of the uneasiness which the idea of tripe sometimes evokes even today.

1 kg cleaned tripe (2 lbs.)
20g paprika powder (½ oz.)
2 cloves garlic
salt, caraway seeds
flour
100g fat (3–4 oz.)
120g onion (4 oz.)
3 green peppers
2 tomatoes
celery leaves

Boil the tripe for 15–20 minutes in water; drain it and wash it in fresh water.

Meanwhile fry the chopped onion lightly in the fat, sprinkle with paprika powder and add 6 tablespoons water. Bruise the garlic and crush about half a teaspoon of caraway seeds and add them to the onion with the tripe.

Cover barely with water, slice in the peppers and tomatoes, cover and simmer for 3–4 hours until the tripe becomes tender.

Mix about 1 teaspoon flour with a little cold water and use this to thicken the *pörkölt* lightly. Bring to the boil again and keep simmering for 10 minutes longer.

Before serving, mix in at least 1 tablespoon finely chopped celery leaves, and serve hot with mashed potatoes or *zsemlegombóc* (*see* p. 116).

Csikós tokány – Cowboy Stew

The other long cooking method which is fairly widely used for meat cut into cubes is the *tokány*, a stew with onion and black pepper as the characteristic flavouring. Paprika is usually involved as well.

The first recipe is basic and the touch of richness is not extravagant: the cooking liquid is reduced and the stew made velvety by sour cream.

700g lean pork, cubed (1½ lbs.)
½ tsp. paprika powder
2 dl sour cream (⅜ pint)
salt and freshly ground black pepper
100g onions (4 oz.)
100g smoked streaky bacon (4 oz.)
2 green peppers
1 tomato
1 tsp. flour

Cut the bacon into thin strips and fry it in its own fat. Add the finely chopped onion and fry it lightly. Sprinkle on the paprika, add 1 tablespoon water and put in the meat. Season with salt, and as liberal a dose of freshly ground black pepper as you can enjoy. Add the sliced peppers and tomato. Cover and braise slowly until the meat is almost tender, stirring occasionally and adding a little water from time to time as necessary.

When the meat is tender, reduce the liquid until only the fat remains and then add the sour cream mixed with the flour. Cook for 5 minutes more, adjust seasoning and serve with *galuskas* or boiled potatoes.

Horány tokány – Horány Stew

Elaborate on these ingredients and you have the next recipe. Horány is the name of a little village up the Danube from Budapest and I think we can be certain its only connection with this *tokány* is that its name rhymes with the name of the method.

250g braising beef (8 oz.)
120g streaky bacon (4 oz.)
120g mushrooms (4 oz.)
20g salt (¾ oz.)
20g paprika powder (¾ oz.)
1 tsp. flour
400g hand of pork (13 oz.)
250g pigs' kidneys (8 oz.)
100g fat (3 oz.)
120g onion (4 oz.)
freshly ground black pepper
2 dl sour cream (⅜ pint)

Cut the meats into finger lengths. Pour boiling water over the kidneys and slice them, too.

Braise the finely chopped onion in the fat, sprinkle the paprika over it and add the meat. Braise until the meat is half done – about half an hour. Season well with salt.

Dice the bacon, fry it golden in its own fat and add the sliced mushrooms and the kidney. Fry quickly, seasoning with salt and liberally with pepper, and add to the beef and pork when they are almost ready.

Reduce the liquid until only the fat remains. Put in the sour cream mixed with a little flour and simmer for 5 minutes before serving.

Erdélyi marhatokány – Transylvanian Beef Stew

700g beef ($1\frac{1}{2}$ lbs.) cubed
150g onion (5 oz.)
salt and pepper
white wine
120g smoked streaky bacon (4 oz)
60g tomato *purée* (2 oz.)
2 cloves garlic
savory

Cut the meat into strips, wash it and drain it well.

Dice and fry the bacon, adding the finely chopped onion. Put in the meat, season with salt and cook for a few minutes over fierce heat, stirring it around all the time. Then add the garlic, a little more pepper than usual, and a very little white wine. Cover and braise very slowly. Stir from time to time and if the liquid evaporates replace it with some more white wine but always in small quantities.

When the meat is about half ready add the tomato *purée* or a fresh tomato, and sprinkle with savory. Continue to braise until the meat is tender. Although the traditional accompaniment is *puliszka* (a sort of porridge made from corn meal, like *polenta*) mashed potatoes with chopped and fried onions mixed in meet with just as much approval. A salad of green peppers preserved in vinegar is also served with this *tokány*.

Tárkonyos bárány – Tarragon Lamb

Any Hungarian inclined to scorn mutton or lamb is himself ridiculed by the very successful tradition of tarragon lamb – I have never seen it in Budapest, but then that could be said about many of the best dishes described in this book. The same division between town and country can be seen in the second of these mutton recipes. What would they know in Budapest about a vintage? The facts, perhaps; and possibly an anticipatory glow. But vintage around the Badacsony or the Mecsek is an air laden with the richest end-of-summer smells, weighty grapes, fresh must, and you are given every encouragement to laze over a special vintage mutton *gulyás*.

1 kg shoulder of lamb ($2\frac{1}{4}$ lbs.)
50g flour ($1\frac{1}{2}$ oz.)
6 tbs. sour cream
1 egg yolk
salt
1 large onion
60g butter (2 oz.)
2 tbs. fresh double cream
20g tarragon ($\frac{1}{2}$–$\frac{3}{4}$ oz.)
tarragon vinegar

Cut the meat into large cubes, wash them and cook them until they are tender in 1 litre (2 pints) salted water, with the onion.

Prepare a light *roux* from the butter and the flour, thin it gradually with some of the liquid in which the meat was cooked. Add this sauce to the meat and bring to the boil.

Mix the finely chopped tarragon with the cream and the egg yolk. Stir a very little tarragon vinegar into the sour cream and add this to the meat and sauce. After this it should not be allowed to boil.

Szüreti ürügulyás – Mutton Gulyás for Vintage

800g lean mutton (1¾ lbs.)
1 clove garlic
1 tsp. paprika powder
3 green peppers
2 tomatoes
salt
60g fat (2 oz.)
1 onion
a few caraway seeds
600g potatoes (1¼ lbs.)
2 dl white wine (⅜ pint)

Cube the mutton, place it in a pan, season with salt and put in the fat. Stirring all the time, fry over moderate heat for about 15 minutes.

Add the finely chopped onion, the chopped garlic, the caraway seeds and finally the paprika. Allow to cook gently for a few minutes more. Pour on enough water to cover and cook very slowly until the meat is tender.

When it is beginning to soften put in the sliced peppers, the tomatoes and the diced potatoes. Add the wine and taste for salt. In the last five minutes or so put in a few small *galuskas* made from 1 egg (*see* p. 127) and serve very hot.

Kunsági birkepaprikás – Cumanian Paprika Mutton

Mutton is a favourite meat in the Great Plain generally but in Cumania, in the centre, there is no getting away from it. *The* lamb stew uses immense proportions of fat and for serving it is topped with ¼–½ pint clotted sheep's milk. Since in Britain we do not normally have access to sheep's milk, here is a spicy mutton stew with more easily obtainable ingredients.

1 kg flank or shoulder of mutton (2¼ lbs.)
1 clove garlic
1 kg fresh cabbage (2 lbs.)
salt
1 chilli
100g fat (4 oz.)
1 onion
1 heaped tsp. paprika powder
60g smoked streaky bacon (2 oz.)
caraway seeds
1 tbs. tomato purée

Dice the bacon finely and fry it a little in the fat, adding the chopped onion. Remove from the heat, mix in the paprika and then the cubed meat. Add the bruised garlic and just a few caraway seeds, season well with salt and braise until it is about half ready.

Mix in the tomato *purée*, the shredded cabbage and the whole chilli, complete with seeds. Add just enough water to cover and then simmer until the liquid is much reduced.

Lakodalmas kása – Wedding Hash

For sheer spectacle and ceremony in Hungary I doubt whether anything can approach a rural wedding. There is no end to the details involved in the order of things and of course the wedding feast is at the centre of it all. Among the wealth of celebratory dishes, each jokingly introduced by a mock-serious rhyme, is the *kása* or hash. At one stage of the feast the cooks appear with their hands tied and plaintively moan that the hash has burnt their hands. The guests put money on to the wooden spoons the cooks hold straight out in front of them– this is called 'the price of the hash' or 'the price of the pot'.

3 goose legs
300g rice (11 oz.)
150g (5 oz.) vegetables (carrot, cabbage, mustard root . . .)
120g mushrooms (4 oz.)
salt and pepper
200g goose liver (6–7 oz.)
150g goose dripping (5 oz.)
1 small onion
90g celery (3 oz.)
a good bunch of parsley

Remove the meat from the leg bones and cube it.

Dice the vegetables and the celery and fry them with the finely chopped onion in 100g (3 oz.) of the dripping. Then add the goose meat, season with salt and freshly ground black pepper, cover and braise gently. Stir it occasionally.

When the meat begins to become tender, mix in the washed and salted rice; mix well. Then add the roughly chopped mushrooms and parsley and pour on water equal to twice the volume of the rice. Bring to the boil and then transfer to a moderate oven until it is ready – 15–30 minutes.

Slice the liver very finely and fry it in the remainder of the dripping. Place these slices on top of the 'hash' and sprinkle with the fat.

Bácskai rízses hús – Rice Hash from Bácska

Rice is done real justice in one bright recipe from Bácska. Hungarian paprika adds a slightly sharper flavour than turmeric or saffron and the colour is very welcoming.

600g lean, boneless pork (1 lb. 6 oz.)
120g onion (4 oz.)
5 green peppers
4 tomatoes
200g rice (7 oz.)
60g fat (2 oz.)
1 tsp. paprika powder
salt

Cube the meat. Chop the onion and fry it lightly in the fat. Sprinkle with the paprika powder, mix well and add 3 tablespoons cold water. Very gradually reduce liquid until only the fat remains and then put in the meat. Stir the meat about a bit and then add approximately 1 dl (¼ pint) water. Cover and let it cook at the slowest simmer.

Just before the meat is quite ready, mix in the rice, the chopped peppers and tomatoes, and water equal to 1½ times the volume of the rice. Season with salt, cover and finish in a moderate oven.

Decorate with fresh tomatoes and serve with lettuce salad.

Imagine blank walls, distempered, probably ochre; in the walls a high solid gate, giving away no secrets. Behind, however, is an open courtyard surrounded by one-storey cottages which, if you once succeed in getting into the courtyard, are as eager to reveal their character as the blank outside walls are to hide it. Verandas, roses, tinkly clatter of water pails, muted thuds from chopping boards.

Multiply by seventy and you have a Hungarian village. For the foreigner the idyll would perhaps be shattered by the sudden squeals escaping from behind the courtyard walls when a pig is being killed. But in the village household economy this is the event of the year – and in the towns they revel at the thought of the parcels which will arrive from the country relatives on such an occasion.

Perhaps even the wedding feast is surpassed by the *disznótor*, the dinner held after a pig has been killed. It has more warmth, and concentration on things culinary is less likely to be beset by distractions in other directions. Each district – or even each family – has its own special recipes for preparing *hurka* and *kolbász*, which are two of the main products of the hard day's work which follows the killing of the pig. *Kolbász* can loosely be translated as sausage: it is a pure mixture of chopped meat and fat, spiced with salt, pepper, paprika and a garlic infusion, and then pressed into the pig's small intestine, the cleaning of which is a particularly complicated operation requiring devoted, meticulous care. The basis of *hurka* can be liver, lung, liver and lung combined, or blood. Each variety is then given a liberal dose of fatty meat, a rice hash, a fatty liquid and spices. The mixture is pressed loosely into the sausage-case, simmered gently for 6–8 minutes to allow it to expand and then it is cooled. When it is to be prepared for eating it is first covered with cold dripping and allowed to warm up very slowly so that the skin will not crack. Then it is fried golden and crisp.

To give one recipe as an example, here is the combined lung and liver *hurka*.

Clean the boiled lung carefully, removing any thick veins and windpipe parts. Mince it together with about twice its volume of liver, which should first be boiled gently in an absolute minimum of water and then drained thoroughly, and some bits of fattier pork. Mix in about one third part boiled rice. The seasoning begins with salt, freshly ground black pepper and fried onion, but the real flavouring includes freshly ground allspice, one or two crushed cloves, 1–2 grated apples, about 50g (2 oz.) sultanas. Add some water in which a small lump of fatty bacon has been boiled to make a fairly mushy consistency, and loosely fill it into a sausage-case. Give it a good steaming and then cool it, or bring it just to the boil in water, remove it from the heat and allow it to cool down slowly.

Use good smoked streaky bacon dripping to fry the *hurka* for eating.

The blood *hurka* is seasoned with crushed dill seeds, savory, marjoram and fried onion, but as far as blood is concerned I have found this simple *pörkölt* recipe more interesting.

Vérpörkölt

blood of 1 goose or duck or 5 dl (1 pint) pig's blood
salt
60g fat (2 oz.)
1 large onion
paprika powder, or pepper

Fry the sliced onion lightly in the fat.

Slice or cube the congealed blood and add it to the onion. Season it with salt and pepper or paprika. Stirring continuously, fry it for 6–8 minutes.

Serve with potatoes which have been boiled and tossed in hot bacon dripping, and accompany with a salad such as cucumber.

Kenőmájas – Liver Paste

(literally means 'spreading liver')

In spite of the popularity in Hungary of the *hurka* and *kolbász*, the real delicacy of the *disznótor* feast is a liver paste.

This is a village recipe which is not simple but it is certainly of value to more experienced cooks. There is a more refined recipe for a liver paste in the Cold Table section.

Cut up the pig's liver into pieces and cook in abundant boiling water for 4–5 minutes.

Clean away any thick veins, etc. and while it is still warm, mince the liver finely twice, together with one third part pure fat (authentically from the pig), or with fatty bacon.

Add a few spoonfuls of water in which fatty bacon has been boiled, and some strained fat in which a finely chopped onion has been fried.

Season with salt and pepper.

Fill a sausage skin fairly loosely with this mixture and simmer it very gently for one hour. Pierce the skin only if and where air bubbles have gathered. The sausage is then usually put in cold water and cold smoked but it can be eaten straight away if you prefer. If it is smoked it will keep for a few weeks.

Pirított máj magyarosan – Hungarian Braised Liver

When a Hungarian cook wants to braise liver she usually chooses chicken livers, preferring to use pig's liver for recipes which require larger slices in one piece. The following recipe is a good way to treat any liver (whichever you choose).

½ kg liver (1 lb.)	120g onion (4 oz.)
½ tsp. paprika powder	60g fat (2 oz.)
freshly ground black pepper	salt
2 large sweet peppers	2 tomatoes

If you use pig or ox liver, cut it into thin strips; chicken livers can be sliced or left whole. Half-fry the chopped onion quickly over high heat, add the meat straight away and season with salt and the paprika. Allow to cook for a few minutes, stirring continuously, taking care that the paprika does not burn.

Clean and slice the sweet peppers, and add them with the sliced tomatoes. Season liberally with freshly ground black pepper. Cover and leave to braise at the gentlest simmer for about 10 minutes.

Serve with potatoes, with lightly fried chopped onion mixed in, and accompany with tomato salad.

Here is another of those surprise balls which sometimes come as an accompaniment floating on the soupier kinds of braised vegetable dishes, but this one also enjoys an individual life of its own and is best accompanied by fluffy rice and a juicy salad.

Májpuffancs – Liver Puff

200g liver (7 oz.)	2 eggs
1 tbs. flour	1 tbs. fine breadcrumbs
1 small onion	120g fat (4 oz.)
salt and pepper	chopped parsley

Grate the liver.

Fry the finely chopped onion lightly in a minimum of fat and add it to the liver with the 2 egg yolks, the flour and the breadcrumbs. Season with salt and pepper, finally putting in some parsley. Mix thoroughly.

Beat the egg whites until they are stiff and fold them into the liver mixture. Put tablespoons of the mixture in the hot fat and fry them until brown on both sides.

Hortobágyi palacsinta – Hortobágy Pancakes

The *palacsinta*, or pancake, is something of a happy refrain in the Hungarian kitchen. Before we go onto the more substantial steaks and chops, we must venture over the plain to the Hortobágy where they have, among other things, a famous 'bridge with nine holes', infinitely skilful horsemen, an even more infinite expanse of sheer flat space, and a very fine traditional pancake. The first three defy all verbal description and one simply has to go to see for oneself. But for the pancakes, here is the recipe.

½ kg veal (1 lb.)
1 level tbs. flour
200g onion (7 oz.)
paprika powder
120g bacon dripping (4 oz.)
2 dl sour cream (⅜ pint)
salt
10 pancakes (*see* p. 132)

Braise the cubed veal in the fat with the chopped onion and a liberal sprinkling of paprika powder. When the meat is tender, drain off the juices and mince the meat finely. Mix in half the juices again. Add 1–2 tablespoons sour cream and cook further in another pan until the mixture becomes like pulp.

Fill the pancakes with this mixture. Roll them up, folding in the ends, place them in a fireproof dish and heat thoroughly in a very hot oven for 5–10 minutes.

To the remaining half of the braising liquid add the flour mixed with the remaining sour cream, bring it to the boil and pour the mixture through a sieve. Pour this sauce over the pancakes and serve very hot in a long shallow dish – the pancakes should not overlap.

To accompany the *Hortobágyi palacsinta*, Hungarians like to reach for one of their best red wines such as *Szekszárdi burgundi*, *Villányi burgundi*, *Soproni kékfrankos* or *Egri bikavér* (Bull's Blood).

Steaks and Chops

The recipes which make up the second half of this chapter are concerned with steaks, chops, *escalopes*, whole pieces of meat. Perhaps when he wants to dine one stage better than 'everyday' but still without making it into a celebration, the average Hungarian would choose a *rántott borda*. This is a pork chop beaten out fairly thinly, given a breadcrumb coat and fried in deep fat. The relationship to the *Wiener Schnitzel* is not hard to notice and even though Hungarians moan nostalgically about the unavailability of veal, they ought to be proud of their pork, which must be the best in the world, and competes very favourably in its golden breadcrumb coat with its more famous Viennese brother. Slices of liver cooked in this way also count as one up on the ordinary, and carp steaks cooked by this method are extremely good.

Pork chop recipes range from the 'peasant style' to that using Tokaj wine, and, as always, Transylvania has its contribution to make.

Sertésborda parasztosan – Peasant Pork Chops

1 kg pork chops (2 lbs.)
120g fat (4 oz.)
150g onion (5 oz.)
1 kg potatoes (2 lbs.)
20g salt (¾ oz.)
1½ tbs. flour
150g smoked streaky bacon (5 oz.)
parsley

Dip the chops in flour and brown them quickly on both sides in the fat. Strain off the fat. Add a very little boiling water to some of the fat. Put this back onto the meat and braise it gently until required for serving.

Heat the remainder of the fat and fry the diced bacon in it. Then put in the chopped onion and fry until both the bacon and the onion are golden brown. Again strain off the fat and fry the raw potatoes in it – they should be cut into small cubes. Remove them from the pan onto kitchen paper to drain and then mix well with the bacon and onion, adding a little chopped parsley.

Place the chops in the centre of a warm serving dish, surround them with the potato mixture, pour the juices over and decorate with any seasonal salad.

Sertésborda hentes módra – Pork Chops Butcher Style

1 kg pork chops (2 lbs.)
20g salt (¾ oz.)
3–4 tbs. flour
tomato purée
half a small cucumber preserved in vinegar
120g smoked fatty bacon (4 oz.)
150g fat (5 oz.)
120g ham (4 oz.)
1 large or 2 medium onions
freshly ground black pepper
chopped parsley

Beat out the chops until they are thin, season with salt and pepper, dip them in flour on both sides and brown them quickly in half the fat.

The recipe requires a relatively large amount of fat – the pork chops do tend to be smothered in it, but the fat becomes very well flavoured and the quantity given should be adhered to. Set aside.

Put a little tomato *purée* (½–1 tablespoon) in the fat, thin it with a little water, bring it to the boil, mixing well, and strain it onto the chops. Then let the meat simmer very slowly.

Cut the bacon, ham and cucumber into thin strips. Fry the onion and bacon a little in the remaining fat, give the ham a toss in the fat and then mix in the cucumber. Add a little chopped parsley and pepper. Place evenly on top of the half-cooked chops and continue to braise them gently until they are tender.

Magyaros Szűzérmék – Hungarian Veal Steaks

One characteristic and rather fiery dish which restaurants tend to excel in is *magyaros szűzérmék* – originally the meat used was small round steaks of veal ('*szűz*' means virgin) but nowadays this is replaced by equally small and much tastier pieces of pork. At its best the dish glistens with pure pork dripping and cooks like to waive restraint here when it comes to chillis. The meat is fried very quickly in abundant dripping and then removed from the pan. A chopped onion and thinly sliced raw potatoes are fried in the same fat, with a liberal sprinkling of paprika powder and chilli powder. To serve, this glowing mixture is heaped over the meat: accompany with thick chunks of strong bread, and a light wine.

Temesvári sertésborda – Temesvár Pork Chops

The two Transylvanian recipes which follow are milder but with very distinct characters of their own. Temesvár is a town in what was Transylvanian Hungary and, like Kolozsvár, lends its name to various dishes, such as this one for pork chops with green beans.

4 pork chops	½ kg green beans (1 lb.)
1 onion	60g fat (2 oz.)
2 sweet peppers	60g smoked streaky bacon (2 oz.)
2 dl sour cream (⅜ pint)	2 tomatoes
½ tsp. flour	salt and paprika powder

Beat the chops out a little, dip them in flour and fry them quickly on both sides until they are lightly browned.

Put the chops aside and fry the finely chopped onion with the bacon, which should be cut into strips. Sprinkle with a little paprika powder and add the green beans, cut in three or four, and the sliced peppers. Season with salt, place the chops on top, put a minimum of water in to prevent sticking and simmer very gently.

When the beans begin to soften, put in the chopped tomatoes.

Once the meat and the beans are quite tender and the liquid much reduced, sprinkle on ½ teaspoon flour and pour in the sour cream. Thin with a little water if necessary and bring just to the boil. Serve immediately.

Székely sertésborda – Székely Pork Chops

With Székely cooking, sour cabbage, sour cream and fresh dill leaves are never far away. Here they all come together to give a completely individual pork-chop dish.

4 pork chops
2½ dl sour cream (½ pint)
1 clove garlic
salt
caraway seeds
flour
60g fat (2 oz.)
¾ kg soured cabbage (*see* p. 85) (1½ lbs.)
1 onion
paprika powder
dill leaves

Salt the chops, dip them in flour and seal them on both sides in the fat. Set them aside in another pan.

Fry the chopped onion in the fat, sprinkle with paprika powder, add a little water and then reduce gradually to fat again over moderate heat. Put in the bruised garlic and a few crushed caraway seeds and pour over the chops. Add a little water, cover and simmer for 10 minutes.

Put in the cabbage and continue to braise until both meat and cabbage are ready. Mix two thirds of the cream with about 1 teaspoon flour and mix this in. Season with salt, and simmer for 5 minutes.

To serve, first set out the chops, heap the cabbage on the chops and pour on the juices. Sprinkle the remaining sour cream on top and finally some finely chopped fresh dill.

Tokaji sertésborda – Tokaj Pork Chops

If you know the price at which the better Tokaj wines sell, you may not even bother to read the next recipe! You can, however, like most people in Hungary, replace 'the king of wines' with a sweet white wine of your own choice and still end up with a good dish. If you do find real Tokaj wine, it is best to use the *szamorodni*, although the *furmint* will disappoint nobody and it is much cheaper.

1 kg small loin pork chops (2 lbs.)
1 tbs. flour
1½ kg red cabbage (3 lbs.)
250g apples (8 oz.)
1 tsp. vinegar
1 onion
60g smoked streaky bacon (2 oz.)
1 tbs. tomato purée
100g bacon dripping (3 oz.)
3 dl Tokaj wine (a good ½ pint)
sugar
salt

Beat out 9 or 10 thin pork chops, salt them and dip them in flour.

Fry them in the dripping (or in oil) over fierce heat to seal them. Set them aside in another pan.

Cook the tomato *purée* in the fat for a minute or two; add, gradually, 2 dl (⅜ pint) cold water and a third of the wine. Bring to the boil, pour over the chops, cover and braise quietly until the meat is tender.

Cut the stem out of the cabbage and shred it finely. Salt it lightly and let it stand for half an hour.

Dice the bacon and fry it crisp in a minimum of fat. Add the vinegar, some chopped onion and a little water. Put in the cabbage, sugar it lightly and braise it. Add the peeled and sliced apples, the remainder of the wine and continue to braise until the cabbage has softened.

Serve the cabbage and the chops on a large plate, sprinkle with the juices and accompany with roast potatoes.

Beef

Slices of beef from the sirloin or rump steak are treated in an attractive variety of ways in the Hungarian kitchen, beginning with the straightforward *Hagymás hátszin*, a lightly floured rump steak with onions. The onions are cut into rings, sprinkled with flour and fried golden in plenty of dripping. When they are ready, they are drained and separated so that they will retain their crispness.

The next three recipes are also based on rump steaks or thick slices of sirloin.

Szegedi rostélyos – Szeged Steak (or *Serpenyős rostélyos* – Pot steak)

4 steaks – about ½ kg (1 lb.)	90g fat (3 oz.)
2 green peppers	1 onion
2 tomatoes	¾ kg potatoes (1½ lbs.)
caraway seeds	paprika powder
sour cream	salt, pepper

Season the steaks with salt and pepper and dip them lightly in flour. Fry them quickly on both sides over fierce heat in a little fat and then remove them from the pan onto a plate.

Add the remainder of the fat to the pan and fry the chopped onion in it lightly. Sprinkle with 1 level tablespoon paprika powder, mix well and thin with a little water. Add a good pinch of caraway seeds, return the meat to the pan, cover and braise slowly.

When the meat is nearly ready, put in the sliced peppers, tomatoes and potatoes. Add water so that the contents of the pan are *half* covered. Simmer until the potatoes are ready.

To serve place the meat on the individual plates first and heap the vegetables on top, finishing with the merest sprinkling of sour cream.

Eszterházy rostélyos – Eszterházy Steak

4 rump or sirloin steaks
1 tbs. flour
3 tbs. white wine
6 tbs. sour cream
1 tbs. French mustard
salt, sugar, parsley, paprika powder
60g fat (2 oz.)
1 small onion
150g vegetables (carrot, parsley root, celery etc.) (5 oz.)
1 bay leaf

Fry the meat quickly, as described in the preceding recipe. Set it aside and fry the chopped onion in the fat. Place the meat on the onions, season with salt and add a very little water so that the meat can be braised. Add the sliced vegetables, a large pinch of paprika powder and the bay leaf.

When the vegetables have softened add the wine and reduce the liquid until only the fat remains. Sprinkle on the flour and mix in well with the sour cream. Add a pinch of sugar and the mustard.

Garnish with parsley and serve with noodles.

Csáky rostélyos – Csáky Steak

4 rump or sirloin steaks
300g tomatoes (10 oz.)
4 eggs
3 dl sour cream (½ pint)
paprika powder
100g fat or oil (3 oz.)
2–3 sweet peppers
2 onions
1 tbs. flour
salt

The following dish was created in memory of Sándor Csáky, an outstanding Hungarian chef.

Use a little of the fat for frying the chopped onions. Add one sliced pepper and all but one of the tomatoes. Braise for 5 minutes.

Beat the eggs and pour them over the vegetables. Allow to cook very slowly until the eggs begin to set without stirring them any more than necessary.

Beat out the meat slices and spread the egg mixture evenly over each slice. Season with salt, roll up the meat and tie with thread.

Heat the remainder of the fat. Brown the meat rolls all over in it and fry a little more chopped onion with them. Sprinkle with paprika, pour on a little bone stock, or water, and cover to simmer gently. Later add 1–2 sweet peppers and 1 tomato, chopped.

When the meat has become tender, reduce the liquid until only the fat remains. Sprinkle on a little flour, mix in the sour cream, bring to the boil and simmer for a few minutes.

Take out the meat rolls and remove the threads. Slice thinly and serve in a shallow dish surrounded by the sauce.

Serve with *galuskas*.

Vadas Bélszín – Steak Game Style

Although a description of how to prepare wild boar would be superfluous, this next recipe is quite straightforward and is called 'Steak Game Style'. This meat dish should be served with *zsemle-gombóc*, roll dumplings (*see* p. 116), with a little chopped fresh parsley worked into the dough.

½ kg porterhouse steak (1¼ lbs.)
2 tbs. flour
2 dl sour cream (⅜ pint)
salt
60g streaky bacon (2 oz.)
60g dripping (2 oz.)
1 tsp. sugar
mustard

For the marinade

200g carrots and parsley root mixed (7 oz.)
1 onion
salt and peppercorns
2 tbs. wine vinegar
1 bay leaf

To make the marinade, slice the vegetables, including the onion, and parboil them in about 1 litre (1¾ pints) water with salt and a few whole black peppercorns. Remove from the heat, put in the vinegar and bay leaf and pour over the meat – in winter while the liquid is still warm, in summer cool it first. Leave the meat in the marinade for 2–3 days in a cold place, covered. Give it a stir occasionally.

When you are ready to cook it, lard the steak with thin strips of the bacon. Smear cold dripping all over the meat and roast in the oven until it is about half cooked.

Then put in the vegetables from the marinade, add a little of the liquid and braise until the vegetables are quite ready and the liquid is reduced so that only the fat remains.

Put the meat aside and prepare the sauce. Sprinkle the flour over the vegetables, let it cook for about 5 minutes, gradually add the marinade liquid and then cook gently for a few minutes.

Roast the sugar until it is brown, add a little water to smooth it out and put it into the sauce. A few drops of vinegar, or a vinegar mustard, are also added for flavour and finally the sour cream.

Slice the meat thickly, place in a serving dish and pour the sauce over it. Macaroni is an acceptable accompaniment, if you do not want to prepare the bread dumplings.

Stefánia marhasült – Stefania Roast Beef

Another recipe using steak in the piece – a roll in which Hungarian cooks sometimes prefer to compromise by replacing the steak by minced meat formed into a roll. The real thing, however, is decidedly the real thing.

1 kg steak in the piece (2 lbs.)
300g mixed vegetables (10 oz.)
5–6 tbs. red wine
1½ tbs. flour
salt, pepper, sugar
3 hard boiled eggs
120g onion (4 oz.)
1 clove garlic
120g fat (4 oz.)
tomato purée

Slice a large horizontal opening in the meat with a very sharp knife. Stuff the chopped eggs tightly inside and fix the opening firmly with small wooden skewers.

Season the meat with salt and pepper and fry it quickly on all sides in the fat. Set aside.

Brown a little sugar in the fat, put in the sliced vegetables, onion and garlic, and fry them for a few minutes. Sprinkle with the flour, season with more pepper and continue to fry gently. Finally add a little tomato *purée* and the wine and add more water if necessary to give a thin sauce. Adjust seasoning, bring to the boil and pour over the meat.

Cover and cook in the oven until the meat is tender.

If you decide to use a mince roll instead, make it from minced beef, breadcrumbs, and bacon, seasoned with some nutmeg and lemon rind as well as the customary salt and pepper. The meat mixture, which must be fairly firm, is rolled out into an oblong. Spread the stuffing over the meat and then roll it up Swiss-roll fashion and pour the sauce over it.

Mustos pecsenye – Steak with Must

For the last beef recipe I return to the vineyards where at vintage time one can always be sure of some must, which lends such a unique character to any dish. This kind of recipe is not very familiar to Hungarians in the large towns but nobody in the country misses the autumn opportunity.

$\frac{3}{4}$ kg rump steak in a piece ($1\frac{3}{4}$ lbs.)
120g smoked streaky bacon (4 oz.)
2 dl red wine ($\frac{3}{8}$ pint)
2 tbs. bilberry jelly
2 tbs. flour
1 tsp. sugar
bay leaf
200g mixed vegetables (7 oz.)
120g onion (4 oz.)
$\frac{1}{2}$ litre must ($\frac{3}{4}$–1 pint)
1 tbs. tomato purée
2 cloves garlic
salt and peppercorns
thyme

Dice and fry the bacon.

Salt the meat and seal it in the bacon fat. Set it aside.

Fry the chopped onion and the sliced mixed vegetables in the fat with the garlic, a few whole peppercorns and a bayleaf. Sprinkle with the flour and cook for about 5 minutes.

Gradually add the must and the red wine.

Lastly add the tomato *purée* and the bilberry jelly, the sugar, and perhaps a pinch of thyme, and then pour the sauce over the meat. Bring to the boil, cover and braise on very low heat until the meat is quite tender and the vegetables cooked through.

Lamb

For lamb and mutton dishes I have not found anything in Hungary to match this subtle combination of roast lamb with asparagus.

Báránycomb spárgával – Roast Leg of Lamb with Asparagus

1 kg leg of lamb (2 lbs.)	600g fresh asparagus (1¼ lbs.)
100g butter (4 oz.)	60g fat (2 oz.)
salt and black pepper	parsley, chives, orange rind, thyme

Have the bone removed from the leg of lamb, leaving only the knuckle. Wash the meat well and dry it. Smear some spices of your own choice into the space left by removing the bone and then re-shape and tie the leg. Season with salt and pepper and perhaps a little thyme, pour the heated fat over it and roast the lamb in the usual way. When it is about half done (after 20–30 minutes, depending on the temperature at which you are cooking it) spread grated orange rind over it.

Meanwhile clean and tie the asparagus in bundles and cook it until it is tender in salted boiling water with a good pinch of sugar. The asparagus will take about 25–30 minutes to cook.

Season the parsley and some chives lightly with salt and pepper, chop them finely together and mix them thoroughly with half the butter. Form into a cylinder and put this in the refrigerator to be-come firm. For serving, place a slice of the butter cylinder on each slice of the hot meat.

Drain the asparagus well, melt the other half of the butter and pour it over the asparagus. Serve with a very mildly vinegared lettuce salad.

Chicken

Although *grillcsirke* – whole chickens publicly and enticingly roasted on rotary barbecues – has become a popular fashion in recent years in Hungary, it can neither oust nor compare with the best of the traditional Hungarian fowl dishes. A fairly everyday delight is *paprikás csirke*, where the chicken pieces are braised with onion and paprika powder in *pörkölt* style; the liquid is then reduced and a good half pint of sour cream mixed in. I have replaced it here with this recipe for a much richer dish based on the same principle.

Csirkeragu – Chicken Ragoût

1 chicken about 2 kg (4½ lbs.)
1 clove garlic
150g fat (5 oz.)
salt
1 tomato
paprika powder
150g onion (5 oz.)
180–200g mushrooms (6 oz.)
2½ dl sour cream (½ pint)
1 sweet pepper

For the galuskas

½ kg flour (1 lb.)
2 eggs
60g butter (2 oz.)

For the salad

¾ kg cucumber (1½ lbs.)
freshly ground black pepper
chives
1 clove garlic
1 tbs. vinegar
1 tbs. oil

Cut up the chicken into pieces, putting the liver aside.

Melt three quarters of the fat in a pan and fry the chopped onion in it with one clove of garlic. Sprinkle with paprika. Put in the chicken pieces, season with salt, cover and braise – give it an occasional stir and add a small quantity of water from time to time as necessary.

Quarter the mushrooms and braise them in a little fat, seasoning them with salt and pepper.

Add the sliced tomato and green pepper to the chicken pieces when they are about half ready.

Prepare the salad, *see* below. For the *galuskas* for this chicken dish it is better to separate the eggs, folding in the beaten whites just before breaking off the *galuskas* into the boiling water they are to be cooked in.

When the chicken is almost ready add the chicken livers, the mushrooms and finally the sour cream. Serve in a hot deep tureen, putting the *galuskas* in a separate heated dish and remembering side dishes for the salad.

Salad

Peel the cucumbers and slice very thinly. Hungarians use the word 'planing' for this – the slices are wafer thin. Salt these slices and set them aside for half an hour. Then press the liquid gently away and mix the cucumber with 1 tablespoon good wine vinegar and 1 tablespoon oil. Place in a wide shallow salad bowl and sprinkle liberally with freshly ground black pepper, finely chopped chives and a little paprika powder. Place the other garlic clove in the centre. Put the salad in the refrigerator until serving and then remove the garlic clove.

Mandulás töltött csirke – Chicken with Almond Stuffing

1 chicken (4 lbs.)
60g fat (2 oz.)
60g butter (2 oz.)
2 dl milk ($\frac{3}{8}$ pint)
ginger
flour
2 rolls
2 eggs
100g almonds (4 oz.)
salt and freshly ground black pepper
tomato purée

Clean the chicken and loosen the skin by moving the fingers very gently in under the breast between the flesh and the skin. Take care that the skin does not become broken at any point during the cleaning or loosening.

Soak the rolls in milk for a few minutes and then squeeze any surplus milk out of them and break them up.

Beat the butter and the eggs together until they are creamy.

Put the almonds in boiling water so that the skin will come off more easily. Drain, skin and chop them roughly. Add the rolls and the almonds to the egg mixture, season with salt, a little black pepper and a good pinch of freshly ground ginger, and mix thoroughly. Press this filling evenly in under the chicken skin. Roast the chick en in the usual way.

Mix 1 teaspoon concentrated tomato *purée* into the fat, whisk in a pinch of flour and let it simmer for a few minutes. Gradually thin with half a glass of water. Season and serve with the roast chicken.

Fatányéros – Wooden Platter

The *fatányéros,* originally a Transylvanian tradition, is a sumptuous meat orgy indulged in and served grandly on its enormous wooden platter by even the most modest of restaurants. It is based on at least two different meats and sometimes also contains liver fried in batter.

300g slender pork chops off the bone (10 oz.)
1½ tbs. flour
150g fat (5 oz.)
300g veal rump steak (10 oz.)
300g sirloin, off the bone (10 oz.)
250g smoked lean bacon with the rind on (8 oz.), salt

Slice the meats thickly and beat them out well. Season with salt, dip them in flour and brown them quickly on both sides in the fat. Put in the bacon, making small incisions in the rind to prevent it from curling.

Round the perimeter of a large serving plate – it must be wooden to be authentic – place preserved red cabbage, peppers, tomatoes, ridge cucumbers and beetroot slices. In the centre of the dish heap freshly fried chips. On the potatoes place the various meats alternately and top with the bacon.

Rablóhús – Robber's Meat

The Hungarian summer is a healthy, dry, flat heat. It is lazing on verandas or rushing to Lake Balaton for week-ends, and, most pertinent of all, it is *szalonna sütés,* which is not only a summer occupation but – mosquitoes permitting – an unparalleled culinary experience.

Thick strips about 4 inches long are cut from a large piece of pure bacon fat, with skin on it but not with meat, and generous incisions make it into something of a cock's-comb. In the garden everyone gathers round a charcoal fire which has already passed the flaming stage. Pinning your strip of fat on a long fork, you hold it close to the glowing embers and when the fat begins to run you let it drip off onto a chunk of bread in your other hand. Then you can bite off the appropriate bit of the bread adding a slice of raw onion and a bite of vinegary cucumber, while you return the bacon fat to the fire to get more drips ready.

An extension of this is to impale thick steaks on the end of long pointed hazel sticks and roast them with onions over the embers. This is given the romantic name of *rablóhús* – robber's meat. As with all outdoor eating, the danger is always present that when things that are meant to be simple begin to become complicated, frustration often wins the day and you are more apt to remember the mosquitoes than the food. But with adequate foresight and preparation there is no reason why bacon should not be roasted very enjoyably in this way – in Britain there are fewer mosquitoes to cope with and you may be lucky enough to have a real summer evening!

Salads

Hungarian salads are always served in a separate individual side-dish for each person. The characteristic feature of the modern Hungarian salads is the juicy dressing which more or less covers the vegetable. Although the general theory is to take one part wine vinegar to two parts water, I have never been given a salad with anything approaching this proportion of vinegar in the dressing. For practical purposes I find the best way of achieving results which are typical is to count 1 teaspoon good wine vinegar to 3–4 tablespoons water for each individual portion. These proportions may vary from family to family but all Hungarian salads are certainly variations on this theme.

The basic seasoning is a good pinch of salt and precisely the same amount of sugar. Freshly ground black pepper is also fairly usual and other ingredients which commonly find their way into the dressing are a very slight proportion of oil (1 teaspoon to 1 tablespoon), chopped onion, paprika powder, chives and sour cream. The slightly tangy salads which this dressing produces are an integral part of any Hungarian meal. A restaurant waiter will always expect you to choose a particular salad to go with whatever meat or vegetable dish you order – which is not without its wisdom since some of the heavier, richer or fierier dishes can only be fully appreciated in the presence of a complete contrast such as the right salad provides.

The basic dressing, then, per individual portion, requires 1 teaspoon wine vinegar, 3–4 tablespoons water, a good pinch of salt to taste and the same amount of sugar. This is what is meant when the recipes which follow refer to 'the dressing'. Any special variation will be found in the individual recipes but one may freely add a good pinch of freshly ground black pepper to the basic dressing whether any particular recipe calls for it or not.

Fejes saláta – Lettuce Salad

Count one quarter of a large lettuce per person. Wash and quarter the lettuce. Place the quarters in individual dishes. Prepare the dressing, adjusting the seasoning to taste. Pour liberally over the lettuce.

Uborkasaláta – Cucumber Salad

Peel ½ kg (1 lb.) cucumber and slice it thinly. Salt it lightly and set it aside for half an hour. Then gently squeeze away the juice.

Place the cucumber slices in individual dishes and pour the salad dressing over it, with very little or no salt in the dressing. There should be enough dressing in each portion for the cucumber to be *almost* covered – aim at creating the effect that the cucumber slices are lightly floating.

Chop half an onion finely and mix it in. Sprinkle the top liberally with freshly ground black pepper and a good pinch of paprika powder.

In some parts of the Great Plain, sour cream is sprinkled over cucumber salad. This salad is customary if the main dish has a fairly heavy fat content.

Paradicsomsaláta – Tomato Salad

Slice as many tomatoes as you need. Chop 1 onion finely. Mix the onion and the tomato slices together and place some of the mixture in the appropriate number of individual dishes.

Pour on the salad dressing, in this case thinned down a little more with additional water. Add about 1 teaspoon olive oil to each portion and mix it in gently.

In tomato salad freshly ground black pepper is given a slight emphasis among the flavourings.

Paprikasaláta – Pepper Salad

Clean the peppers and slice them into thin rings. Salt them lightly and set them aside for about 1 hour.

Pour on the dressing, from which the salt should be omitted in this case. Keep chilled for about 1 hour before using.

If the peppers are strong don't rinse them in boiling water for a minute as is often suggested: it is much better to salt them, leave them for 10–15 minutes and then gently squeeze away the juice and salt. This way they lose their strength but not their taste.

Sültpaprika saláta – Roast Pepper Salad

This is an unusual speciality for which you need the fleshiest kind of peppers. Wash them and without removing the seeds place them whole on a hotplate, stems and all, moving them about until the peppers are soft and the outer skin loosens. Dip each in cold water for a moment and then pull off this outer skin.

Make the salad dressing with a little more water than usual and add a little oil. Pour it over the peppers and leave for half an hour before serving.

Slices of tomato are often used as decoration in this salad.

Káposztasaláta – Cabbage Salad

Shred the cabbage, season evenly with salt and set aside for an hour. Squeeze away the juice gently.

Prepare the dressing, bring it quickly to the boil and pour it immediately over the cabbage. Mix in 1 chopped onion and at least ½ teaspoon caraway seeds. Chill before serving.

If red cabbage is used it should first be drenched well in boiling water.

For a different salad using cabbage, soured cabbage is mixed with onion rings and caraway seeds and then sprinkled with pure sunflower seed oil. This goes particularly well with drier vegetable dishes and potato dishes.

Céklasaláta – Beetroot Salad

Wash the beetroot and cook them in boiling water as usual – or, better still, bake them in a slow or moderate oven. Plunge them into cold water and remove the skins. Slice the beetroot and pour on the dressing with more than the usual amount of vinegar. Flavour liberally with caraway seeds and a little grated horseradish. This salad can be bottled and kept for several days.

Burgonyasaláta – Potato Salad

Boil and slice $\frac{1}{2}$ kg (1 lb.) potatoes. Place the slices in a large serving dish.

Mix 1$\frac{1}{2}$ tablespoons French mustard with 1 teaspoon castor sugar and 2–3 tablespoons tarragon vinegar. Season with salt and thin with a little water, adding 1 tablespoon sour cream. Pour this mixture over the potatoes and leave for 1–2 hours.

Decorate with slices of hard boiled egg.

Karfiolsaláta – Cauliflower Salad

600g cauliflower (1$\frac{1}{4}$ lbs.)	6 tbs. oil
120g tomato purée (4 oz.)	1 lemon
6 tbs. white wine	1 small onion
salt and freshly ground pepper	1 clove garlic
thyme	basil

Separate the cauliflower into its individual sprigs, wash them well and bring them to the boil in salted water. Drain well.

Meanwhile fry the chopped onion lightly in the oil. Add the chopped garlic and the tomato *purée*. Allow the mixture to heat through and then thin with the wine, seasoning immediately with salt, pepper, thyme and a very little basil. Add a small piece of lemon rind and a little lemon juice.

Put in the cauliflower, cover and simmer as gently as possible until the cauliflower is completely cooked. Chill and serve decorated with parsley.

Vegetables

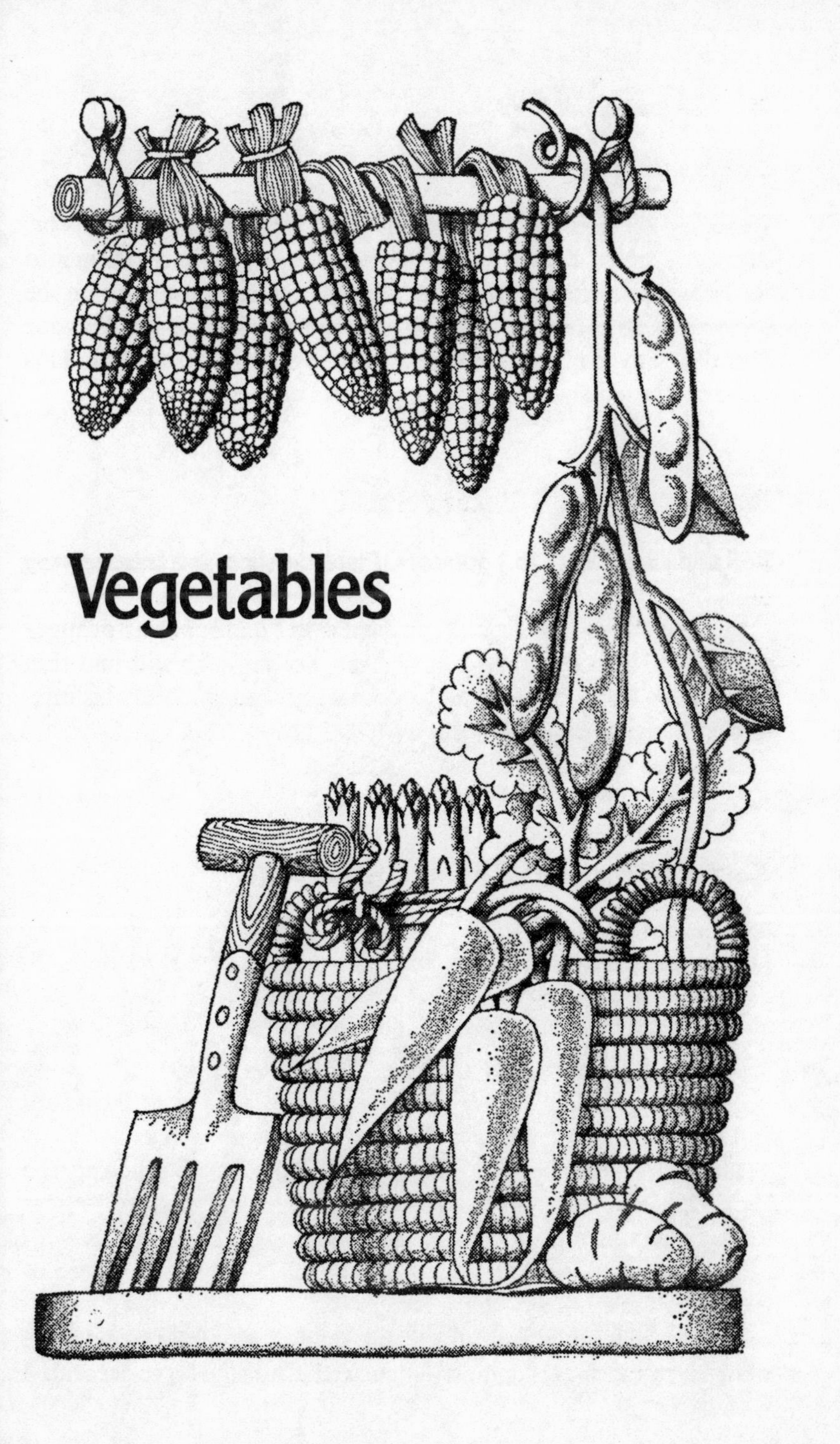

We are nowadays fully aware that food involves science, its preparation is considered an art, and eating it ought as often as possible to be centred on a sense of occasion. This enthusiasm is seldom lacking in Hungary, and combined with a fine sense of simplicity it makes even the most summary meal a real experience. Hungarians tend to consider everyday *British* ways with vegetables not a little monotonous – I think the variety of their own everyday vegetable recipes offers some truly wonderful ideas to prove their point.

The basic Hungarian way of cooking any vegetable is, first, to fry it lightly in bacon dripping. A little water is then added and the vegetable simmered until it is completely cooked. A light *roux* is mixed in and the dish served with a slice of meat, usually pork, floating on top. Other accompaniments occasionally replace the slice of pork and some of these are described at the end of this chapter.

Cauliflower

Kirántott karfiol – Cauliflower Fritters

Separate out the individual flowers of a large cauliflower and cook them in boiling salted water, taking care not to overcook them, so that they can still be handled easily.

Drain them well, season them lightly with salt and dip each sprig in flour, beaten egg and then breadcrumbs. Fry in abundant hot fat until the breadcrumbs are brown.

Set the cauliflower fritters out on a serving dish, sprinkle with a little grated cheese and serve with rice.

Karfioltekercs – Cauliflower Roulade

This recipe I found a bit tricky at first: it tastes good, however, even if it falls to bits. Perseverance helps towards making it look as good as it tastes.

First prepare the filling.

Filling

½ kg cauliflower (1 lb)	6 tbs. sour cream
1 tbs. grated cheese	50–60g finely chopped ham (2 oz.)

Cook the cauliflower in boiling salted water. Once it has just softened, drain it, chop it and break it down finely. Mix it with the finely chopped ham, about 2 tablespoons of the sour cream, and the cheese.

Roll

50g butter or bacon dripping (2 oz)	80g flour (3 oz.)
3 eggs	½ litre milk (1 pint)
salt	

Make a thick white sauce from the fat, flour and milk. Allow it to cool; then mix in the egg yolks. Beat the egg whites until they are stiff and fold them into the sauce mixture. Spread this about half an inch thick on a well greased and floured baking sheet and bake in a hot oven for 10–15 minutes. The baking must be fast to prevent the mixture from drying out and becoming brittle. Lift it carefully out onto a damp cloth, spread it with the filling and roll it up. The filling should cover no more than three quarters of the baked base. Return the roll to the oven for a few minutes for the filling to heat through. Serve on a long dish and cut into thick slices. Over these sprinkle the rest of the sour cream.

Kelvirág vajas morzsával – Cauliflower with Fried Crumbs

To return to individual cauliflower sprigs, here is a gritty sort of dish which does a lot to emphasize the texture as well as the taste of the vegetable.

1 kg cauliflower (2 lbs.)
3 tbs. fine breadcrumbs
90g unsalted butter (3 oz.)
20g salt ($\frac{1}{2}$–$\frac{3}{4}$ oz.)

Separate the cauliflower into its individual sprigs, boil them in salted water until they are almost soft. Place them in a greased fireproof dish.

Fry the breadcrumbs deep golden in half the butter, sprinkle them over the cauliflower and heat through in a moderate oven for 10 minutes, seasoning well with the salt. Before serving, dot the rest of the butter on top.

Karfiolpörkölt – Braised Cauliflower

Karfiolpörkölt represents application of a basic Hungarian method to a vegetable which is, I think, less suited to cauliflower than mushrooms, for example: but since it is so basic it is well worth including it.

1 kg cauliflower (2 lbs.)
1 small onion
salt
60g bacon dripping (2 oz.)
1 heaped tsp. paprika powder

Separate the cauliflower into its individual sprigs and clean them.

Fry the finely chopped onion lightly in the fat until it becomes transparent. Sprinkle on the paprika and let it fry gently for a few minutes, stirring it about all the time. Then put in the cauliflower sprigs, season with salt and mix well to get the cauliflower well covered with the paprika and fat.

Add the minimum of water – a few tablespoons – to the pan and braise the cauliflower until it softens. If necessary add one or two tablespoons of water while the cauliflower is cooking.

Serve with rice.

Rakott karfiol – Layered Cauliflower

1 kg cauliflower (2 lbs.)
50g dripping (1$\frac{1}{2}$ oz.)
1 tsp. chopped onion
salt
400g lean pork (13 oz.)
2 dl tomato juice ($\frac{3}{8}$ pint)
1 level tbs. flour
2 dl bone or beef stock ($\frac{3}{8}$ pint)

Separate the individual flowers of the cauliflower and cook them in a little boiling salted water until they just begin to soften.

Mince the pork. Fry the onion lightly in 20g ($\frac{1}{2}$ oz.) of the dripping, and then add the meat. Cover and braise the meat in its own juices, adding an occasional tablespoonful of water if necessary, until it is tender.

In a greased fireproof dish make alternate layers of the cauliflower sprigs and the minced meat.

Prepare a *roux* from the rest of the fat and the flour and add the tomato juice. Thin the sauce with about 2 dl ($\frac{3}{8}$ pint) bone or beef stock, and pour the sauce over the layers in the dish.

Heat through in a hot oven for about 10 minutes.

Cauliflower and Potatoes

Since I found this next recipe, I have kept cauliflower cheese solely as an accompaniment. For an independent dish this Hungarian combination of cauliflower and potatoes has definite advantages.

$\frac{1}{2}$ kg potatoes (1 lb.)
5 eggs
100g grated cheese (3–4 oz.)
salt

$\frac{3}{4}$ kg cauliflower ($1\frac{1}{2}$ lbs.)
2 dl sour cream ($\frac{3}{8}$ pint)
50g fine breadcrumbs ($1\frac{1}{2}$ oz.)
50g butter ($1\frac{1}{2}$ oz.)

Separate the cauliflower into its individual sprigs and cook them in lightly salted boiling water. Boil the potatoes in their skins and boil three eggs hard.

Beat the other two eggs and add the sour cream to them, seasoning with a little salt.

Slice the peeled potatoes and the hard boiled eggs thinly. Grease a fireproof dish with some of the butter and sprinkle the surface with breadcrumbs. Fill the dish with a layer of potatoes, a layer of egg slices and a layer of cauliflower on top. Sprinkle each layer liberally with grated cheese and then pour on the cream and egg mixture once the top layer has been put on and given its cheese coating.

Bake in a fairly hot oven for 20–30 minutes until the top is golden brown. Just before serving dot knobs of the remaining butter on top.

Cabbage

In Hungary cabbage as often as not means *soured* cabbage. Although it is now possible to buy good sour cabbage in Britain, the best is undoubtedly that prepared at home. Since it was Mária Széchenyi who initiated me into the whole process of souring cabbage, you will find below not precisely what the Hungarian cookery books suggest – which I have not tested – but what she incontestably lays down – which I have. *Savanyú káposzta*, sour cabbage, from Vecsés has something of the reputation within its own sphere which Parma has for ham, but, since you will probably not want to sour cabbage by the barrel (and, in accordance with Hungarian tradition, put your smallest child into the barrel to stamp down the layers one by one), use an open-mouthed sweet-jar for the purpose.

Savanyú káposzta – Souring Cabbage

Strip off any outer fading leaves and remove the thick hard inner stem from one or two white cabbages. Shred the cabbage – it should be firm and mature. First of all into the jar put a layer of raw potato slices in the bottom. Then to every 1 kg (2 lbs.) cabbage count 30g (1 oz.) salt, mix them well together and press this salted cabbage evenly and firmly down into the jar layer by layer. To taste, put a few bay leaves, peppers, peppercorns, caraway seeds and dill seeds in between the layers. Mária Széchenyi puts a good big piece of horseradish in the middle, about 3–4 inches long – she claims the cabbage keeps longer this way.

On top place a whole cabbage leaf: since not all of us live on the edge of a quarry this is easier than coping with the large flat stones which are traditionally set to press down the cabbage. Once it is salted the cabbage should give out enough juice to cover itself, but if at any time there is not enough liquid to cover the cabbage during the maturation process, make it up with lightly salted water, first boiled and then allowed to cool before pouring it on.

Every day it is necessary to remove the scum or foam that will form at the top under the whole cabbage leaf; some people put in a thick slice of bread to collect this. Four or five days in a warm room

– in Hungary everyone has a whole army of jars, bottles and barrels of souring cabbage out at the door to mature in the more or less completely dependable Hungarian sun – and it is ready for using. You can, however, leave it for much longer in a cooler place where it will mature more slowly: but don't forget to remove the scum week by week.

When you come to use it, taste it and if it is too sour, wash it in running cold water until it suits your taste.

Now we can return to the *gulyás* family – to those of the Székelys, and the Csángós. If you would prefer to try the Kolozsvár variation the method is similar but uses equal weight quantities of beef and *fresh* cabbage, with some sweet peppers, a couple of tomatoes and the customary paprika powder, caraway seeds, salt – and a good dash of marjoram.

Székelygulyás

½ kg shoulder of pork (1 lb.)
150g chopped onion (5 oz.)
salt, paprika powder
1 clove garlic
2 sweet green peppers
½ kg pork ribs (1 lb.)
80g fat (2½ oz.)
caraway seeds
4 dl sour cream (¾ pint)
1 tbs. flour
1 kg soured cabbage (2 lbs.)

Cut the meat into chunks. Melt the fat and fry the onion in it. Add the paprika, garlic and a good pinch of caraway seeds, and then pour in a very little water. Reduce this liquid slowly almost to the fat and add the meat. Season with salt, cover and braise for about 40 minutes, adding small amounts of water from time to time if absolutely necessary – cabbage and meat both provide juice and the sour cream also eventually thins the *gulyás* so be careful to keep the liquid to the bare minimum.

Wash the cabbage and the sliced peppers. Add them to the *gulyás* and pour on enough water to cover. Stirring occasionally, cook gently until the cabbage softens – about an hour altogether. When this is ready, stir in a mixture of half a pint of the sour cream and the flour. Simmer for about 5 minutes longer.

Serve in a deep wide dish and sprinkle the remaining cream over the top.

Csángógulyás

800g chuck beef (1 lb. 10 oz.)
150g onion (5 oz.)
½ kg soured cabbage (1 lb.)
caraway seeds
60g rice (2 oz.)
90g fat (3 oz.)
1 clove garlic
paprika powder, salt
4 dl sour cream (¾ pint)
2 sweet peppers (in season)

Dice the beef into 30g (1 oz.) cubes and wash them. Slice the onion into rings and fry lightly in the fat, adding the garlic, a good pinch of caraway seeds and about 1 dessertspoon paprika powder. Mix well and put in a very little water, letting the ingredients cook together for a few minutes. Add the meat, season with salt, cover and braise slowly for about 1¼ hours, adding a small quantity of water from time to time if necessary.

Then put in the washed sour cabbage and sliced sweet peppers and add enough water to cover. Once both the meat and the cabbage begin to soften add the washed rice and cook for 15–20 minutes longer, on very low heat.

Before serving in a deep dish, mix in the sour cream.

Rakott káposzta – Layered Cabbage

There are several villains in Hungarian cooking. Villain in chief must be *rakott káposzta.* It tends to look evil before, during and after cooking. Nothing in the world except Marika Kostyál's brilliant cooking would have induced me to attempt this dish, but once I summoned the courage to attack I found the flavour holds all the rewards one could wish for: after all, only a stage villain.

¾ kg soured cabbage (1 lb. 10 oz.)
120g rice (4 oz.)
2 dl sour cream (⅜ pint)
150g smoked sausage (5 oz.)
350g shoulder of pork (¾ lb)
½ onion
80g fat (2½ oz.)
salt, pepper

Braise the soured cabbage in 30g fat (1 oz.) or in oil, until it softens.

Mince the pork, chop the onion and fry them together in the remainder of the fat.

Prepare boiled rice in the usual way, simmering it until it is not quite soft.

Drain if necessary and mix in with the meat.

Place alternate layers of the cabbage and the meat mixture in a greased fireproof dish, sprinkling each layer liberally with soured cream, and slipping in circles of smoked sausage if available, but this last ingredient is not necessary.

The final layer should be cabbage; pour on the remaining sour cream, thinned with some of the fat over from frying the meat.

Heat thoroughly in a hot oven for 20 minutes.

Savanyú káposzta almával és rizssel – Sour Cabbage with Apple and Rice

1 kg soured cabbage (2 lbs.)
1 kg apples (2 lbs.)
2 tbs. oil
2 dl sour cream (⅜ pint)
1 level tbs. sugar
½ cup apple juice or cider
200g rice (6–7 oz.)

Braise the cabbage in the oil with the apple juice. Add the sliced apples and the sugar and braise for a few minutes longer until the apples soften. Meanwhile prepared boiled rice and then, in a greased dish, layer it alternately with the cabbage and apples, sprinkling each layer with soured cream. Heat through in a hot oven for 15–20 minutes.

Savanyú káposzta burgonyával – Sour Cabbage and Potatoes

1 kg soured cabbage (2 lbs.)
1½–2 tbs. tomato juice
2 dl sour cream (⅜ pint)
½ kg potatoes (1 lb)
2 tbs. oil

Fry the shredded cabbage lightly in the oil – but not for too long – keep it crisp. Boil the potatoes in their skins, then peel and slice them. Add these slices to the cabbage and mix in about 2 tablespoons thick tomato juice. Simmer for a few minutes and pour on the sour cream just before serving.

Töltött káposzta – Stuffed Cabbage

Any Hungarian menu – and this book – would be guilty of a serious omission if they did not include *töltött káposzta*: Hungarians honour this by making it the dish for the day after Christmas Day, but it is a culinary masterpiece which they adore eating at any time of the year.

400g lean minced pork or a mixture of pork and beef (13 oz.)
1 kg soured cabbage leaves (2 lbs.)
1 small onion
50g flour (1½ oz.)
300g pork ribs (11 oz.)
100g rice (3 oz.)
60g fat (2 oz.)
salt
pepper
3–4 dl sour cream (¾ pint)

Fry the rice and chopped onion quickly in half the fat and mix them with the minced meat. Season with salt and pepper. This filling can be made easier to handle by adding one beaten egg or a handful of finely cut sour cabbage.

Remove any coarse veins from 10–12 soured cabbage leaves and fill with the meat mixture by placing a heaped spoonful of it on the middle of each leaf and folding it in from all sides.

Cut the remainder of the sour cabbage finely and place half of this with the rest of the fat in a saucepan. The rib bones and any bits of meat and skin may also be placed in the bottom of the pan. Then put in the stuffed cabbage leaves, the ribs, and finally the remainder of the shredded cabbage. Cover with water and simmer gently for about 1¾–2 hours until everything is cooked and tender.

Remove the meat and the stuffed leaves. Discard the bones and skin and pour the mixture of the sour cream and the flour onto the cabbage in the pan, adding a little water if necessary, to thin.

To serve put the shredded cabbage in a dish, then the stuffed leaves, and surround them with the meat. Sprinkle on a little more sour cream.

If you have no large soured leaves, use ordinary fresh cabbage leaves for that part of the recipe – the rest really has to be soured cabbage.

For the Székely variation of this dish, use

300g (10 oz.) smoked meat, ½ kg (1 lb.) good lean beef; ½ kg (1 lb.) leg of pork with the skin on it, and 300g (10 oz.) minced pork. Follow the same procedure, but include a good bunch of both savory and dill.

Fresh cabbage

My emphasis on sour cabbage may give the impression that Hungarians have forgotten what *ordinary* cabbage tastes like; the following recipes show what they like to do with it apart from leaving it for weeks in barrels to sour!

Párolt káposzta – Braised Cabbage

1 k[illegible] or white cabbage (2 lbs.)
2 tbs. chopped onion
¼ tsp. salt
60g dripping from smoked streaky bacon (2 oz.)
vinegar
sugar, caraway seeds

Shred the cabbage, salt it and leave it for 10–20 minutes. Then squeeze the surplus moisture out of it gently.

Fry the chopped onion lightly in the dripping, add the cabbage, cover and braise it in its own juice very slowly for 10–15 minutes. Add a pinch of sugar and a good large pinch of caraway seeds.

When the cabbage is about half ready put in a couple of drops of vinegar to help prevent the cabbage from becoming mushy, and continue the braising until the liquid evaporates.

To produce extraordinary results from ordinary cabbage, add 4 tablespoons good white wine just before removing the pan from the heat to serve. Serve as an accompaniment.

Vöröskáposzta almával – Red Cabbage with Apple

1 kg red cabbage (2 lbs.)
30g butter (1 oz.)
6 tbs. sour cream
1 kg apples (2 lbs.)
10g salt (¼ oz.)

Shred the cabbage finely, sprinkle half a teaspoon of salt over it and leave it for 20–30 minutes. Peel the apples and cut them into thin slices.

Heat the butter. Squeeze the liquid out of the cabbage gently and then braise both the cabbage and the apples slowly in the butter for about half an hour. Pour the sour cream over the mixture just before serving.

This is served as a dish on its own and is excellent cold as well – and a few raisins 90–100g (2–3 oz.) are usually put in when the cabbage is being braised.

Paradicsomos káposzta – Cabbage in Tomato Sauce

1 kg cabbage (2 lbs.)
50g dripping ($1\frac{1}{2}$ oz.)
1 onion
$\frac{1}{4}$–$\frac{1}{2}$ tsp. salt
1 kg tomatoes (2 lbs.)
50g flour ($1\frac{1}{2}$ oz.)
1 heaped tbs. sugar

Shred the cabbage roughly, chop the onion finely and cook both in salted boiling water until they soften.

Prepare a golden *roux* from the fat and the flour. Peel and chop the tomatoes, add them to the *roux*, breaking them down as they soften. Cook this sauce for 10 minutes. Then adjust seasoning and add the sugar.

Pour the tomato mixture over the cabbage, heat well together and serve with pork or smoked meat or ham.

Káposztás kocka – Cabbage and Noodles

Káposztás kocka, a satisfying mixture of boiled squares of dough and braised cabbage, is generally considered 'very good' in Hungary – with an air about this vague enthusiasm that suggests 'if there's nothing better about'. In fact it is an excellent dish, but I promise that it is so only if you can merely suspect the cabbage in among the squares of dough; once the cabbage begins to dominate the dieticians may be delighted and our figures may be saved, but all subtlety of flavour will be lost. If you can get a red cabbage so much the better. Once it is cooked it looks, authentically, much dirtier and earthier and more last-resortish – which is roughly the general Hungarian attitude to it – and brings that much greater surprise when you taste it. A similar but slightly more elaborate recipe using potatoes with the squares of dough can be found on p. 126.

400g flour (13 oz.)
800g cabbage (1 lb. 10 oz.)
1 tsp. sugar
1–2 eggs
80g fat (2½ oz.)
salt, freshly ground black pepper

Shred the cabbage and then chop it up very finely. Salt it lightly and leave it for 20 minutes.

Meanwhile, prepare the dough. Work the flour together with 1, 1½ or 2 eggs, and adding as much water as is necessary – a little at a time – make a very firm dough. Divide this into two lumps, roll each out separately, and leave the two flat sheets to dry out a bit. (You can, of course, use bought dough but then look for *fresh* pasta from an Italian delicatessen. In Hungary it is part of the ceremony that the dough is made at home in a whirl of rolling out over vast expanses of kitchen table.) And a word about shapes – I used to think dough was dough whatever the shape; but there was simply no comparison with the real thing when I tried this recipe using bought spaghetti or macaroni. There really is something about those flat squares.

Press the juice lightly from the cabbage. Brown the sugar in the fat and then fry the cabbage in it, mixing it about all the time. Cut the dough into inch squares and cook them in abundant boiling water with a knob of butter in it.

When you have cooked the dough squares, drain them well and toss them about in the cabbage pan to get the dough well touched with the hot fat and to make a combination which should be predominantly pale golden squares with dots of cabbage everywhere – not the other way round, remember.

Dose liberally with freshly ground black pepper.

Many Hungarians replace the pepper seasoning with 1–2 tablespoons castor sugar or a slightly tart apricot jam for each helping.

Káposztabomba – Cabbage Bomb

1 medium cabbage
150g rice (5 oz.)
1 small onion
2 dl sour cream ($\frac{3}{8}$ pint)
$\frac{1}{2}$ tsp. salt
$\frac{1}{2}$ kg leg of pork (1 lb.)
1 egg
100g fat or oil (3 oz.)
100g toasted breadcrumbs ($3\frac{1}{2}$ oz.)
$\frac{1}{4}$ tsp. pepper

Mince the meat and fry it gently with the chopped onion in 30g (1 oz.) of the fat.

Wash the rice in cold water and fry it in 30g (1 oz.) of the fat, then add twice its volume of water and let it cook at the slowest possible simmer for about 15 minutes.

Remove the outer leaves from the cabbage and parboil it *whole* in simmering salted water. Lift it out of the water, drain it well and open out the softened outer leaves (about a dozen). Cut out the centre of the cabbage, which should still be raw, and chop it up finely. Fry this in the remaining 30g (1 oz.) fat, occasionally adding a very little water if necessary, until the cabbage softens.

Mix the meat, the rice and shredded cabbage together, add one beaten egg and season with salt and pepper. Place this filling all together in the centre of the cabbage. Draw the cabbage leaves together again so that the filling is covered and the cabbage pretends to resume its original shape. Tie it up tightly in a fine cloth, hang it on the handle of a wooden spoon and cook it for about 40 minutes in boiling salted water.

Lift it from the pan, drain it well and place it with its stem upwards so that the thick stem can be cut out neatly with a sharp knife. Then place the serving dish on top of it and turn the whole thing the right way up.

Just before serving, sprinkle it with the sour cream and then the toasted breadcrumbs.

Savoys

Savoys may indeed be a kind of cabbage but in Hungary they are emphatically savoys. Of the three savoy dishes which follow, the first is the everyday dish, the second a very fine combination of savoy and curds, and one might think the third rather gaudy and out to make an impression, but it is really quite a simple though inventive way of making a whole course in one bundle, as it calls itself.

Kelkáposztafőzelék – Braised Savoy

1 kg savoy (2 lbs.)
50g fat (1½ oz.)
1 tbs. chopped onion
300g potatoes (10 oz.)
2 level tbs. flour
1 clove garlic, chopped
salt, freshly ground black pepper, caraway seeds, dill, paprika powder

Clean and cut up the savoy. Boil it gently in enough salted water to cover it, and sprinkle with a few caraway seeds and a little green dill. When the savoy is half cooked, add the peeled and diced potatoes and cook for about 10–15 minutes longer.

Meanwhile prepare a fairly dark *roux* from the fat and the flour, add the finely chopped onion and the garlic and sprinkle some paprika powder over it. Cook gently for 5 minutes and then add the mixture to the savoy, stirring constantly. Season with the pepper and bring to the boil again. Serve with sour cream.

Túróval töltött kelkáposzta – Savoy with Curd Stuffing

1 kg savoy (2 lbs.)
2 dl sour cream (⅜ pint)
1 tbs. chopped fresh dill leaves
1 egg
½ kg curds (1 lb.)
50g butter (1½ oz.)
salt
breadcrumbs

Separate the savoy leaves and cook them in boiling salted water. Put the curds through a sieve to make them thoroughly smooth and combine with the beaten egg, the sour cream, the dill and the salt.

Cut out any coarse veins in the savoy leaves. Give each some of the curd filling and roll up like a pancake, but don't close in the ends.

Place the rolls in a greased fireproof dish lined with breadcrumbs, sprinkle with a little extra sour cream, dot with butter and bake quickly in a hot oven until the top just begins to brown.

Kelgöngyöleg – Savoy Bundle

½ kg lean boiled beef (1 lb.)
2 eggs
2½ dl sour cream (½ pint)
3 tbs. fine breadcrumbs
salt and pepper
60g fat or oil (2 oz.)
1 roll
a 1 kg savoy (2 lb.)
1 onion
milk

Fry the onion lightly in 50g (1½ oz.) of the fat. Add the beef to heat it, and then mince this mixture. Soak the roll in milk, squeeze out any surplus liquid gently and break up. Add the egg yolks and the roll to the mince. Season with freshly ground black pepper and mix in 1 tablespoon sour cream. Combine well and then add the firmly beaten whites of the eggs.

Separate the savoy leaves and boil them in salted water until they are almost ready. Cut any coarse parts out of them. Grease a cloth and place the savoy leaves on it, one on top of the other, spreading each one in turn with the filling. Finish with a leaf. Fold up the cloth and tie the ends together. Boil in the cloth for three quarters of an hour.

Remove the 'bundle' from the cloth, place it on an oblong dish and slice it vertically. Sprinkle with breadcrumbs, fried golden in the remaining fat, and then with sour cream.

Serve with horseradish sauce.

Spinach

Apart from making it into a vegetable dish in the characteristic way with a *roux* and sour cream, Hungarian cooking has several more attractive ways of treating spinach.

The first is to prepare a spinach *roulade* on the same lines as the cauliflower *roulade* described at the beginning of this chapter. And although the same filling is used for this spinach roll as that given in the earlier recipe, quite justifiably when you consider the balance of flavours, you can change the filling to suit yourself – try, for example, a ham and cheese filling prepared in a similar way from 200g (7 oz.) cooked ham; 50g (1½ oz.) butter; 1 level tablespoon flour; 5–6 tablespoons milk; 30g (1 oz.) grated cheese.

The second recipe is a spinach pancake with an egg filling – light, full of colour and tasty.

Parajtekercs – Spinach Roulade

400g spinach (13 oz.)
3–4 tbs. sour cream
pinch salt
3 eggs
3 tbs. flour

Boil the spinach and when it is cooked, break it through a sieve. Mix in the egg yolks, 1 tablespoon of the sour cream, and the flour. Beat the egg whites until they are stiff and fold them into the spinach mixture. Spread out on a greased and floured baking sheet and bake for 10–15 minutes in a hot oven.

Use the same filling as in the recipe for the cauliflower roll on p. 82 – or otherwise, as you choose.

Return the roll to the oven to heat through. Serve on a long dish, slice thickly and pour the remaining sour cream over the whole.

Parajpalacsinta – Spinach Pancake

4 eggs
250g spinach (8 oz.)
80g fat (2½ oz.)
30g grated cheese (1 oz.)
100g flour (3½–4 oz.)
3 dl milk (about ½ pint)
2 tbs. sour cream
salt

Mix 1 egg with 100g (3½–4 oz.) flour and gradually add enough milk to make a thin pancake batter.

Cook the spinach in boiling salted water until it is reduced and soft. Press it through a sieve and add it to the pancake batter. Fry the pancakes from this mixture and keep them warm – above boiling water or in the oven.

Mix 1 tablespoon of the sour cream with three beaten eggs and make scrambled eggs from this mixture, using the fat for frying. Spread the cooked eggs on the pancakes, roll them up and place them in a fireproof dish. Sprinkle with sour cream and heat through thoroughly in a fairly hot oven for 10 minutes. Just before serving sprinkle with the grated cheese.

Carrots

The carrot is not something Hungarians take very seriously: they stick it in and perhaps even pull it out again – the flavour, yes, they'll have that . . . but it is never given the care and elaboration which is lavished on the mushroom or the cabbage. On the rare occasions when it is allowed to revel in its own colour and display its ability to be independent, this is the dish which results. Not, they will say, boiled carrots – followed by a deal of earthy jocularity about health, hydration and Englishmen!

Sárgarepafőzelék – Braised Carrots

700g carrots (1½ lbs.)
1 tbs. flour
parsley
6 tbs. sour cream
60g fat (2 oz.)
1 level tbs. sugar
salt and pepper

Clean and slice the carrots very thinly and braise them in hot fat until they soften, adding a very little stock or water from time to time and seasoning with salt and the sugar. When the liquid is well reduced and the carrots ready, stir and sprinkle with flour. Then add a very little water or possibly milk. Mix in 1–2 tablespoons chopped parsley, and season liberally with freshly ground black pepper.

The sour cream may be added just before serving – but Edith Néni wouldn't hear of it and there is no denying she coped better with carrots than anyone else I met in Hungary.

Green Beans

Green beans do not bring any dazzling variety in Hungary – but one dazzling dish, most definitely. That is, if a taste and a texture can dazzle; what meets the eye is less significant.

Zöldbab sajtos mártással – Cheese Beans

700g green beans (1½ lbs.)
1 egg
6 tbs. sour cream
salt
thick white sauce made from 30g butter (1 oz.), 1 level tbs. flour and 2 dl milk (⅜ pint)
100g smoked cheese (4 oz.)

Cook the beans in boiling salted water, but don't allow them to become over-soft.

Prepare the white sauce and when it is ready remove it from the heat and mix in the sour cream and the beaten egg.

Grease a fireproof dish and make alternate layers of beans and sauce, sprinkling each layer with grated cheese, and finishing with cheese. Heat through thoroughly in a hot oven for 5–10 minutes until the cheese on top begins to brown.

If you can't get a good smoked cheese use a ham flavoured one or a fatty cheese with bits of ham in it.

Sólet

Hungarians have no more than two uses for barley. One is to feed it to horses and the other has already disappeared into the past: it was roasted and brewed to give the cleverest wartime coffee in the world. But combine barley with beans and you get *sólet*, not to be translated, and one of the finest and most typical lunch dishes for everyone in Hungary. The dish is of Jewish origin and both the fat used for frying at the beginning of the recipe and the meat cooked in the bean mixture came from goose. Hungarians, however, are quite happy to make anything and everything food-wise their own and now it is just as common to find *sólet* in the company of smoked knuckle bone or pork ribs.

400g smaller white or spotted beans (13 oz.)
250g goose (8 oz.) with plenty of fat on it – or 250g (8 oz.) piece of smoked streaky bacon
1 tbs. flour
a little paprika powder
100g lightly crushed barley ($3\frac{1}{2}$ oz.)
200g pork ribs, preferably smoked (6–7 oz.)
80g fat ($2\frac{1}{2}$ oz.)
1 onion

Soak the beans overnight or for a few hours in ample water. Drain well and mix with the barley.

Chop the onion finely and fry it lightly in the fat.

Sprinkle with paprika powder, fry a few minutes longer and keep stirring it about.

Cut the meats into cubes and put them into a large pan (it should be large vertically rather than horizontally). Mix in the beans, barley and onions, and sprinkle with 1 tablespoon flour. Pour in enough water to cover and bring to the boil. Continue the cooking in a moderate oven – it will take at least two hours, maybe even three, before the beans will soften and the meat become tender. By the time both are ready relatively little liquid remains – but see that the mixture does not dry out too quickly.

Cucumber

The multitudinous quantities of cucumbers present in season, and nowadays out of it as well, seem out of all proportion to the variety of uses they can be put to. I pick up a cucumber with some sense of expectancy, because if there are so many of the things they must be useful for *something*, and then I'm at a loss. I can salad it, sandwich it or pickle it – but I've done all that hundreds of times before. Stuff it? Hungarians make a delicious salad from fresh cucumber which I have described elsewhere (*see* p. 76), but this stuffed cucumber recipe is something quite special.

Töltött uborka – Stuffed Cucumber

4 short fat cucumbers, about 8 inches long	1 roll
2 tbs. oil	milk
6 tbs. sour cream	1 egg
1 small onion	1 tsp. flour
250g lean pork (8 oz.)	stock
	salt, pepper, and dill leaves

Fry the chopped onion in half the oil. Add the meat and braise with the lid on the pan, seasoning liberally with freshly ground black pepper.

Peel the cucumbers, cut them in two lengthwise and scrape out the seed part.

Mince the braised meat and onion, and to this add the roll, which should first be soaked in milk, squeezed lightly to remove the surplus milk, and then crumbed. Add the beaten egg and mix well. Use this mixture to fill the spaces in the cucumbers. Tie the halves together in pairs with thread so that they look like whole cucumbers again.

Grease a fireproof dish and place the cucumbers in it. Pour on a little bone stock and, covering the dish, cook for 30–40 minutes until the cucumber becomes clear and soft.

Mix the flour and the sour cream and pour this over the cucumbers, cooking the whole together for a few minutes longer. Before serving sprinkle with freshly chopped dill.

Lentils

This next dish is another rather muddy looking bowlful which presents another fascinating taste surprise. In Hungary it is the large black lentils that are used and in this dish they are combined with lemon juice and a little sour cream. Top the dish with a couple of slices of good roast pork.

Lencsefőzelék – Lentils

400g black lentils (13 oz.)
50g flour (1½ oz.)
rind and juice of 1 lemon (or a little wine vinegar)
salt and sugar
30g dripping (1 oz.)
1 onion
6 tbs. sour cream
sage
paprika powder

Wash the lentils well under running water. Boil them in enough water to cover until they soften.

Prepare a light *roux* from the flour and the fat. Add the finely chopped onion, a mere sprinkling of paprika and season well with salt. Mix thoroughly and then pour the mixture slowly into the lentils, stirring all the time. Flavour with the grated lemon rind and juice, a good pinch of sugar and a good pinch of sage.

Add the sour cream just before serving.

Grated horseradish is commonly served with lentils. It may be given on a separate plate or mixed in before serving. For me the lemon juice is enough and I prefer the same accompaniment as most Hungarians – a thick chunk of bread.

Corn

For a Hungarian the only way to eat corn is to be lured by the plaintive two-note melody of the gipsy as she stands by her steaming basket, crying her beautiful medieval cry over and over until her basket is empty: suddenly everyone in the street is gnawing at hot *kukorica* (corn on the cob) held firmly in both hands. Although in Britain little opportunity presents itself for us to march along the street munching freshly boiled corn on the cob, the food itself is not unknown, so it is more interesting to find new ways of working with this colourful piece of autumn. Why not serve it with sour cream? This is a recipe I *learned* in Hungary, which means I must admit, nobody ever presented the dish to me. I suspect it amounts to a sort of theory which probably exists to be laughed at by the crowds who are fully satisfied with the simplicity they have the chance to enjoy from the gipsy's basket.

Kukoricafőzelék – Corn with Cream

8 corn cobs (or about 450g – 1 lb. cooked loose corn)
6 tbs. sour cream, or fresh cream
60g butter (2 oz.)
1 tbs. flour
milk
salt, sugar

Boil the corn in the usual way until it softens and remove it from the cobs.

Prepare a light *roux* from the flour and the butter. Thin by adding a little milk and then some of the water the corn was cooked in. Season with salt and a pinch of sugar, and simmer until it forms a soft thin creamy consistency. Then put in the corn and bring back to the boil for a few minutes.

Finally add the cream, bring it back to the boil and remove it from the heat straight away. Adjust seasoning and serve with roast chicken or turkey.

Asparagus

There would be no sense in pretending that Hungarians eat this next dish every day. Although asparagus is plentiful and of excellent quality, it is more inclined to appear in accompanying sauces and less likely to be allowed its own glory. There would likewise be no sense in denying that if Hungarians do decide to make a central attraction of asparagus, they certainly know how to.

Spárga magyarosan – Hungarian Asparagus

1 kg asparagus (2 lbs.)
6 tbs. sour cream
½ tbs. flour
sugar, salt
30g butter (1 oz.)
1 egg yolk
about 20g fine breadcrumbs (½ oz.)
½–1 tsp. paprika powder

Cook the cleaned asparagus in boiling water with salt and a little sugar for 20–30 minutes. Dry it with a cloth and place it in a fireproof dish.

Mix the sour cream with the flour and the egg yolk, season with salt, a good pinch of sugar, and a little paprika. Pour this over the asparagus, sprinkle with breadcrumbs, dot with knobs of butter and bake in a fairly hot oven until the breadcrumbs are golden brown.

Peppers

The pepper has a long tradition in Hungary since the Turks introduced it; but in the last hundred years particularly it has tended to steal the Hungarian show for foreigners. Apart from boasting more vitamin C than, for example, lemons, the pepper or Capsicum, in all its many forms, is simply a very beautiful vegetable, with a taste to match. If you see the wide range of varieties growing in the flat steady heat of the Great Hungarian Plain, you can only think they are there to mock man, dangling lightly with their wax shapes – full-fire suns, mellower moons, deep green shadows.

They are not all rage and mischief. There are indeed chillis in the family and there are cherry paprikas – *cerasiforme* – but there are also the sweeter kinds which have no trace of sharpness. One primrose-yellow beauty is eaten as a treat on thickly buttered bread and sprinkled with salt – there are several varieties: best known are the *Cecei édes* and the *Keszthelyi fehér*. The flattish, round tomato-paprikas make regular appearances in Britain every autumn, but I have never seen the whitish-yellow triangular varieties here yet – and that is an unfortunate omission.

In spite of their reputation and their variety, peppers are not the actual foundation of many dishes in Hungary. They get into nearly everything in a discreet sort of way but are less inclined to step into the limelight. But when they do, we have two superb dishes: *Töltött paprika* and *Lecsó*.

Töltött paprika – Stuffed Peppers

½ kg minced pork (1 lb.)
1 kg tomatoes (2 lbs.)
60g onion (2 oz.)
1 level tbs. sugar
1 egg and 1 egg yolk
parsley and celery leaves
salt, pepper
8–10 large sweet green peppers, or the yellow ones if you can find them
80g fat (2½ oz.)
2 tbs. flour
100g rice (3½ oz.)
1 clove garlic, chopped
marjoram

Remove the seeds and the inner veins from the peppers: that is where you find the nippy *capsicin* which excites, among other things, the liver, and should be avoided whenever possible.

Simmer the rice until it is half cooked (about 7–10 minutes), drain it and set it aside to cool.

Mix the minced meat with the rice in a large bowl.

Fry half the onion in 30g (1 oz.) of the fat and add this with some freshly chopped parsley to the meat and rice. Beat well together with the egg and the extra yolk. Season with salt and freshly ground black pepper and, if you like, sprinkle with marjoram. Add the garlic and mix well.

Fill the peppers with this meat stuffing – loosely, so that the rice will still have room to swell.

To make the tomato sauce, chop up the tomatoes and cook them gently with the remaining onion and a couple of chopped celery leaves in a minimum of water. Make a light *roux* with the flour and the remaining fat, and add this to the tomatoes when they have softened, stirring constantly. Bring to the boil and, continuing to stir, cook for five minutes. Add sugar and salt to taste.

Simmer the stuffed peppers in this sauce until they have become tender.

Serve with boiled potatoes.

Lecsó

Lecsó is a bright mixture of mild peppers and tomatoes – eaten alone, with frankfurters or smoked sausage, with eggs, with potatoes, with *tarhonya* (tiny pellets of dough the size of salmon ova when cooked – first fried and then allowed to swell in a little water), and it can also be preserved for winter use and eaten with any of these things all over again. A tablespoon of preserved *lecsó* (*see* p. 225) finds its way into many winter dishes and sauces, but it is at its colourful best when freshly made.

1 kg sweet peppers (2 lbs.)
60g smoked streaky bacon (2 oz.)
1 onion
paprika powder
250g rice (8 oz.)
½ kg tomatoes (1 lb.)
80g fat (2½ oz.)
salt
250g smoked sausage, or good frankfurters (8 oz.)

Fry the chopped onion in 50g (1½ oz.) of the fat until it is transparent. Chop up the bacon finely and fry it with the onion. Sprinkle lightly with paprika powder.

Peel the tomatoes and clean the peppers, removing the seeds.

Slice them up and add them to the pan. Stirring frequently, cook over a strong heat for 5–6 minutes. Then simmer until the peppers soften. Add the smoked sausage or frankfurters about 5–10 minutes before serving.

Serve with rice, which should be fried in the remaining fat and then simmered in twice its volume of salted water for about 15 minutes.

Mushrooms

In Hungary's capital city it is a joyous Sunday afternoon outing to go hunting mushrooms in the Buda hills on the outskirts of the city. And when you return with your finds there are special stalls in the markets and busy centres where experts will tell you whether you can go home to a scrumptious supper or whether you have merely gathered a bagful of delirium or even death-producing poison.

There is scarcely any such thing as 'a mushroom' in Hungary – that would be like saying you have 'some flowers' in your garden: it is the individual kinds that are well known and consciously appreciated, the favourites being the *csiperke* (the common *Psalliota campestris*), the yellow *rókagomba* (literally the 'fox mushroom', the chanterelle), the red and brown *vargánya* (*Boletus edulis*), the *kucsmagomba* (the morel – literally the 'fur-cap mushroom') and the *szegfügomba* (the fairy-ring mushroom, *Marasmius oreades*). I have scarcely ever seen anonymous cultured mushrooms in Hungary.

This variety is reflected in the ways mushrooms are presented as food – nothing reveals the ceremonious excitement of a real 'find' so proudly as the mushroom-fritter variations which must come first here.

Kirántott gombafejek – Mushroom Fritters

600g mushrooms (1¼ lbs.)
2 dl oil (⅜ pint)
200g fine breadcrumbs (7 oz.)
150g rice (5 oz.)
2 eggs
100g flour (3–4 oz.)
salt

Do not skin the mushrooms unless they are discoloured – just wash them lightly in running hot water before using them, pull out the stems and dry the flat heads with a cloth. Sprinkle them with salt, but only immediately before they are to be fried. Dip them in flour, then in beaten egg and finally in breadcrumbs. Fry them immediately in the oil – not too quickly so that even the larger mushrooms will have time to become cooked right through.

Prepare boiled rice in the usual way. Fry the mushroom stems in a little fat and then mix them with the boiled rice.

Set the rice out on a hot dish and place the mushroom heads on top.

Serve with tartare sauce.

The beery variation which follows is the ultimate in fluffiness. The melting texture of the fried batter blends lightly with the mushrooms. I think this version is particularly useful if the dish is served as a gentle opener and you have less gentle intentions for later courses.

Gombafejek sörtésztában – Mushrooms in Beer Batter

For the batter:

2 eggs	2 dl beer (⅜ pint)
100g flour (3–4 oz.)	1 tbs. oil
salt	

Mix the egg yolks and the flour. Then add the beer gradually to make a batter somewhat thicker than for pancakes. Beat the egg whites stiff, fold them into the batter and finally add the oil.

Salt the cleaned mushroom heads. Dip them immediately in flour and then in batter. Fry in ample fat or oil until they are crisp and golden on both sides.

Prepare the rice as above, mixing in the fried mushroom stalks. Sprinkle with a little chopped parsley, set out the mushroom heads on top and serve with tartare sauce.

Rántott gomba májjal – Mushroom Fritters with Liver Stuffing

Although this recipe is successful with any of the large flat edible *Agaricus* mushrooms, such as *A. campester* or *A. arvensis,* but *not A. xanthodermus,* greater effect is achieved by using the morels *Morchella esculenta* or *M. conica,* or the *Mitrophora samilbera* mushroom. These last three all have a shell with a holey surface on the outside and are completely empty inside, which makes them particularly suitable for filling.

700g large mushrooms (1½ lbs.)	salt and pepper
60g butter (2 oz.)	rum
250g liver (8 oz.)	1 lemon
2 egg yolks	1 egg
½ cup milk	breadcrumbs
½ onion	deep fat for frying
flour	

First prepare a liver paste. The best liver for this recipe is considered to be lean goose liver, failing which use duck liver, failing which use chicken liver, failing which forget the recipe.

Slice the liver thinly. Fry the finely chopped onion lightly in the butter. Add the liver and braise it until it is tender, seasoning with salt and freshly ground black pepper. Sprinkle with flour and, gradually adding half a cupful of cold milk, mix it together smoothly and bring it to the boil. Thicken with two egg yolks and flavour with a thimbleful of rum. Simmer gently, stirring regularly, and once the mixture has become thicker, press it through a very fine sieve.

Cook the mushrooms in a minimum of salt water with the juice of 1 lemon. Then cool. Drain well and dry with a cloth. Take pairs of mushroom heads and stick them together with a tablespoon of the cold liver paste in between. Dip them in flour, beaten egg, and then breadcrumbs, and fry them in deep fat until they are golden brown all over. Serve at once, with a brown sauce thinned with a little Bull's Blood. Accompany with boiled rice mixed as above with the fried mushroom stalks.

Gombapaprikás – Braised Mushrooms

In Hungary you will still pay more for mushrooms in restaurants even when they are merely braised or roasted than for many meat dishes. *Gombapaprikás* is inclined to look squirmy, if not evil, but the situation is saved by *galuskas*: although the deep warmth of the combined flavours is by no means matched by the appearance, the colour contrast and texture harmony make for eventual success. For this dish the best mushroom to use is the *bolete* (*Boletus edulis*).

½ kg mushrooms (1 lb.)
6 tbs. sour cream
paprika powder
60g dripping from smoked streaky bacon (2 oz.)
1 onion
salt

Fry the chopped onion gently in the fat and sprinkle it generously with paprika powder. Mix the ingredients well together and add the sliced mushrooms and season with salt. Cover and braise slowly until the mushrooms become quite soft and the liquid is reduced.

Remove from the heat and mix in the sour cream. Serve with *galuskas* (*see* p. 127).

An excellent variation is to omit the sour cream: it is in this variation that the chanterelle (*Cantharellus cibarius*) comes into its own in Hungarian cooking.

Sült gombafejek – Baked Mushrooms

½ kg mushrooms (1 lb.)	paprika powder
60g butter (2 oz.)	parsley
salt and pepper	fresh dill leaves
60g good bacon dripping (2 oz.)	chives

Wash the mushroom heads. Place them with the open part upwards – saucer wise – in a baking dish smeared thickly with the bacon dripping. Season each with salt, freshly ground black pepper and paprika powder.

Chop equal bunches of fresh parsley, chives and dill together and place at least half a teaspoon on each mushroom. Finally dot each with butter and bake for 8–10 minutes in a very hot oven.

Serve with rice – and into the boiled rice mix the stems of the mushrooms, which should be fried with a little chopped onion in butter.

Although the everyday accompaniment to the everyday vegetable dish (braised and then thickened) is the unceremonious slice of pork slung on top, other accompaniments show more originality and more finesse. Try this 'mushroom pie', for example – with dishes described earlier, such as *paradicsomos káposzta*, (p. 91) *lencsefőzelék*, (p. 100) or with spinach, for example. For this recipe the best mushroom is *Marasmius oreades*, the fairy-ring mushroom.

Gombás lepény – Mushroom Pie

½ kg mushrooms (1 lb.)	3 eggs
2 rolls	salt and pepper
parsley	breadcrumbs
60g fat (2 oz.)	milk

Clean and slice the mushrooms, and fry them in hot fat, seasoning them with salt and pepper and two tablespoons of chopped parsley. Cook until the liquid from the mushrooms is reduced completely. Set aside to cool a little.

Soak the rolls in milk and then gently squeeze any surplus liquid out of them. Break them up and beat with the egg yolks until smooth. Add the braised mushrooms and finally the beaten whites of the eggs.

Grease an ovenproof dish, line it with breadcrumbs and bake the mixture in this until it sets and becomes firm. Cut into squares and use as an accompaniment to vegetable dishes.

Potatoes

The potato is certainly the Hungarians' favourite vegetable, and their favourite way of presenting it is probably *paprikás krumpli.*

I have never met anyone in Hungary who actually denied the genius of this dish: they merely object that it is a 'peasant dish', and 'so plain'. Which is, of course, no more than one way of looking at it.

To translate this title into 'Paprika Potatoes' is like comparing the Tátra with Ludgate Hill. There is an indulgence, a joy in things earthy in *krumpli,* the unliterary word for potato, and the long wide 'aash' sound at the end of *paprikás* has all the fire and sparkle of the Hungarian kitchen, which disappears into dull blobs in the English translation. But it is not titles and words we have to concern ourselves with: the masterpiece itself – or plain dish for peasants, if you prefer – has a sharp contrast which must not be lost sight of.

You need some feeling for the split personality to make an authentic success of *paprikás krumpli.* The potatoes and paprika powder are quiet and innocuous and once you have combined them with good, salty, smoked bacon-dripping – butter would be too bland here – a lightly smoked sausage and chilli powder, it is possible to forget about any apparent schizophrenia in the ingredients: the result will be well adjusted.

Paprikás krumpli – Paprika Potatoes

1 large onion
1–2 tbs. paprika powder
¼–½ tsp chilli powder
¼–½ tsp. caraway seeds
90g dripping from smoked streaky bacon (3 oz.)
1 tsp. salt
700g potatoes (1½ lbs.)
180–200g smoked sausage (6–7 oz.)

Melt the dripping and fry the finely chopped onion in it until it is transparent. Lower the heat and mix in the paprika and chilli powder. Cook gently for a few minutes, stirring it about all the time.

Peel and slice the potatoes. Turn them about in the onion and paprika to get them well covered with the fat. Put in the salt and caraway seeds, add enough water to cover and simmer for 20–25 minutes, or until the potatoes are cooked. Add circles of smoked sausage (or good frankfurters will do) about 10 minutes before serving.

Serve with thick chunks of bread.

To add 1 tablespoon sour cream to each individual portion is to alter the whole idea of the dish, and Hungarians would consider it cheating, but this variation undoubtedly has its value.

Burgonyafőzelék – Potatoes with Sage and Sour Cream Sauce

Remaining with the potato, the tart, sourish tradition produces a much cooler flavour – and colour. I prefer – heresy – to omit the vinegar; Edith Raskó prefers to use sage rather than the marjoram which all the cookery books dictate, and as usual she's right.

1 kg potatoes (2 lbs.)
6–7 tbs. sour cream
1 tbs. vinegar
salt and pepper
50g fat (1½ oz.)
50g flour (1½ oz.)
1 tsp. sage

Peel and slice the potatoes. Put them on to boil in just enough water to cover them barely.

Prepare a light *roux* from the fat and the flour. Add a little cold water and then the sage, stirring constantly to keep it smooth. Add this gradually to the potatoes when they are half ready and season with salt and pepper. Then continue to simmer until the potatoes are quite cooked. Remove from the heat, add the vinegar, mix thoroughly and finally, just before serving, mix in the sour cream.

Rakott burgonya – Layered Potatoes

A layered dish presents delightful opportunities for sneaking in all kinds of things. *Rakott burgonya*, however, has a habit of remaining surprisingly unadulterated. If you want to use it as a cheap and convenient dish on its own, include the sausage layer described.

1 kg potatoes (2 lbs.)
8–9 tbs. sour cream
salt
5 hard boiled eggs
90g bacon dripping (3 oz.)
breadcrumbs

Boil the potatoes in their skins. Then peel and slice them. Slice the hard boiled eggs, too.

Place a layer of potato slices in a greased fireproof dish. Season this layer with salt and sprinkle it with sour cream and a little melted dripping. On this, place a layer of egg slices and season with salt. Continue alternating the two kinds of layer and each time sprinkle with sour cream and some melted fat on the potatoes, not forgetting to season each layer with salt.

Most Hungarians include a sparse layer of smoked sausage cut into thin slices. This certainly makes all the difference even if you are only using the dish as an accompaniment: if you are serving it as an independent course the sausage is indispensable, but you don't need any more than 6 ounces.

Once the ingredients are all used up, sprinkle breadcrumbs liberally on top and bake for 20–30 minutes in a moderately hot oven until the breadcrumbs become golden brown.

Burgonyaropogós – Potato Croquettes

There is nothing particularly Hungarian about potato croquettes, but the way Hungarians approach them is none the less worth some emphasis.

850g potatoes (1¾ lbs.)	60g butter (2 oz.)
3 eggs	salt and nutmeg
flour and breadcrumbs for covering	deep fat for frying

Peel and slice the potatoes and cook them in boiling salted water until they are ready. Drain thoroughly and return to the heat for a minute or two, stirring constantly, to dry them. Mash them well, allow them to cool a little and then add the yolks of the eggs, seasoning with salt and freshly grated nutmeg. Mix well and then form small cylinder shaped croquettes from the mixture on a floured board. Allow to cool more, then dip in flour, the beaten egg whites, and finally in breadcrumbs, and fry in deep fat until golden.

Aubergines

The aubergine – one of the names Hungarians give it is the blue tomato – is not by any means a characteristic part of either their agriculture or their menu, but this next recipe shows their admirable bent for taking what is available and applying their own familiar methods to it.

Rakott padlizsán – Layered Aubergines

4 aubergines (700–800g – 1½–1¾ lbs.)	100g dripping, or oil (3½ oz.)
300g lean pork (11 oz.)	1 onion
2 eggs	6 tbs. sour cream
2 tbs. flour	salt and pepper

Fry the finely chopped onion in 1 tablespoon oil or fat. Mince the pork and add it to the onion. Season with salt and pepper, mix well and braise until the meat is tender, adding a small amount of water if necessary, finally reducing the liquid until only the fat remains.

Peel the aubergines and cut them into very thin slices. Salt them lightly and leave them to sweat for twenty minutes. Wipe off any moisture, dip them in the flour, and fry quickly on both sides in the remaining oil or fat so that they are not quite completely cooked. Place the aubergine slices and the meat in alternate layers in a greased fireproof dish. One or two tomatoes may also be sliced, fried and slipped in between the layers.

Beat the eggs and mix with the sour cream and pour over the contents of the casserole. See that the egg mixture gets right in through the ingredients as evenly as possible. Bake for 20 minutes in a hot oven.

Dishes to Serve with Vegetables

There are a number of recipes for dumplings and other accompaniments for vegetable dishes. Sometimes they are eaten as a snack on their own, but usually they are served with vegetable dishes, particularly the basic braised vegetables.

First two potato dishes.

Burgonyahab – Creamed Potatoes

600g potatoes (1¼ lbs.)
1–2 tbs. sour cream
salt and pepper
2 dl milk (⅜ pint)
30g bacon dripping (1 oz.)

Boil and mash the potatoes in the usual way.

Make the fat hot and add the potatoes. Heat the milk and add it to the potatoes gradually. Beat well with a whisk. Season with salt and pepper and mix in the sour cream.

For potatoes whose jackets are not elegant enough for serving, remove them and combine the potatoes with onion – this is particularly useful for potatoes which do not have much to offer even under their jackets in terms of flavour.

Hagymás burgonya – Onion Potatoes

Boil 700g potatoes (1½ lbs.). Skin them and break them down a bit into pieces, crumbling them without mashing them.

In a separate pan fry a large onion, chopped finely in 60–80g (2–3 oz.) dripping from smoked streaky bacon until it is just transparent. Add the potatoes all at once, toss them around in the fat, season with salt and serve.

Although the self-service restaurants in Budapest tend to consider their art complete by dropping that summary slice of pork on *főzelék* dishes – the basic kind of dish where any appropriate vegetable is braised and then finished with a *roux* – elsewhere this predictability is roundly dispelled by a bundle of balls, 'poles' and dumplings which form a firm island for vegetarians to feel at home on. Many of them can be eaten on their own but their original purpose is to float decoratively in a sea of braised, creamed or *puréed* vegetables.

Spenótos labdacs – Spinach Balls

250g spinach (8 oz.)	2 eggs
2 tbs. flour	120g bacon dripping (4 oz.) ,salt

Boil the spinach in salted water until it is reduced, drain it and then press it through a sieve. Add the yolks of the two eggs, the flour and then the stiffly beaten egg whites.

Make the dripping hot. Shape spoonfuls of the spinach mixture into balls and fry them quickly all over.

Burgonyalabdacs – Potato Balls

2 potatoes	1 egg
half an onion	1 tbs. flour
salt, pepper and parsley	120g bacon dripping (4 oz.)

Grate the raw potatoes and drain them in a sieve, or toss them in a cloth to dry.

Chop the onion very finely and fry it lightly in 30g (1 oz.) of the fat. Remove the pan from the heat, add the potato, mix in the egg yolk, the flour and some parsley, and finally fold in the stiffly beaten white of the egg.

With a greased spoon form rounds from the mixture and fry them golden in the remainder of the fat.

Several of these recipes for accompaniments use semolina. It is as simple as flour to cook with and its crumby texture gives it a variety of uses: Hungarian cooking exploits these to the full and different kinds of semolina recipes can be found dotted about this book. The Semolina Poles which follow are excellent; roasted semolina is good for pecking at and irresistible to children who refuse semolina pudding, and with potatoes added it is well above the snack rank.

Dararúd – Semolina Poles

100g semolina (3½ oz.)
2 eggs
100g bacon dripping (3½ oz.)
½ litre milk (scant 1 pint)
100g breadcrumbs (3½ oz.)
salt

Bring the milk to the boil and cook the semolina in it until it thickens well.

Allow it to cool and then mix in the beaten eggs. Work the mixture together and season with salt.

Form fingers from the mixture and dip them in breadcrumbs. Fry them golden in plenty of hot fat.

Pirított dara – Roasted Semolina

Count 50–60g (1½–2 oz.) semolina and a scant 10g (¼ oz.) bacon dripping per person.

First roast the semolina in a dry frying-pan over gentle heat moving it about all the time. When the semolina begins to change colour, add the fat gradually, continuing to stir. Let it become brown, but beware burning, season well with salt and then gradually add warm water in teaspoons or tablespoons so that the semolina can swell. The final consistency should be slightly dry and crumbly – not sauce-like! – and the kitchen will be pervaded by the same mealy aroma as when oatcakes are being baked.

A more substantial variation is to roast the semolina as above, using somewhat more fat: 50g (1½–2 oz.) semolina to 20g (¾ oz.) dripping per person. When it is ready, mix in cubed boiled potatoes. Put in a heated serving dish and throw in one chopped and fried onion.

Serve with any of the salads described earlier.

Zsemlegombóc – Roll Dumplings

Zsemlegombóc is what traditionally accompanies braised tripe in Hungary and also goes along with boiled meats which are served with a sauce.

3 dry rolls
2 dl milk (⅜ pint)
1 egg
50g bacon dripping (2 oz.)
350g flour (12 oz.)
1–2 boiled potatoes, grated

Cube the dry rolls and fry them gently in the dripping. Sprinkle with about two thirds of the milk.

Mix the flour and the egg, thin gradually with water and the remaining milk, and add the grated potato to make a light dough.

Mix in the fried rolls and work the mixture together until it is smooth; it is easiest to do this by hand.

With a spoon dipped in cold water form dumplings from the mixture and cook them in boiling salted water for about 15 minutes.

Szalonnás gombóc – Bacon Dumplings

To the ingredients given for Roll Dumplings above add 180–200g (6 oz.) smoked streaky bacon.

Fry the bacon and then the diced rolls in the fat from the bacon. Chop the bacon up finely, and then continue as above.

If you want to serve these dumplings as a separate dish, fry some breadcrumbs and roll the cooked dumplings in them and then sprinkle with grated cheese.

Bundás kenyér – Bread in a Jacket

It is perhaps the Hungarians' glee over a surprise that makes them cover things up and produce, for example, golden globes which turn out to be juicy mushrooms in a breadcrumb coat, and when they extend this to giving an egg jacket to a slice of bread, nobody can accuse them of not making the most of things.

Bread slices (use slightly dry bread)	1 egg
milk	100g bacon dripping (3–4 oz.)

Dip each slice of bread first in milk, then beaten egg, and fry immediately on both sides in hot fat.

It is better not to be too conscientious about beating the egg – if it is not very thoroughly done it will coat the bread more thickly.

Burgonyafánk – Potato Doughnuts

300g mashed potatoes (11 oz.)	100g flour (3½ oz.)
2 egg yolks	30g fat (or butter) (1 oz.)
10g yeast (¼ oz.)	6 tbs. milk
salt	120g fat for frying (4 oz.)

Warm the milk to blood heat and start the yeast working in it.

Beat the egg yolks and the butter to a cream.

Mix the potatoes and the flour, season with salt, and add the other ingredients, working everything together thoroughly with a wooden spoon, until the dough produces blisters on the surface.

Rest it for a good half hour in a warm place.

Roll the dough out to half-inch thickness on a floured board and cut rounds from it with a pastry cutter. Set them aside in a warm place to rise for 5–10 minutes more.

Fry them in the hot fat – which should, nevertheless, not be smoking hot.

Dumplings, Pancakes and Noodles

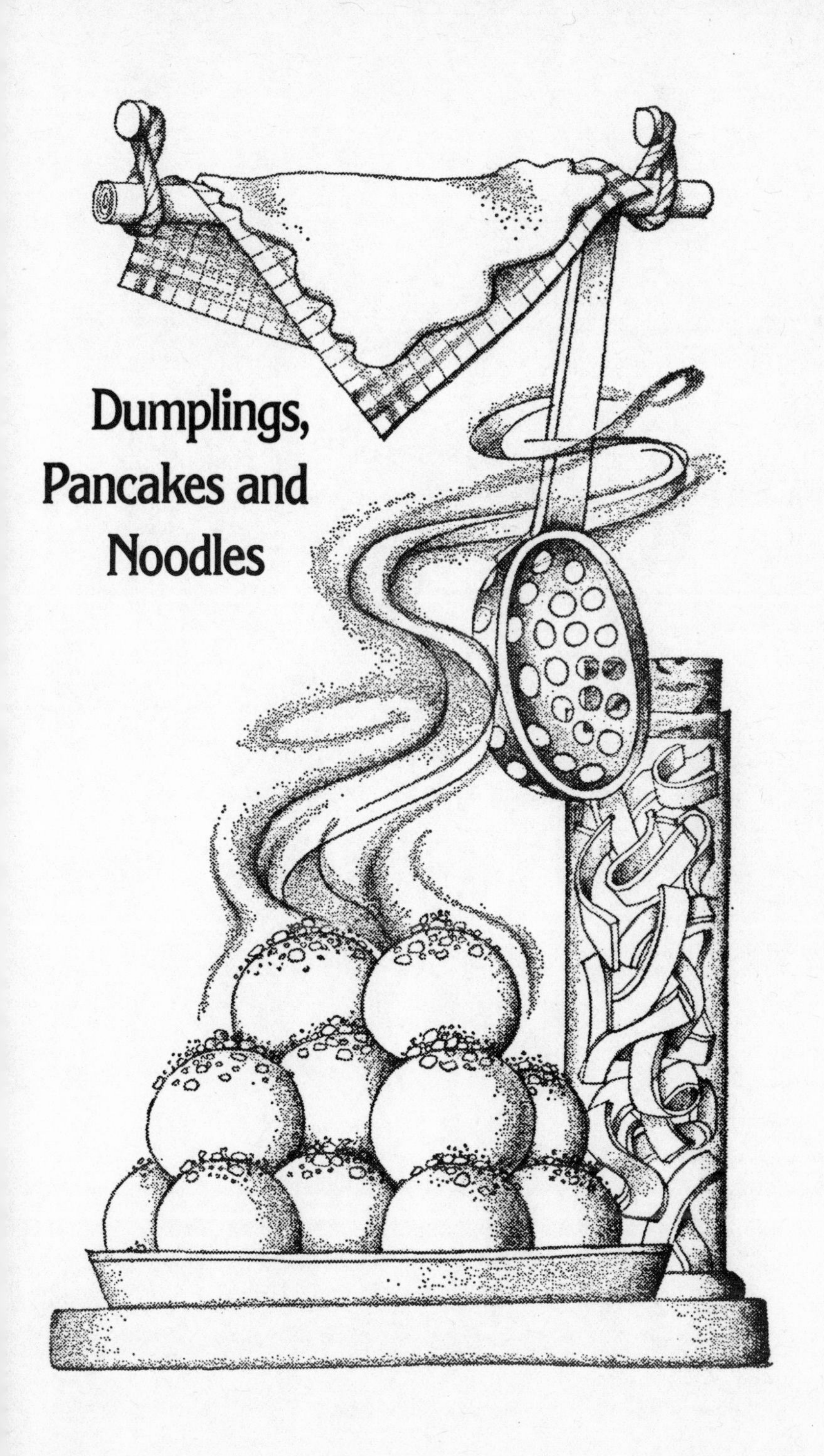

This is a section of Hungarian cooking which Hungarians themselves never tire of decrying – nor, fortunately, do they ever tire of eating the dishes involved. Eaten in moderation they will widen and enhance the diet. There is a clear link with Italy, which probably began in the fifteenth century when Beatrix, the wife of the Hungarian King Mátyás, brought with her from her homeland not only cheese, onions, garlic and aniseed but chestnuts, which became naturalized and have remained firm favourites ever since. The boiled dough recipes begin with pasta dishes, and these are followed by *galuskas* made from a slightly softer dough which is much easier to work with. Then there are two richer variations of the basic doughs: one uses potatoes as its main ingredient and the other uses curds.

Basic Boiled Dough

Although you may prefer to use the convenient ready-made *pasta* preparations which are available, not even the best buy can match fresh home-made dough.

For each person take 100–120g flour (3½–4 oz.) and 1–2 eggs for each ½ kg (1 lb.) of flour.

The appropriate quantities for four people are given in each recipe, but to prevent unnecessary repetition, here is the basic method for preparing the dough as it is made by Hungarians.

Place the sifted flour in a deep bowl, make a hollow in the centre and break the egg(s) into this hollow. Add water, the volume of the water being the same as that of the egg. You may need more but, since the dough has to be firm, it is better not to overdo the water at the beginning. Work the ingredients thoroughly together with the fingers to make a stiff dough. Continue working it on a baking board. Divide the dough into two or three lumps, cover them with a cloth and leave them to rest for 5–10 minutes.

No salt is included in the dough since it tends to soften it.

Roll out each lump of dough separately, using the absolute minimum of extra flour to prevent sticking. The thickness will depend on the recipe, but varies between that of paper and that of a match.

Once the dough has dried enough so that it is no longer in the slightest sticky, roll a sheet of the dough onto the rolling pin, cut it lengthwise down the middle and then cut pieces of whatever size and shape you need.

To cook them, bring a large pan of salted water to the boil, putting in only a few of the pieces of dough at a time so that the water does not at any point stop boiling.

Once the pieces rise to the surface of the water they are ready to be drained, rinsed quickly in warm water, and tossed in a little moderately hot fat. Home-made dough will take considerably less time to cook than bought *pasta.*

Each person's portion of the boiled strips, squares or curls is then given the accompaniment which provides the particular dish with its name and its character. The accompaniment can be mixed in all at one go before dividing the material into individual portions, but most Hungarians prefer to heap an appropriate amount of the accompaniment on each person's individual portion and serve the dish like that. These accompaniments are inexhaustible in their variety, beginning with crumbly curds or grated cheese, and below I have chosen some of those which may strike a new note to British ears. Novelty, however, is not in itself enough to secure success, and one special point to remember in presenting these boiled doughs is that thoroughly heated serving dishes are of primary importance. These recipes provide the dishes which follow meat courses in a full dinner, but they are also frequently eaten by Hungarians as one-course lunches.

Darás metélt – Semolina Noodles

400g flour (13 oz.)	1 egg
80g semolina (3 oz.)	100g fat (3–4 oz.)
salt	

Form a firm dough from the egg and the flour with some water as described above. Roll out the dough to matchstick thickness and cut it into strips about half an inch in breadth.

Brown the semolina evenly in the fat. Add 1 tablespoon of water so that it will swell, then add another – until the semolina grains separate and you have a loose mealy mixture. Season with salt.

Meanwhile, cook the dough strips in salted boiling water. Drain them well and then mix them carefully with the semolina. Taste for salt, return the whole to the heat, mixing it about constantly to make it evenly hot, and serve immediately.

Sonkás kocka – Ham Noodles

½ kg flour (1 lb.)	3 eggs
2 dl sour cream (⅜ pint)	200g smoked ham or smoked meat (7 oz.)
60g fat (2 oz.)	
breadcrumbs	

Work the flour and 1 egg to a firm dough with water, roll it out and cut it into inch squares. Boil these as described above, drain them and toss them in 30g (1 oz.) hot fat.

Beat the remaining 2 egg yolks with 30g (1 oz.) fat or butter, mix in the minced ham and then the sour cream. Finally fold in the two stiffly beaten egg whites. Pour this mixture over the cooked squares and mix thoroughly but carefully. Grease an ovenproof dish and line it with breadcrumbs. Pour in the mixture and bake in a fairly hot oven for 25–30 minutes.

Túrós metélt kaporral – Curd Noodles with Dill

½ kg flour (1 lb.)	200g sheep's curds (7 oz.)
1 egg	60g fat (2 oz.)
fresh dill	6 tbs. sour cream

Prepare the dough from the flour and the egg as above, cut it into strips and cook these in the usual way. Drain them well and toss them in the heated fat.

Crumb the curds (use ordinary curds from cow's milk if it is impossible to find sheep's curds, or use a good pure curd cheese). Mix the curds with the cooked noodles and serve immediately. At the table, top each portion with a full tablespoon of sour cream and then sprinkle liberally with freshly chopped dill leaves.

Mákos metélt, diós metélt – Poppy Seed Noodles, Walnut Noodles

Prepare the dough from 400g (13 oz.) flour and one egg as described above.

Cook it, drain it and toss the noodles in 40g fat (1½ oz.).

Take 120g (4 oz.) poppy seeds or ground walnuts, mix them with 100g (3 oz.) castor sugar or honey and mix into the noodles.

To serve decorate the top with more poppy seeds or walnuts.

Rakott metélt – Layered Noodles

Dough from ½ kg (1 lb.) flour and 1 egg
200g apricot jam (7 oz.)
80g ground walnuts (3 oz.)
80g sugar (3 oz.)
60g fat (2 oz.)

Cut the dough into strips, cook them, drain them and toss them in the heated fat as in the preceding recipes.

Mix the walnuts with the sugar.

In a greased dish place alternate layers of the noodles, the walnuts, and the jam. A thick somewhat tart jam is best here.

The last layer should be strips of dough.

Bake in a moderate oven for 30–35 minutes.

Poppy seeds mixed with sugar may also be included in this dish.

Lekváros derelye – Jam Pockets

This next dish is popularly known as *barátfüle* – Friend's Ears – but the official title is less suggestive!

½ kg flour (1 lb.)	60g fat (2 oz.)
300g thick, stiff plum jam (11 oz.)	100g fine breadcrumbs (3½ oz.)
cinnamon	60g sugar (2 oz.)
2 eggs	salt, white of egg

Mix the flour thoroughly with the lightly beaten eggs and as much water as you need to produce a very firm dough. Roll it out thinly and divide it into two.

Working quickly so that the dough will not dry out, place small spoonfuls of the plum jam 1½–2 inches away from each other on one of the sheets of dough. Brush the spaces between the dots of jam with white of egg. Place the other sheet of dough on top, pressing it down carefully between the dots of jam. With a fluted cutter – they are traditionally square in Hungary – separate out into individual 'pockets'.

Drop these pockets into a large pan of boiling salted water and keep them boiling for somewhat longer than the usual cooking time for *pasta* forms.

Meanwhile fry the breadcrumbs golden in the fat, adding a good pinch of salt. Drain the jam pockets thoroughly when the dough is cooked, and mix in the breadcrumbs carefully. Before serving sprinkle with the sugar mixed with a little cinnamon. The sweetness of the cinnamon must be firmly contrasted in the combination of flavours by the salt seasoning – the final flavour is perhaps better described as biting than sweet.

Túrós derelye – Curd Pockets

These are made in the same way as the jam pockets described above but the plum jam is replaced by a curd mixture as a filling.

Filling	60g sugar (2 oz.)
300g well drained curds (11 oz.)	2 eggs

Break down the curds with a fork and mix with the eggs and the sugar. Place little islands of the curd mixture on the dough, making the pockets a little larger than in the preceding recipe.

To serve mix as above with salted fried breadcrumbs and sprinkle lightly with sugar.

A country variation of this recipe omits the sugar and bread-crumbs are not mixed in. The pockets are boiled as usual and then they are liberally sprinkled with sour cream and bacon fat which has been diced and fried until it is crisp.

Gránátos Kocka – Potato Noodles

It is interesting to notice the way in which at least one Hungarian reacts to one of the most popular 'fillers' in his national cuisine. The compiler of the only available Hungarian–English dictionary begins his description of *Gránátos kocka* with the strange condem-nation – 'an inferior dish . . .' This may not stem so much from snobbery as from a genuine concern, because the Hungarian diet contains such an endless variety of doughs and potato dishes, but as long as one keeps the 'doughs in moderation' attitude in mind, this dish, far from being inferior, is of outstanding value.

A similar very popular recipe can be found in the vegetable chapter in the cabbage section: chopped red cabbage is mixed with the squares of dough and strongly flavoured with black pepper (*see* page 91).

dough made from ½ kg (1 lb.) flour and 1 or 2 eggs
½ kg potatoes (1 lb.)
paprika powder
80g fat (3 oz.)
1 onion

Make the dough and cut into one inch squares and cook as de-scribed above.

Boil the potatoes in their jackets, peel them and break them up roughly without mashing them.

Fry the onion lightly in the fat, sprinkle with a little paprika powder and put in the potatoes, stirring them about until they are well covered with the fat, paprika and onion. Then mix in the cooked squares carefully.

Serve with any of the fresh salads described earlier – preferably cucumber.

Galuskas

Galuskas are made from a dough which is similar to the basic 'boiled dough' recipe, but it is softer. The dough is not rolled out and so these *galuska* recipes are quicker and easier to make.

Basic galuska dough

600g flour (1¼ lbs.)
6 tbs. milk
salt
1–2 eggs
30g melted fat (1 oz.)
water

Mix the beaten egg, or eggs if you can spare more than one, with the fat and the milk. Work in the flour and enough water gradually to make a medium dough, not too soft and not too hard. This *galuska* dough is much softer than the firm dough for rolling out described earlier – although the basic ingredients are the same more water is used. To get a really light dough, mix it with no more than the minimum of stirring, and prepare the dough only immediately before it is to be cooked.

Although there are several ways of dividing the dough into *galuskas* the simplest and most common method is to place the dough (dividing it into two if necessary to make it easier to handle) on a small cutting board and cut off marble-sized pieces into boiling salted water, first dipping both board and knife in water. The shape of each *galuska* is irregular so there is no need to shape carefully. They are ready when they rise to the surface of the water. Drain them, rinse them by pouring a kettle or pan of hot water over them and put them in a deep serving bowl with a little very hot fat. Stir them about so that all the *galuskas* become coated in the fat and serve as described in the following recipes.

Somogyi galuska – Somogy Galuskas

Somogy is a strongly individual county to the south of the Balaton as consciously traditional as, for example, the Palóc area in the north. This recipe is for *galuskas* in the Somogy style.

Prepare the *galuskas* as described above and then mix them about in this sauce.

Chop 1 onion and fry it lightly in 60g (2 oz.) fat. Sprinkle with a good pinch of paprika powder and pour in 2 dl ($\frac{3}{8}$ pint) sour cream. Bring to the boil, mix with the cooked *galuskas* and serve immediately.

Tojásos galuska – Galuskas with Eggs

Prepare and cook the *galuskas* as above.

Melt 60g (2 oz.) fat. Mix 4 beaten eggs with 6 tablespoons of milk or sour cream. Pour this mixture into the fat, stir it about as for scrambled eggs. When the eggs just begin to set (don't let them dry out), mix them in with the *galuskas*. Serve with lettuce salad.

Sztrapacska

Sztrapacska is a Hungarian dish from the highland part of the old Hungary, now in Czechoslovakia.

1 kg potatoes (2 lbs.)
60g fat (2 oz.)
150g curds, traditionally sheep's curds (5 oz.)
1 egg
400–500g flour ($\frac{3}{4}$–1 lb.)
9 tbs. sour cream

Peel the potatoes and grate them finely. Mix in 20g ($\frac{3}{4}$ oz.) melted fat, the egg and enough flour to give a dough slightly firmer than the usual *galuska* dough. It is necessary to work quickly with this dough or it will tend to become brown because of the raw potatoes. Cut off small *galuskas* into abundant boiling water and cook for about 10 minutes. Drain, rinse quickly with hot water and stir about in a little hot fat.

Crumb the curds, mix in with the *galuskas* and serve sprinkled with the sour cream.

Juhtúrós galuska – Sheep's Curd Galuskas with Dill

400g flour (13 oz.)	2 eggs
2 dl sour cream (⅜ pint)	60g smoked streaky bacon (2 oz.)
200g fresh sheep's curds (7 oz.)	30g butter (1 oz.)
large handful chopped fresh dill	salt

Prepare the dough from the flour, eggs and a little water, adding a good pinch of salt. Break off thumb-sized twirls into boiling salted water and cook as in the preceding recipes. Drain them well.

Dice the bacon, fry it lightly and mix in among the *galuskas.* Season with a little salt and add half the sour cream and half the dill. Mix well together and place in a greased fireproof dish. Crumb the curds over the *galuskas*, pour on the remaining sour cream and sprinkle with the other half of the dill. Lastly sprinkle the melted butter on top and bake in a moderate oven for 8–9 minutes. Serve immediately.

Potato Dough

The recipes which follow are prepared from a dough in which mashed potatoes are used as a basic material along with flour. The dough is sometimes boiled, sometimes fried, and in any form is considered finer than the more 'ordinary' dishes made from boiled doughs.

To make the basic dough use 1 kg potatoes (2 lbs.); about 200–300g flour (7–10 oz.), depending on how mealy the potatoes are; 1 heaped tablespoon semolina; 30g (1 oz.) fat; 1 egg; salt.

Boil the potatoes in their jackets. Peel them, mash them and mix them thoroughly with the fat, flour and semolina. Season with salt and work in the egg.

Burgonya-sodrott – Potato Twists

Divide the dough into two or three to make it more manageable and roll each lump in turn to finger thickness. Cut into small strips about 1 inch long and less than ½ inch wide. Flour these strips well and with one movement of the palm roll up each strip on the table into a small cylinder shape. Boil them in abundant salted water for 10–12 minutes, drain them well and turn them about carefully in 120g (4 oz.) breadcrumbs which have been fried golden in 100g (3–4 oz.) fat. Heat through and serve immediately.

These twists are served with sugar or with salt, as you choose, but if you prefer the savoury idea, season the breadcrumbs with a little salt when frying them.

Szilvás gombóc – Plum Dumplings

Each section of Hungarian cooking seems to include its own special surprise in the form of a dumpling or something subtly concealed within a batter or breadcrumb coating. The plum dumpling is an unrivalled *pièce de résistance* which again hints at the salty-sweet concept encountered earlier in 'Friend's Ears'.

I have never known any lack of plums in Hungary – if not fresh, then the most beautiful preserved fruit – and although in times of stress the substitution of thick plum jam for the whole plum is theoretically permitted, I think the recipe is so good that it deserves the best possible ingredients.

Prepare the potato dough as above and roll it out until you have a large sheet about half an inch thick (not less). Cut it into 4-inch squares. In the middle of each square place a stoned plum – some people like to replace the stone with cinnamon. Fold the corners of the square together and shape into a ball. Cook these balls in boiling water until the dumplings rise to the surface. Then remove the pan from the heat and leave them for a minute longer. Drain the dumplings and roll them about in 60–80g (2–3 oz.) breadcrumbs which have been fried golden in fat and seasoned with a little salt. To serve sprinkle the dumplings with castor sugar mixed with cinnamon.

Hússal töltött burgonyagombóc – Meat Dumplings

Prepare the basic potato dough as described above.

Filling

250–300g pork or veal (8–10 oz.)
60g fat (2 oz.)
2 dl sour cream (⅜ pint)

Braise the cubed meat in the fat and its own juices until it is tender and then mince or chop it up finely. Cut the dough into 3-inch squares, place a little of the filling on each and then form them into balls. Cook as in the preceding recipe in boiling salted water and then drain them.

Add the sour cream to the juices remaining from the braising, bring to the boil and then roll the dumplings around in this mixture.

Serve immediately, garnished with fresh chopped parsley.

Curd Doughs

Fresh curds form the basis of a large number of Hungarian dishes and here I have included the two favourite recipes where curds are used to form a dough. The first recipe is an 'everyday' treasure which manages to seem rich and yet remain very light – a perfect finish to any full meal.

Túrógombóc – Curd Dumplings

600g fresh curds (1¼ lbs.)
2 eggs
6 tbs. sour cream
50g breadcrumbs (1½–2 oz.)
salt
100g semolina (3½ oz.)
2 tbs. flour
30g fat (1 oz.)
30g butter (1 oz.)

Press the curds through a sieve or put them through a mincer. Mix in the eggs, semolina, a pinch of salt and the flour. Dip a knife or spoon in water and use it to form balls from the dough about half the size of an egg.

Have a large pan of water ready boiling and cook the dumplings in it for about 5 minutes. Take one out and cut it in two – if it is spongy right through, the dumplings are ready.

Drain them well and roll them carefully in a dish with the hot fat. Pour on the sour cream and then sprinkle with the breadcrumbs which have been fried golden in the butter, rolling the dumplings about to get them coated all over with the crumbs.

These dumplings are served seasoned with salt or sugar: both are placed on the table and you can choose whichever you prefer.

Styriai metélt – Styrian Noodles

½ kg curds (1 lb.)
40g butter (1¼ oz.)
3 dl sour cream (½ pint)
2 tbs. castor sugar
salt
200g flour (7 oz.)
4 eggs
rind of half a lemon
50g sultanas (1½ oz.)
breadcrumbs

Prepare a dough from the finely broken curds, 1 egg, the flour, a good pinch of salt and 1 tablespoon sour cream. Roll it out to matchstick thickness and cut it into noodles about half an inch broad and a little over an inch long. Cook them in boiling salted water as in the preceding recipe and drain them well.

Beat the butter with the yolks of the three remaining eggs until creamy, mix in the sugar and the sour cream and again beat well. Add the grated lemon rind, the sultanas and finally fold in the stiffly beaten egg whites.

Mix this cream very carefully with the cooked noodles and place in a dish which has been greased and lined with breadcrumbs.

Bake in a moderate oven for 35–40 minutes. Turn it out and sprinkle with castor sugar.

Pancakes

Hungarian cooks make perfect pancakes. Apart from filling them with their characteristic tart apricot jam or with ground walnuts, they have the special Hortobágy pancake already described earlier (*see* p. 57), a wonderful fish pancake, and the recipes which follow. These include the fillings which are best known in Hungary and also some other ways of treating pancakes.

To make enough batter for about 12 pancakes, use the following proportions:

1 egg
150g flour (5 oz.)
3 dl milk (½ pint)
6 tablespoons soda water or water, a pinch of salt, sugar – use 1 tablespoon if the filling is to be sweet, but even if not put in 1 teaspoon.
For frying you will need abut 60g fat (2 oz.)

Mix the egg with the flour, add the sugar, salt and then the milk – very gradually so as to keep the mixture smooth. Stir and beat until smooth after each small addition of milk. Add the soda water – enough to make a very thin mixture, like cream.

To fry, brush an omelette pan with fat, make it very hot and put in two tablespoons of the mixture, moving the pan so as to make the dough spread evenly. Lower the heat immediately and let the pancake brown on one side, turn it over and finish the frying by turning the heat up a little once more.

If it is necessary to make a lot of pancakes, cook them in two pans simultaneously.

Of the multitude of fillings common in Hungary, some of the following may be new and attractive to British readers. My own favourite is certainly *túrókrémes palacsinta* – curd cream pancakes – which I first met in the *Paksi Halászcsárda*, an unassuming but warm and friendly restaurant where the cooks seem to know everything there is to know about making the most everyday dishes sparkle with freshness, flavour and the feeling they are made specially for you – which, in fact, they nearly always are.

Túrókrémes palacsinta – Curd Cream Pancakes

Filling for 12 pancakes
200g curds (7 oz.)
60g vanilla sugar (2 oz.)
rind of half a lemon
1 egg
2–3 dl sour cream (¼ –½ pint)

If they are dry and crumbly, break the curds through a sieve, mix in the egg yolk, 1–2 tablespoons sour cream, the grated lemon rind, and finally fold in the stiffly beaten egg white. Fill the pancakes with this mixture, roll them up, set them out in a well greased fireproof dish large enough to give them plenty of room, and sprinkle sour cream over each pancake. Put the dish in a very hot oven for a few minutes for the filling to heat through, sprinkle with the vanilla sugar and serve immediately.

Another recipe which uses a curd filling is more on the savoury side. For the filling:

150g (5 oz.) sheep's curds mixed with a little paprika powder
1 heaped tbs. fresh chopped dill
1 egg
a white sauce made from 20g (¾ oz.) butter, 20g (¾ oz.) flour and about 6 tbs. milk

Break down the curds if necessary, mix with the white sauce, the egg yolk, the dill and finally fold in the stiffly beaten egg white.

This filling is usually put on the pancakes in a different way. When the first side of each pancake is ready, it is turned as usual and then the pan is removed from the heat. Spread half the browned side of the pancake with some of the filling, fold the other half over on top of it and then return to the heat to brown on both the still unbrowned half-sides. Serve immediately.

If fresh dill is not available, try this recipe with fresh parsley in the filling instead, mixed if possible with a little fresh mint.

Apart from filling them, Hungarians have other excellent ways with pancakes, some of which are described below, beginning with the straightforward idea of adding something extra to the batter, in this case grated cabbage.

Káposztás palacsinta – Cabbage Pancakes

pancake dough as above
80g fat (3 oz.)
200g cabbage (7 oz.)
salt

Grate the cabbage finely, salt it lightly and set it aside for about 10 minutes. Then press away the liquid and mix well with the pancake batter. The batter should be a little thicker than the usual pancake batter as the juices from the cabbage tend to have a thinning effect.

Fry the pancakes in the customary way, and then fold each in four. Serve with freshly ground black pepper and serve.

Rakott palacsinta – Layered Pancakes

12 pancakes
120g sugar (4 oz.)
120g ground walnuts (4 oz.)

Lay the pancakes, unfolded, in a greased dish, sprinkling each one with the walnuts mixed with the sugar. Finish the pile with a pancake.

Heat thoroughly in a hot oven for 10–15 minutes. Sprinkle with vanilla or castor sugar and serve by cutting into slices vertically.

A variation of this which, in my experience, is more general in Hungary is to use different fillings in the same dish, the commonest being to spread one pancake with thick home-made apricot jam, the next with the walnut and sugar mixture, and so on alternately.

A further and richer variation is to prepare the pancakes with 3 egg yolks instead of 1 whole egg. Then layer them in a greased dish alternately with jam and nuts as above. Beat the egg whites until they are stiff, add 100g (3½ oz.) sugar, 2 tablespoons apricot jam, a few drops of lemon juice and then beat well. Pour the resulting 'foam' over the pancakes, smoothing the top with a knife. Just before serving bake for 10–15 minutes in a moderate oven until the top becomes brown. Serve by slicing vertically.

There is also a savoury dish which uses the above method. For 12 pancakes prepare a filling from the following ingredients:

200g minced cooked ham, or smoked meat (7 oz.)
2 tbs. sour cream
1 egg
a thick white sauce made from 20g butter (¾ oz.), 20g flour (¾ oz.) and about 6 tbs. milk
30g grated cheese (1 oz.)

Mix the minced ham into the white sauce and then fold in 1 tablespoon sour cream, the egg yolk and finally the stiffly beaten egg white. Place the pancakes in a greased dish, spreading each with the ham mixture. Have a pancake on top and bake for 20–25 minutes in a fairly hot oven. To serve, turn out onto a heated serving plate or leave in the baking dish – in either case sprinkle with 30g (1 oz.)

grated cheese and the remaining sour cream. Slice vertically as in the preceding recipes.

A somewhat stronger and richer flavour may be obtained by a variation of this last recipe which uses minced pork. For 12 pancakes you will need:

300g lean pork (11 oz.)
a white sauce made from 20g butter (¾ oz.), ½ tbs. flour and about 6 tbs. milk
60g fat (2 oz.)
2 tbs. sour cream

Braise the pork in the fat, using a minimum of water, until tender. When it is cooked mince or cut up the pork finely. Mix a little of the meat juices with 1 tablespoon of the sour cream and then mix it with the minced meat and the white sauce. Spread this filling on the layered pancakes and over the top pour the rest of the meat juices mixed with 1 tablespoon of sour cream. Bake and serve as described in the ham dish above.

Spenótos palacsinta felfújt – Spinach Pancake Soufflé

12 pancakes
400g spinach (13 oz.)
2 tbs. sour cream
120g finely chopped ham (4 oz.)
60g grated cheese (2 oz.)
3 eggs

Boil the spinach in the usual way and then press it through a sieve. Add the yolks of the 3 eggs, the sour cream, half the cheese and the ham. Fold in the stiffly beaten egg whites.

Layer the pancakes with this mixture in a well greased oven-proof dish and bake in a moderately hot oven for 45 minutes until the mixture begins to rise. Turn it out, sprinkle with sour cream and the remaining cheese, and slice.

This recipe is varied by using cauliflower crushed and mixed with sour cream as a filling, or chopped mushrooms with sour cream – and even a combination using a cream of cauliflower and spinach.

Csúsztatott palacsinta – Slipped Pancakes

4 eggs
2½ dl (or more) milk (½ pint)
100g vanilla sugar (3½ oz.)
salt
60g butter (2 oz.)
100g flour (3½ oz.)
200g apricot jam (7 oz.)
80g fat for frying (3 oz.)

Cream the butter, add the eggs one by one, sprinkling each with a little flour, fold in the remaining flour and add a pinch of salt. Thin gradually with the milk, mixing very thoroughly. Finally fold in the stiffly beaten egg whites. Fry the pancakes on one side and when they are nicely browned on one side do not turn them over but slide them into a greased round dish with the browned side downwards. Sprinkle the other side with vanilla sugar, spread thinly with jam and slip the following pancake on top. Repeat until all the batter is used up and put the last pancake on top with the browned side upwards. Sprinkle with vanilla sugar and serve immediately.

Pancake batter is also used as a covering in which to deep-fry various vegetables and meat slices. For this purpose the batter is made thicker than for ordinary pancakes – that is, using less milk. A small amount (10g–¼ oz.) of yeast may be added, in which case the batter is allowed to rise and treated further in the way customary with yeast doughs.

Puddings and Desserts

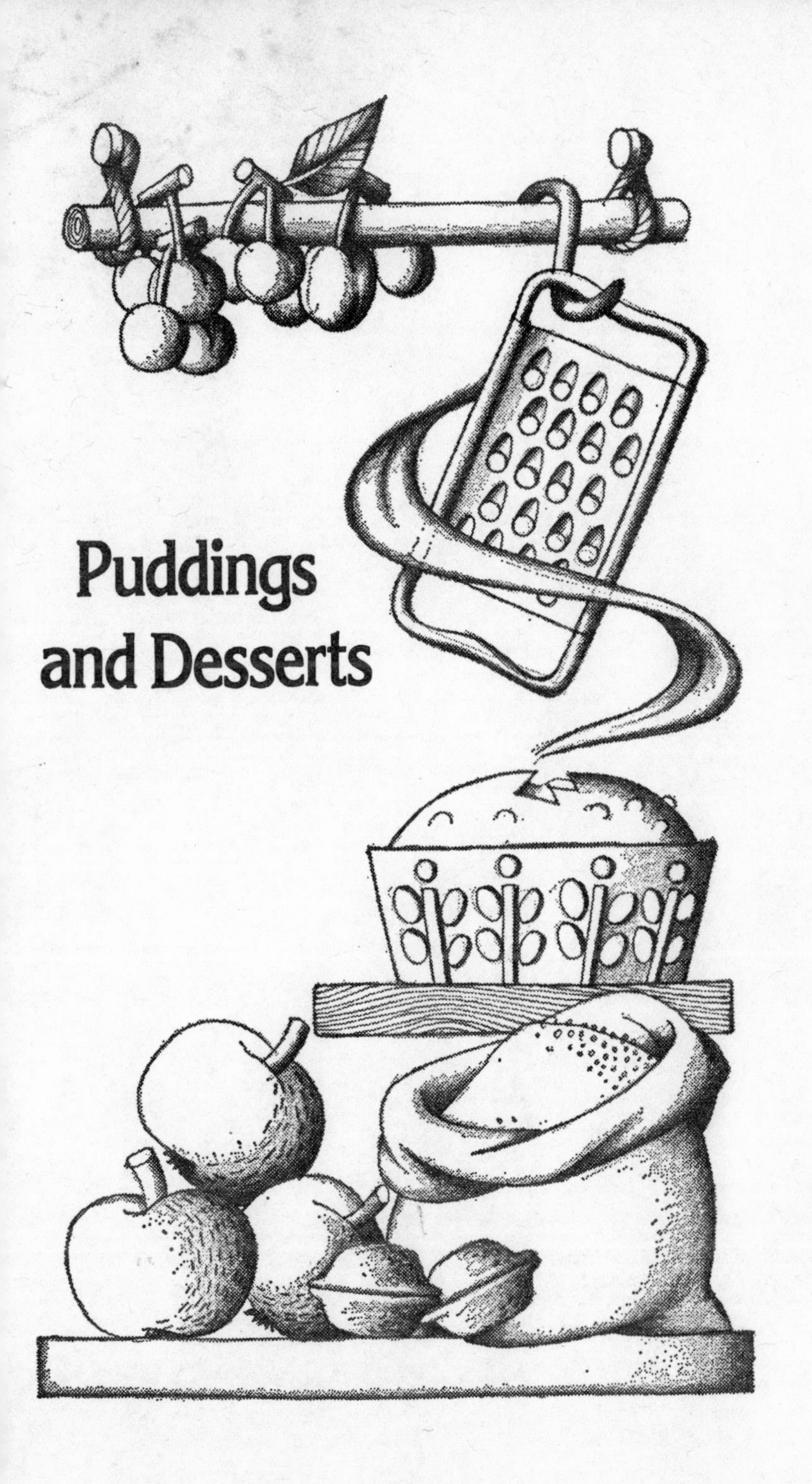

Hungarian desserts range from a few unusual yeast puddings through curd and apple *soufflés* to a wide variety of chilled creams. But in this section the Hungarian kitchen's finest contribution to any international collection of recipes would probably be the *rétes* (*strudel*): a wafer-thin pastry with various fillings, often served cold when eaten as a dessert. The *rétes* recipes come at the end of the chapter. First come the puddings – these are usually accompanied by sauces, some simple and thin, some very rich.

Aranygaluska borhabbal – Golden Galuskas with Wine Sauce

½ kg flour (1 lb.)
2 egg yolks
60g butter or margarine (2 oz.)
200g shelled walnuts (7 oz.)
20g yeast (½–¾ oz.)
3 dl milk (½ pint)
250g sugar (8 oz.)
50g fat or margarine for brushing (1½ oz.)

Warm 6 tablespoons of the milk slightly, add 1 teaspoon from the sugar and put in the yeast. Sprinkle 1 tablespoon from the flour over this, stir it lightly once and leave in a warm place until the mixture rises – about 10 minutes.

Cream 60g (2 oz.) sugar and the egg yolks and beat them until light and fluffy. Gradually pour in the rest of the milk with a pinch of salt. Sift the flour, make a hollow in the middle and pour in the sugar-egg mixture and then the risen yeast mixture. Work thoroughly together with a wooden spoon until blisters begin to show on the surface. Then add the melted butter and again work together well. Leave in a warm place for at least 1 hour to double in size.

When it has risen put the dough out on a floured board, knock it down and then roll it out lightly until it is about 1 inch thick. With a very small cutter cut out rounds from the dough and place a row of these over the bottom of a greased tin, brushing each round lightly with the melted fat or margarine. Then mix the remaining sugar with the ground walnuts and sprinkle the layer generously with some of the mixture.

Repeat this whole process with another layer of dough rounds and cover again with the walnuts and sugar – the top layer should be dough.

Leave in a warm place once more to double in size and then bake for 30–40 minutes in a slow-moderate oven until deep brown on top.

Turn out on to a serving dish, sprinkle with vanilla sugar: to serve, *aranygaluskas* are not cut but pulled apart with tongs – the originally separate rounds will have joined together in the baking but they can easily be pulled apart again.

Although the *kugelhopf* (a deep circular fluted mould) is traditional for baking these *galuskas* in Hungary, there is no reason why you should not use an ordinary cake tin or baking dish for this recipe.

Vanilla sauce accompanies it on ordinary days; but where *aranygaluskas* are concerned Hungarians like to think of every day as a celebration day and serve this delicious, and expensive, wine sauce with it.

Borhab – Wine Sauce

Just over 6 dl (1 pint) white wine
200g sugar (7 oz.) – less if you use a sweet wine
1 tbs. flour
4 dl water (¾ pint)
6 eggs
rind of half a lemon

Mix the wine, water and grated lemon rind.

Mix the sugar with the flour, add the eggs one by one and beat until smooth and frothy.

Pour in the liquids, mix until just smooth and then above a pan of boiling water whisk continuously until the whole mixture is light and thickly frothy.

Although the quantities given above are those used by Hungarians, I have found half quantities to be more than adequate for five people.

Daramorzsa – Semolina Crumbs

100g semolina (3½ oz.)
50g sugar (2 oz.)
grated rind of half a lemon
½ litre milk (1 pint)
3 eggs
50g fat or butter (1½ oz.)

Pour the cold milk over the semolina and set it aside for 1 hour.

Cream the egg yolks with the sugar and lemon rind and combine with the semolina. Beat the egg whites until they are stiff and fold them into the mixture as well.

Heat the fat in a frying-pan, pour in the mixture and allow it to brown in one piece without stirring it. Once the bottom has browned, break it up roughly with a fork and mix the whole around until it has all browned a little.

To serve, heap onto individual plates, sprinkle with castor sugar – mixed with some ground walnuts if you like – and put 1 heaped tablespoon of jam of a less sweet kind, preferably apricot, at the side of each person's helping.

Máglyarakás – Hungarian Bread Pudding

200g light milk bread (7 oz.)
100g sugar (4 oz.)
30g butter (1 oz.)
about 4 tbs. rum
½ kg apples (1 lb.)
3 eggs
½ litre milk (1 pint)
100g ground walnuts (4 oz.)
100g sultanas or preserved sour cherries (4 oz.)
3 tbs. apricot jam

Cut the bread, which should be 1–2 days old, into small slices. Hungarians use *croissants* which are much better, because they have more crust, and the dough is thus much less uniform.

Cream the egg yolks with the sugar and mix in the melted butter. Add the milk and pour the mixture over the sliced bread or *croissants*. Set aside for the bread to become thoroughly soaked.

Grease a broad fireproof dish and place a layer of the soaked mixture in the bottom. Soak the sultanas or sour cherries in a little rum and sprinkle on a layer of these with some of the ground walnuts.

Slice the apples thinly and cover the top with that, sticking them vertically into the dough. Bake for 30 minutes in a moderate to hot oven.

Meanwhile beat the egg whites stiff, add the apricot jam and pour over the baked mixture. Smooth with a knife. Return to the oven for 10–15 minutes, reducing the heat to slow, until the cream rises well and browns a little. To serve cut into large blocks.

Forgácsfánk or *Csöröge* – Doughnut Shavings or Rattles

This crisp doughnut variation gets its names – the English translations are absolutely literal – because they are a little hard on the outside and tend to look like shavings or bits left over from something else and they rattle against each other on the plate.

250g flour (8 oz.)
50g butter (1½ oz.)
50g vanilla sugar (1½ oz.)
200g apricot jam (7 oz.)
pinch salt
100g vanilla sugar for sprinkling (3 oz.)
4 egg yolks
10g yeast (¼–½ oz.)
6 tbs. sour cream
1 tbs. rum
fat for frying
milk

Cream the yeast with 1 tablespoon lukewarm milk.

Crumb the butter into the flour. Mix in the yeast, egg yolks, salt, 50g (1½ oz.) vanilla, sugar and sour cream and work well together to give a smooth, fairly firm dough. Set aside to rise for about half an hour.

Roll out the dough very thinly and cut it into 4–5 inch squares. Inside the squares make two or three cuts but leave a band intact all round the outside edges: then fold the corners in and out through the slits to make an entirely irregular shape.

Take a large quantity of fat, heat it until it just begins to smoke and fry the 'shavings' until brown and crisp. Take them out onto paper to drain. To serve, sprinkle while they are still hot with vanilla sugar and place spoonfuls of apricot jam mixed with a little rum on each person's plate.

Somlói galuska

Somlói Galuska is one of the richest surprises among Hungarian sweets. The pastry-shops and coffee-houses seem to compete with each other as to who can produce the most enticing and delicious *Somlói.* It consists of a light sponge, a nut and raisin filling, a cream and a chocolate sauce.

For the cream

½ litre milk (1 pint)
2 tsp. powdered gelatine
4 egg yolks
1 tbs. flour
vanilla
100g sugar (3½ oz.)

Chocolate sauce

6 tbs. fresh double cream
2 egg yolks
100g sugar (3½ oz.)
1–2 tbs. rum
pinch of flour
2 dl milk (⅜ pint)
30g cocoa (1 oz.)
60g plain chocolate (2 oz.)
vanilla

Syrup

250g sugar (8 oz.)
grated lemon and orange rind
6 tbs. rum
vanilla

Filling

60g sultanas (2 oz.)
100g apricot jam (mashed smooth if necessary) (4 oz.)
100g ground walnuts (4 oz.)
20g cocoa (½ oz.)

Sponge

9 eggs
10g cocoa (¼ oz.)
60g ground walnuts (2 oz.)
200g sugar (6½ oz.)
200g flour (6½ oz.)

To serve

100g vanilla castor sugar (3½ oz.) — ½ litre whipping cream (1 pint)

First prepare three layers of sponge. Cream the yolks of the 9 eggs with the 200g (6½ oz.) sugar. When the cream becomes quite white, add the stiffly beaten egg whites and the flour. Divide the mixture quickly into three – one to be baked as a straightforward sponge; into the second mix the ground walnuts and into the third the cocoa. Bake each sponge separately in a shallow flat tin (preparing the tins in the usual way) in a moderately hot oven (about 375°F, gas 5) for 12–15 minutes. If a deep cake tin is used the baking may take up to 25–30 minutes. Allow the sponges to cool.

For the cream, bring the milk to the boil with half the sugar and a small piece of vanilla. Meanwhile beat the egg yolks with the remaining sugar until white, add the flour and the gelatine, and mix it into the milk, whisking quickly all the time. Stir and mix over very low heat or in the top of a double boiler until it thickens. Remove the pan from the heat and leave to cool. Do not let the cream come to the boil at any time – just keep it warm enough to give off steam, letting it thicken very slowly. Remove the vanilla pod.

To make the chocolate sauce put the milk on gentle heat with a small piece of vanilla, the sugar, and the broken chocolate. Meanwhile mix the egg yolks with the cream, cocoa and flour until smooth. Whisking continuously, mix into the hot milk. Before it comes to the boil, remove it from the heat, mix in the rum and then leave it to cool. Remove the vanilla pod.

Make a syrup from the ingredients given.

Take the cocoa sponge and soak by pouring some of the rum syrup over it. Spread on half the cream, sprinkle with half the ground walnuts and half the sultanas.

On top of this put the walnut sponge and soak this, too, with rum syrup. Then put on the remainder of the cream and sprinkle again with walnuts and sultanas.

Finish by placing the plain sponge on top and soaking with the remainder of the rum syrup. Spread this top layer with apricot jam, sprinkle with cocoa powder and leave in the refrigerator for at least 12 hours.

To serve, dip a spoon in warm water and spoon out large *galuskas* onto chilled plates. Whip the cream, flavouring it with the vanilla sugar. Pipe over the sponge *galuskas* and finally pour on the cold chocolate sauce.

These quantities give enough for about ten people. Half quantities are also practicable but less than that would be unrealistic and would detract from the quality.

Vargabéles – Cobbler's Curds

Vargabéles is a baked pudding which has a curd cream filling mixed with noodles between two thin layers of a rich short pastry.

180g flour (6 oz.)
6 tbs. sour cream
120g butter (4 oz.)
pinch of salt

To make the pastry, sift the flour and salt and rub in the butter. Mix in the sour cream to make a soft dough. Leave the pastry in a cold place for 2–3 hours.

Divide the dough into two and roll out each lump as thinly as possible. One sheet of the pastry goes to line the bottom of the baking tin, while the other is placed on top of the filling.

Filling

120g flour (4 oz.)
3 level tbs. castor sugar
400g curds (13 oz.)
salt
3 eggs
6 tbs. sour cream
50g sultanas (1½ oz.)

Make a firm dough from the flour and 1 egg. Roll this out as thinly as possible and cut it into strips. Cook these, like spaghetti, in boiling salted water, drain them thoroughly in a colander and rinse them quickly in running water. Toss them about in a tablespoon or two of melted butter.

Prepare a curd cream by breaking the curds down smoothly (if necessary) and mixing in the sour cream, the yolks of the 2 remaining eggs, the sugar and the sultanas. Beat the egg whites until they are stiff and fold them into the cream.

Once the boiled noodles have cooled to no more than lukewarm, mix them gently into the curd cream.

Line a baking tin with one of the sheets of pastry. Ideally, if you manage to roll each ball of pastry out thinly enough you should be able to use two or three layers of it at the bottom and likewise at the top, sprinkling each layer with a little melted butter. If you can't do this, simply line the tin with one layer, spread the filling over it and cover with the other sheet of pastry. Sprinkle the top with a little melted butter.

Bake for 30–40 minutes in a moderate oven – about half the time at 360°F, gas 4, and then more slowly if the pastry browns too quickly. While it is still hot, cut it into squares in the tin and before serving sprinkle the top liberally with castor or icing sugar. Serve with a thin jam sauce.

This pudding is even better when it is prepared with the 'folded pastry' described later.

Cseresznyés lepény – Cherry Pie

6 eggs
200g sugar (7 oz.)
½ kg stoned cherries (1 lb.)
60g butter (2 oz.)
120g fine breadcrumbs (4 oz.)
rind of half a lemon

Cream the egg yolks with the butter and half the sugar until you have a thick, fluffy mixture. Add the grated lemon rind.

Beat the egg whites very stiff, add the remainder of the sugar and beat until smooth.

Gradually add the breadcrumbs alternately with the beaten egg whites to the yolk mixture.

Pour the mixture into a greased tin.

Squeeze the juice gently from the cherries and set them out on top of the mixture, pressing them in a little. Bake for 25–30 minutes in a moderate oven, 360°F, gas 5. Cut into squares in the tin, sprinkle with sugar and serve hot.

Rízsfelfújt – Rice Soufflé

120g rice (4 oz.)
100g sugar (3½ oz.)
20g butter (½ oz.)
½ tsp. flour
½ litre milk (17 fluid oz.)
6 tbs. water
2 eggs
lemon rind or vanilla
50g raisins (1½ oz.)
breadcrumbs
castor sugar

Mix the water and milk and bring to the boil with half the sugar, a little piece of lemon rind or vanilla pod and the butter. Put in the washed rice, bring to the boil again, and leave just beside low heat until the rice swells (about 15–20 minutes) and absorbs the liquid. Remove the lemon rind or vanilla pod. The latter can be rinsed and dried and kept for further use.

Cream the egg yolks with the remaining sugar until white. Mix in gently to the cooled rice, then add the flour and finally fold in the stiffly beaten egg whites. Add the raisins.

Grease a deep 2-litre (5-pint) dish and sprinkle with fine breadcrumbs. Pour in the mixture and bake in a moderate oven for about 30 minutes. To serve, turn out and sprinkle with castor sugar. Serve with chocolate sauce, or the wine sauces given on page 142 or 151.

Almafelfújt – Apple Soufflé

6–8 apples
100g flour (3½ oz.)
½ litre milk (scant 1 pint)
1 lemon
1–2 tsp. cinnamon
200g sugar (7 oz.)
60g butter (2 oz.)
4 eggs
apricot jam
a few sultanas
breadcrumbs

Peel and halve the apples. Scrape out the core and cook the halves for a few minutes in a very little water with a touch of sugar and lemon juice.

From the butter, flour and milk prepare a white sauce and allow it to cool a little. Mix in the sugar, the grated lemon rind, the egg yolks and finally the stiffly beaten egg whites.

Into a greased dish lined with breadcrumbs pour a layer of this mixture ½–1 inch deep. Sit the apple halves in this, having filled the spaces left by the removed cores with apricot jam and a couple of sultanas. Pour on the remainder of the sauce mixture and bake in a moderate oven for 30–40 minutes. 10 minutes before the end of cooking take the dish from the oven and sprinkle with the sugar mixed with the cinnamon. Return the dish to the oven. This may be served in the same dish as it is baked in, or turned out and sprinkled with more cinnamon sugar. It is also good cold.

Some Sweet Sauces

Vanilla Sauce

To ½ litre (1 pint) milk count:
2 egg yolks
10g butter (¼ oz.)
¼ vanilla pod (or about 1 dessertsp. vanilla sugar)
50g sugar (2 oz.)
1 tsp. flour

Mix the egg yolks with about 1 dl (¼ pint) of the milk. Whisk in the sugar and the flour.

Bring the rest of the milk to the boil with the vanilla and pour immediately onto the egg mixture. Put on gentle heat and stir constantly until it begins to thicken: do not allow it to come to the boil. It is ready once it no longer drops off the spoon.

Remove the pan from the heat and add the butter, stirring it in until the mixture shines. Remove the vanilla pod.

This sauce can be served hot or cold. If it becomes very thick in cooling it can be thinned later by gradually adding a little single cream or milk.

Ideally this sauce, and those which are based on its method, should be thickened in a double saucepan or above steam and not on direct heat. With care, however, it is perfectly possible to prepare the sauce as described above.

Chocolate Sauce

For chocolate sauce add 20g (½–¾ oz.) cocoa powder with the flour, or put 30–60g (1–2 oz.) plain chocolate to melt with the milk when it is being brought to the boil.

Lemon Sauce

Omit the vanilla when boiling the milk. When it has cooled mix in the rind of 1 lemon (grated) together with the chopped flesh and the juice of half the lemon.

Caramel Sauce

For ½ litre milk (1 pint) count
60g sugar (2 oz.)

Roast the sugar in a dry pan until it becomes a light golden brown. Make it into a syrup by mixing it with a little water. Add this to the milk, flavour with vanilla and continue as for the vanilla sauce above.

Sodó

Sodó is the Hungarian name given to the creamy, frothy kind of sauce prepared by including not only the yolks of the eggs but also the beaten whites. A *sodó* is usually served hot and should be made just before serving. Here is the recipe for a wine sauce which is the most popular of the sauces prepared in this way.

Borsodó – Wine Sauce

About 3 dl (½ pint) liquid made up of 2 parts white wine, 1 part water
2 eggs
grated rind and juice of ½ lemon
½ tsp. flour
100g sugar (3½ oz.)

Heat the liquid with the lemon rind and juice.

Cream the egg yolks with 80g (2½ oz.) of the sugar; add the flour and a little of the warm liquid.

Bring the wine just to the boil and pour it into the egg mixture, stirring all the time. Cook over the gentlest possible heat until the mixture thickens.

Beat the egg whites with the remaining sugar until stiff and pour in the hot sauce, stirring constantly. Mix for a few minutes longer with a whisk and stand over hot water until required for serving.

The recipe which follows is for a thin sauce to accompany *soufflé* puddings, thick creams, or dry sponge puddings. This kind of sauce is called an *öntet* in Hungarian, which literally means 'something poured'. It is used both hot and cold.

Baracköntet – Apricot Sauce

½ kg apricots (1 lb.)
80–90g sugar (2–3 oz.)
1–2 tbs. rum

Peel and stone the fruit and chop it up finely (or mince it). Bring the apricots to the boil with the sugar and stir in the rum.

Cream Desserts

The literal translation of the next recipe's title is 'bird milk': it is a vanilla cream with foamy *galuskas* floating on top – a favourite Sunday dessert in Hungary.

Madártej – Floating Islands

2 litres milk (3¾ pts.)
4 eggs
150g sugar (5 oz.)
½ vanilla pod
½ tsp. flour

Beat the whites of the eggs with 3 tablespoons of the sugar until the mixture becomes very stiff.

In a large (3-litre–6-pint) pan bring 2 litres (3–4 pints) of water to the boil and place separate spoonfuls (*galuskas*) of the beaten egg whites onto the surface of the gently simmering water. Don't put too many in at once as there must be room for the *galuskas* to expand. Once each has risen well, turn them over carefully and then let the other side cook for about 30 seconds. Spoon them out very carefully onto a large sieve to drain.

Now prepare the vanilla cream with the milk and vanilla, the egg yolks, the remaining sugar and the flour (follow the method given in the next recipe). Pour the cream into one large dish or into individual dishes, place the *galuskas* on top of the sauce and serve cold.

Vaníliakrém tejszínhabbal – Vanilla Cream with Whipped Cream

2 dl milk (⅜ pint)
¼ vanilla pod
10g gelatine (¼ oz.)
50g vanilla castor sugar (1½ oz.)
2 egg yolks
120g sugar (4 oz.)
3 dl fresh cream (a good ½ pint)

Bring the milk to the boil with the vanilla pod and half the sugar.

Cream the rest of the sugar with the egg yolks in a heavy pan or the top of a double boiler. Slowly pour the hot milk onto the egg yolks, stirring constantly, continuing to stir all the time while the mixture thickens over the gentlest possible heat. Remove from the heat and continue to stir until the mixture is just lukewarm. Remove the vanilla pod.

Add the gelatine, dissolved in 2 tablespoons water. Mix it in well.

Whip* the fresh cream with the vanilla sugar and add little by little to the cooked cream, retaining 4–5 spoonfuls for decoration. Pour into glasses or moulds. The cream may be served in these or dipped for a moment in hot water and then turned out. If the cream is to be served in individual glasses the gelatine may be omitted.

This recipe is used as a basis for other creams, of which here are some useful examples.

Coffee Cream

Replace half the quantity of milk by *very* strong black coffee.

Chocolate Cream

Melt 50g (2 oz.) plain chocolate in the milk.

* To whip cream successfully use only cream which has 25–30 per cent fat content. Keep it refrigerated for at least 12 hours at +3°C (37°F). During this time it goes through a maturing process and cream which has been kept in this way can be safely whipped to twice its original volume. It should then be used as soon as possible.

Fruit Cream

Mix two glassfuls of fruit into the cooked and cooled cream (without vanilla) – half of the fruit should be minced or liquidized, the other half cut up roughly. Raspberries, strawberries and apricots are the most suitable. With fruit creams the gelatine is virtually essential.

Babpüré – Bean Purée – Mock Chestnut Purée

250g mottled or red beans (8 oz.)
50g ground walnuts ($1\frac{1}{2}$–2 oz.)
2 tbs. rum
120g vanilla castor sugar (4 oz.)
6 tbs. milk (or cream)
2 dl fresh cream ($\frac{3}{8}$ pint)

Soak the beans overnight, boil them until they are quite soft and press them through a sieve. Mix in the sugar, milk, rum, and walnuts and beat well.

Whip the cream until it is stiff, and light, and then fold it carefully into the mixture. Pour into glasses and decorate with grated chocolate.

Boszorkánykrém – Witches' Cream

1 kg apples (2 lbs.)
150g sugar (5 oz.)
1 egg white
1 tbs. rum

Bake the apples in a hot oven or stew them quickly in a minimum of water. Press the cooked apple through a sieve and add the sugar immediately. Mix in the egg white and whisk for 20–25 minutes until the mixture stiffens. Finally whisk in the rum.

Pour it into glasses, decorate with a very little fresh or preserved fruit, and serve with dry sponge fingers.

Cakes, Pies, Pastries and Gâteaux

Hungarian *pâtisserie* began with Italian and French experts who visited or settled in Hungary. These foreign sources were then moulded according to the ingenuity of the Hungarians, who quickly formed an individual and original art which today has deep professional roots and traditions of its own.

Things have moved a long way since Ferenc Zelena's *National Cookery Book* appeared in Kassa in 1830. Among the numerous *pâtisserie* and confectionery recipes, we find, for example, a chocolate cream made by mixing half a pound of chocolate in a pint of boiling milk, to which five crushed hen's gizzards and some sugar were added and the mixture pressed through a hair sieve. The cream was then covered and placed on warm ashes with a couple of weak embers on top. Finally it was put in the cellar to clot.

Modern Hungarian baking and pastry cooking presents a colourful range of products without being gaudy; the concept of simplicity is never really lost sight of in the Hungarian kitchen. This, however, does not mean that many of the recipes do not require considerable care and hard work!

Hungarian baking recipes are distinguished by the kind of dough (yeast, crumbed, creamed, etc.) and the way it is worked (folded, mixed, kneaded, etc.). It would be impossible to give a systematic description of all of these methods in a book of this size, together with all the regional variations, but I have tried to include recipes for most of the cakes, pies, tarts and savouries most widely baked in Hungary today. You will find some titles repeat themselves, appearing in more than one section, but that is only because there are various ways of producing, say, a Hazelnut Pie, and it is worth trying each recipe to discover which you favour most. On the other hand I have not given individual recipes for each of the many *tortas* as this would have led to a quite unnecessary amount of repetition.

Rétes – Pastries

The most characteristic form of pastry in Hungary is the *rétes* or *strudel.* These pastries are served warm or cold as part of a full meal but they are also very popular cold in the pastry shops with coffee. The pastry is paper-thin, feather-light, and worth every bit of the concentration and energy required to prepare it. This complicated ceremony was held worthy of recording even by one of Hungary's finest writers, Mór Jókai.

It is a sheer art the way in which two girls, pulling in different directions, stretch out on extended tables a fistful of dough until it is as big as the tablecloth itself, so that a woman of ancient Rome could wear it as a cloak. In Hungary, however, they sprinkle it with sour cream, fat, almonds, and sultanas; then they roll it up to form a cylinder, lay it in a tin in boa constrictor form, brown it with Spanish Inquisition cunning in a slow heat, and pity the barbaric peoples who do not know this food.

In the towns in Hungary it is becoming increasingly customary to sell *rétes* dough which is half ready, but as yet there is fortunately no lack of home-bakers who are still proud enough to serve *rétes* which they have worked and rolled and stretched themselves.

One prerequisite for successful *rétes* is flour with a high gluten content. If the quality of the flour you have is doubtful, the addition of an egg helps.

Sift 300g (10 oz.) flour and crumb in a knob of fat (about 20g – ¾ oz.). Make a dip in the middle and pour in 2 dl – ⅜ pint warm salted water (or just a little more). These quantities give enough dough for about 5 portions, but can still be managed in one bout of stretching. Work the ingredients together to make a soft dough. Work it well on a floured board for about 15 minutes until it becomes quite smooth and elastic. Brush the lump of dough with melted lard or butter and cover it with a warm saucepan, leaving it to rest for 15–20 minutes.

Put a large tablecloth on a large table, sprinkle lightly with flour and place the lump of dough in the middle. First of all, roll it out in square or rectangle form according to the shape of the table. Then brush with melted fat and continue the stretching by hand. Put your hands under the dough and stretch it over the backs of them without making any holes. Move round the table while doing it so that the dough is stretched from all sides. The pastry has to be as thin as paper. Stretch it until the edges of the pastry hang over the edges of the table and then trim by hand to the outline of the table. Leave the pastry to dry for a few minutes. Sprinkle evenly, but thinly with melted lard or butter.

Sprinkle one third of the pastry with fine breadcrumbs and then put on the filling. Now, lift the edge of the tablecloth and roll up the pastry and filling, not tightly – it should be slightly flat rather than cylindrical and quite loose. Cut into lengths to fit the baking sheet, brush with melted fat and place them on a greased baking sheet. Leave plenty of room between each roll. Bake in a moderately hot preheated oven (380°F, gas 5) until crisp and well browned – but beware burning on the top. When cool, sprinkle with castor sugar.

Rétes pastry fillings

Many kinds of fillings are used for *rétes* pastry and the quantities given below are enough for the amount of pastry in the basic recipe above.

Apple Filling

1 kg apples (2 lbs.)
½ tsp. cinnamon
100g sugar (3–4 oz.)

Core the apples but do not peel them. Grate and stew them lightly until all the juice has evaporated. Sweeten with sugar and stir in the cinnamon.

If the apples are very soft and mealy, it is possible to use them without stewing them. Slice them thinly, sprinkle them with sugar and cinnamon and leave them for 20 minutes. Then press out the juice lightly and spread over the pastry, but for raw apples use slightly more breadcrumbs.

Sour-cherry Filling

Stone 1 pound morello cherries, press out the juice and spread evenly on the breadcrumbed pastry. Sprinkle with sugar.

Curd Filling

300g curds (10 oz.)
1 egg
1 tbs. semolina
50g sultanas (1–2 oz.)
1 tbs. sour cream
2 tbs. sugar
rind of ½ lemon or 1 tsp. vanilla sugar

Press the curds through a sieve to smooth them out and mix with the sour cream, sugar, semolina and egg yolk. Add the sultanas and then fold in the beaten egg white. Finally flavour with lemon rind, or the vanilla sugar. Sprinkle the pastry lightly with semolina and then spread on the curd mixture.

Poppy Seed Filling

150g ground poppy seeds (5 oz.)
2 tbs. sour cream
100g sugar (3½ oz.)

Mix the poppy seeds with the sugar and spread the mixture evenly over one third of the pastry. Sprinkle lightly with the sour cream.

Cabbage Filling

800g (1½ lbs.) cabbage (white or red)
salt
freshly ground black pepper
50g fat (1½ oz.)
sugar

Shred, or – better still – grate the cabbage, salt it lightly and set it aside for half an hour. Then press away the liquid gently.

Heat the fat and braise the cabbage in it – to begin with use 1–2 tablespoons water and keep the lid on the pan, but once the cabbage begins to soften, remove the cover. Season with a liberal amount of pepper – or, as many people prefer it in Hungary, flavour the cabbage filling with sugar. Spread the filling over the pastry, bake, and serve hot.

Plums, apricots, grapes and grated marrow are also among the fillings used for *rétes*. You can surprise by choosing your own fillings, remembering to keep them fairly free of juice.

Many chicken, meat and fish mixtures are also very suitable for filling this kind of pastry, as well as the sweet fillings described above.

Soproni mandulás rétes – Almond Strudel

This final recipe from Sopron, near the border with Austria, uses *rétes* pastry with an almond filling.

300g flour (10 oz.)
7 eggs
150g ground almonds (5 oz.)
salt
150g red-currant or raspberry jam (5 oz.)
120g sugar (4 oz.)
120g fat (4 oz.)

Make the pastry from the flour, 1 egg, a little of the fat and about 2 dl (⅜ pint) water. Spread the red-currant jam thinly on the pastry.

Cream the yolks of 6 eggs with the sugar until white. Add the ground almonds and then fold in the stiffly beaten whites of the 6 eggs. Mix until smooth and spread evenly on the pastry. Sprinkle liberally with melted fat and roll the *strudel* up. Bake until crisp and golden, and serve hot.

Yeast Baking

Fresh yeast is as everyday a matter in the Hungarian kitchen as sour cream, paprika or eggs. It is always available in all the grocery shops in little half-ounce packets and is used in the home to make a fine range of breads, cakes and pies. This section includes recipes for some of these and also some which do not contain yeast but which bear a certain resemblance to those which do.

Fonott kalács – Braided Kalács

Kalács is a light sweet bread which makes a scrumptious change spread with fresh butter and accompanied by hot cocoa. It is not quite bread and not quite cake.

1 kg flour (2 lbs.)
100g butter (3 oz.)
½ tsp. salt
80g sugar (2½ oz.)
9 dl milk (1⅔ pints)
30g yeast (1 oz.)

Sift the flour. Dissolve the yeast in 6 tablespoons lukewarm milk, sprinkle with 3 tablespoons flour and leave it in a warm place to rise for 15–20 minutes.

Dissolve the sugar and the salt in the rest of the milk. Mix this with the risen yeast mixture and pour it straight away into the sifted flour. Mix well and leave the dough to rise for 20–30 minutes.

Melt the butter and work it into the dough. Lift the dough out of the bowl and sprinkle the bowl with a little flour. Put back the dough, sprinkle it, too, with flour, and cover with a damp cloth. Set it aside to rise for at least an hour, until it has grown to treble its volume.

Lift the dough onto a floured board, shape it lightly and divide it into two. Roll out each piece into a long cylindrical strip. Brush with a little melted butter and place one strip crosswise on top of the other and then twine the two together into a plait.

Place it on a greased baking sheet and leave it to rise in a warm place for at least half an hour. Brush the top with a little beaten egg mixed with a little sugar. Bake the *kalács* in a slow oven for three quarters of an hour. If the top becomes too brown too early, place a sheet of foil or paper over it and continue to bake.

Ízes bukta – Jam Rolls

½ kg flour (1 lb.)	20g yeast (½–¾ oz.)
2 egg yolks	3 dl milk (½ pint)
60g fat or butter (scant 2 oz.)	50g sugar (1½ oz.)
pinch salt	250g jam for filling (8 oz.)

Dissolve 1 teaspoon of the sugar in 6 tablespoons of the milk. Mix in the yeast. Cover with 3 tablespoons of the flour and set aside in a warm place to rise for 15–20 minutes.

Meanwhile cream the egg yolks with the sugar. Gradually mix in the milk, in which the salt should previously be dissolved.

Sift the flour. Pour the egg and milk mixture into a hollow in the flour and add the yeast mixture. Work the dough together thoroughly with a wooden spoon until it is blistery on the surface. Then mix in the melted butter, working it in well. Set the dough aside to rise, covered, in a warm place for at least 1 hour.

Lift the risen dough out onto a floured board, punch it down lightly and roll it out until it is about $\frac{3}{4}$-inch thick. Cut out squares with sides about 3–4 inches, put 1 tablespoon rather stiff jam in the centre of each square and roll them up. Place them side by side on a greased baking sheet. Brush the tops with melted fat and leave to rise again for about half an hour. Bake in a moderately hot oven for 25–35 minutes. When they are ready, remove the rolls from the baking sheet onto a wire tray to cool but pull them apart from one another only when you are serving them – they will stick together during baking.

Serve sprinkled with sugar.

This dough is also filled very successfully with curds or a mixture of poppy seeds and sugar.

Darázsfészek – Wasps' Nests

400g flour (13 oz.)
2 egg yolks
1 rounded tbs. sugar
20g yeast ($\frac{1}{2}$–$\frac{3}{4}$ oz.)
40g butter ($1\frac{1}{4}$ oz.)
$2\frac{1}{2}$ dl lukewarm milk ($\frac{1}{2}$ pint)

Filling

140g vanilla sugar ($4\frac{1}{2}$ oz.)
100g butter ($3\frac{1}{2}$ oz.)

Dissolve the yeast in 6 tablespoons of the lukewarm milk. Cream the egg yolks with the sugar and melt the butter. Add all the ingredients to the sifted flour and work the mixture thoroughly with a wooden spoon. Leave to rise for 1 hour.

When it has risen well, roll it out to a thin rectangle on a floured board. Beat the sugar for the filling into the butter and spread the dough with this mixture. Roll up the dough rectangle into a cylinder form and from this cylinder cut slices about 1 inch thick.

Put the rounds, about an inch away from each other, on a greased baking sheet. Brush the tops with beaten egg, sprinkle with sugar and leave to rise for half an hour.

Bake golden brown in a moderate oven for 25–35 minutes. Serve hot with vanilla sauce (*see* p. 150).

The filling is sometimes varied to a crumbed mixture of 150g (5 oz.) sugar, 100g ($3\frac{1}{2}$ oz.) butter and 150g (5 oz.) ground walnuts. For this filling use 70g or a good 2 oz. butter for the dough.

Túrós lepény – Curd Pie

½ kg flour (1 lb.)	3 dl milk (½ pint)
20g yeast (½–¾ oz.)	2 egg yolks
100g butter (3½ oz.)	60g sugar (2 oz.)
pinch of salt	semolina
	beaten egg

Crumble the yeast into a little lukewarm milk with 1 teaspoon sugar in it.

Sift the flour, and when the yeast has dissolved pour it into the flour, add the egg yolks, sugar and salt and then gradually add the lukewarm milk. Finally melt the butter and work it into the dough. Work the dough thoroughly with a wooden spoon. Set it aside to rest for 10–15 minutes.

Divide the dough into two, roll out one piece and line a greased baking tin with it. Roll out the other half of the dough and leave it to rest on the board. Cover both sheets of pastry dough with a cloth.

Filling

1 kg curds (2 lbs.)	1 dl (¼ pint) sour cream
400g sugar (13 oz.)	50–60g sultanas (1½–2 oz.)
4 eggs	60g butter (2 oz.)
rind of half a lemon	pinch of salt

Cream the butter and sugar until white and fluffy. Add the egg yolks singly and beat them in well. Mix in the sultanas, the grated lemon rind, a pinch of salt, the sour cream and the semolina. Press the curds through a sieve to make them smooth and add them to the mixture. Beat the egg whites until they are stiff and fold them in very carefully.

Sprinkle the pastry already in the tin with a little semolina and spread the filling over it evenly. Cover with the other pastry sheet and brush the top with a little beaten egg.

Bake for 35–40 minutes in a good moderate oven.

My own favourite curd pie, which I was introduced to by Marika Kostyál, comes without the top layer of pastry. The curds are well brushed with beaten egg and look irresistible. This pie is a nourishing and delicious meal in itself and was always specially made if the family went on picnics or long train journeys. You will need to use only half quantities for the pastry since no top cover is placed over the curd mixture.

The next recipe is a country speciality which dispenses with yeast and uses dill leaves as further flavouring.

Dill Curd Pie

300g flour (11 oz.)
20g salt (¾ oz.)
2 dl sour cream (⅜ pint)
small bunch fresh dill leaves
260g butter (8½ oz.)
6 eggs
1 kg fresh curds (2 lbs.)

Make a soft pastry dough from the flour, 180g (6 oz.) of the butter, a pinch of salt, 2 eggs and 9 tablespoons of the sour cream. Roll the dough out to finger thickness and line a baking tin with it, turning it up a little at the edges as well.

For the filling mix the sieved curds with the remaining melted butter, 4 egg yolks, a pinch of salt and finely chopped fresh dill leaves to taste. Mix in the stiffly beaten whites of the 4 eggs, spread this filling on to the pastry, brush the top with the remaining sour cream and bake until golden brown in a good moderate oven.

Rákóczi Curd Pie

This final foam-topped variation of curd pie is one of the best known and most popular in Hungary and, like the preceding recipe, does not require yeast. It is called Rákóczi Curd Pie after Ferenc Rákóczi, a great Hungarian politician who lived from 1676 to 1735.

Pastry

100g flour (3½ oz.)
50g sugar (1½ oz.)
3 tbs. sour cream
80g butter (2½ oz.)
1 egg
good pinch of baking soda

Filling

½ kg curds (1 lb.)	150g sugar (5 oz.)
25g semolina (¾ oz.)	2 eggs
6 tbs. sour cream	

Topping

3 egg whites	90g sugar (3 oz.)

Make a pastry dough from the ingredients given above, roll it out, line a pie plate or baking tin with it, and half bake it. Remove it from the oven.

To prepare the filling, mix the curds with the sugar, the semolina, the yolks of the 2 eggs and the sour cream. Beat the egg whites until they are stiff and fold them into the mixture. Spread this filling evenly over the pastry. Brush the top with beaten egg and bake until light golden.

Remove the pie from the oven. Beat the egg whites for the topping with the sugar until very stiff and form a criss-cross pattern with this foam over the curd filling. Return to the oven for a few minutes for the top to become browned. To serve, sprinkle liberally with vanilla castor sugar.

Sörkifli – Beer Kiflis

Recipes abound in Hungary for very tiny savouries to go with drinks or tea or coffee or just to peck at between meals. They are easy and inexpensive to make and they are at their best when eaten not merely fresh but hot straight out of the oven.

The title of the first of these recipes is an indication that these particular savouries are intended to go with beer, and not that they contain it! The Hungarian word *kifli*, as I have explained in the Introduction, has always something to do with a crescent shape. The *butter kiflis* described later (see p. 175) are *croissants*. You will find recipes for other small savouries later – Sour Cream *Pogácsa* (*see* p. 178), Potato *Pogácsa* (*see* p. 179), Butter *Pogácsa* (*see* p. 179) and Cheese Fingers (*see* p. 192).

½ kg flour (1 lb.)	60g butter (2 oz.)
20g yeast (¾ oz.)	salt, 1 teaspoon sugar
caraway seeds	3–4 dl lukewarm milk (½–¾ pint)

Start the yeast working in 3–4 tablespoons of the milk with 1 teaspoon sugar until the yeast rises to the surface of the milk. Pour it into the flour, add the salt and enough lukewarm milk to make a rather soft dough.

Work it together thoroughly, at first with a wooden spoon and then with the hands. Divide the dough into 4 pieces. Roll each piece into a thin round and spread each with the butter. Divide each into 8 small wedges like a cake, and roll up each of these triangular wedges starting from the wide end. Bend them slightly into crescents and place them on a greased baking sheet, leaving room between them. Mix some caraway seeds with a little salt (home-ground if possible) and sprinkle over the *kiflis*. Leave them for about 2 hours in a warm place to rise.

Bake the *kiflis* for 10–15 minutes in a hot oven until they are lightly browned.

Lángos – Fried Puffs

This is a Hungarian institution. If you have worked from six or seven in the winter morning until ten or eleven, you stop and eat *lángos*. If you have gone on a 2-hour train journey (or indeed a 2-minute one!) and you arrive at your freezing destination, you eat *lángos*. There is certain to be a stall selling *lángos* wherever you arrive.

It is a yeast dough fried in deep fat, served straight out of the fat in a nominal piece of paper supposed to keep your fingers clean (or possibly the *lángos*). You sprinkle it liberally with salt and feel immediately warm, recovered, secure and all good things. To make a mountain of *lángos* – to give *one* to anyone would instigate immediate rebellion – use

400g flour (14 oz.)
20g yeast (¾ oz.)
10g salt (¼ oz.)
warm water
oil for frying
pinch sugar

Start the yeast working in 6 tablespoons of lukewarm water with a good pinch of sugar.

Sift the flour, make a dip in the middle and pour in the yeast mixture. Add enough lukewarm salted water to give a medium soft dough. Knead and beat it well. Sprinkle a little flour over the dough, cover it with a damp cloth and leave it in a warm place to rise for at least 1 hour. When the dough has doubled in size, make a pan of deep fat or oil hot – it is possible, however, to cook *lángos* perfectly successfully in an ordinary frying pan with about 2 dl (¼ pint) of oil. Dip a tablespoon and your hands in cold water, take out 1 tablespoon of the mixture and with your hands pull and tug the dough out gently until it is thin and roughly the size which will cover the bottom of the pan. Place the *lángos* in the hot fat, cover the pan and once it is quite brown on one side, turn it over and continue the frying without the lid on the pan until the other side is golden and the whole *lángos* is crisp. If you wet your hands it helps the dough to fry crisply.

Variations are abundant. And good.

Sometimes dill *lángos* are made by sprinkling finely chopped fresh dill onto the dough when it is in your hand. Then fold the dough over in half and stretch it out again and fry it as before. Another filling is curds: a small knob of fresh curds is folded into the middle of the tablespoon of dough, before it is stretched and fried.

To make potato *lángos* about 200g (7 oz.) cooked mashed potatoes (or grated raw potatoes) are mixed into the dough, which should be made a little firmer than for the original recipe.

My one-time landlady, Edith Néni, preferred not to fry the *lángos* but to cook it in the way girdle scones are cooked in Scotland on a griddle over an open flame; her griddle was wrapped with wire mesh on which the *lángos* sat and this prevented any risk of sticking. This sort of dry *lángos* makes an excellent breakfast with strong white coffee.

Lángos are quickly made and cheap – and in smaller quantities the dough rises more rapidly. They are excellent accompaniments to vegetable dishes.

Női szeszély – Lady's Caprice

50g butter (1½ oz.)	300g flour (11 oz.)
4 eggs	6 tbs. milk
10–20g yeast (½ oz.)	100g hazelnuts (4 oz.)
100g raspberry jam (4 oz.)	salt
50g + 250g (1½ oz. + 8 oz.) sugar	

Beat the butter and 50g (1½ oz.) sugar until the mixture is frothy. Add the yolks of the 4 eggs singly.

Mix the yeast in a little warm milk and add with the flour, then a pinch of salt, and the remainder of the milk, adding more if necessary to give a soft, light, easily beatable dough. Beat it well and then spread the mixture in a layer not more than half an inch thick on a baking sheet. Leave it in a warm place for half an hour. Bake in a moderate oven until lightly browned.

Mix the jam with chopped hazelnuts and spread this mixture on the baked pastry.

Beat the whites of the eggs until they are firm, mix in the 250g (8 oz.) sugar gently, smooth over the jam and nuts and return the whole to the oven for about 10 minutes to become firm. Cut into squares when warm.

Gerbaud szelet – Gerbaud Cake

No visit to Budapest would be complete without a visit to the 'Gerbaud'. Although since the end of the Second World War this great pastry-shop has been renamed the 'Vörösmarty' after a distinguished nineteenth century Hungarian poet, everyone still refers to it as the 'Gerbaud'. Émile Gerbaud went to Budapest from Geneva in 1884 and some months later took over the establishment in what was then Theatre Square, now Vörösmarty Square. There is in the furniture and atmosphere something relaxed and relaxing which gives one a strong feeling of slipping far into the past, but there is no doubt that the pastries served in the 'Gerbaud' are in their quality and in their variety as up to date as they are excellent.

350g flour (12 oz.)
50g sugar (1¾ oz.)
3 tbs. milk
good pinch baking powder
1 egg and 1 yolk
150g margarine (5 oz.)
10g yeast (¼ oz.)
6 tbs. sour cream

Filling

120g ground walnuts (4 oz.)
200g jam (7 oz.)
120g castor sugar (4 oz.)

Start the yeast working in the lukewarm milk with a good pinch from the sugar. Leave it in a warm place for 10–15 minutes.

Rub the flour and margarine together, add the sugar, the egg and yolk, the baking powder, the sour cream and the yeast mixture. Work the dough together with a wooden spoon and then divide it into three. Roll out each part into a rectangle to fit a tin about 14 × 10 inches in size, but the dough should not quite reach the edges of the tins – it will need room to expand.

Over the bottom sheet of dough spread some jam and sprinkle half the mixture of nuts and sugar onto this. Cover with the second sheet of dough and then spread this second sheet with jam and the remaining nuts and sugar. The third sheet should be slightly larger. Place it on top and let the edges come down to cover the sides as well.

Leave the cake to rise for about 1 hour in a warm place. Pierce the top here and there with a fork and bake in a moderate or somewhat slower oven until the top is light golden (about 25–30 minutes). While the cake is still warm, ice with a fondant prepared from 200g (7 oz.) sugar and 30g (1 oz.) cocoa.

Puff pastry and other folded doughs

Unlike yeast doughs, the recipes in this section require that the butter and flour and the water used with them should be very cold.

To make the basic puff pastry dough use ½ kg (1 lb.) plain flour; ½ kg (1 lb.) butter (or margarine); 2½ dl (scant ½ pint) cold water; 10g (¼ oz.) salt; wine vinegar or lemon juice. Apart from these quantities about 100g (4 oz.) flour is needed for sprinkling.

1. Set aside 60g (2 oz.) from the butter. Take 60g (2 oz.) of the

flour and mix it with the *remainder* of the butter, forming it into a flattish square. Set this aside in a cold place.

2. Rub the 60g (2 oz.) butter which has been set aside into the remaining 440g (14 oz.) flour. Pour some of the water into the centre, add the salt and the juice of half a lemon or a good teaspoon of vinegar. Mix these ingredients together and then add the remainder of the water to give a fairly firm dough and work it until it comes away from the hands and the board and is spongy inside. Make cuts in the top of the dough and set it aside in a cold place to rest for 20–30 minutes.

3. Roll out the dough very thinly into a rectangle. Place the butter block in the centre, fold in the dough from all sides and cover the butter well.

4. Roll out the dough once more into rectangular form. Fold it in three with the folds at right angles to the side of the table where you are standing (once from the right and once from the left), and then roll it out again. Fold it in three again – but now the folds should be parallel with your edge of the table. Roll out the dough once more and refold: this time once from the right to the middle, then from the left to the middle and then from bottom to top to give a small pack of dough. Leave it in a refrigerator for 20 minutes to rest.

Roll it out again and fold as for the last folding described above. Leave it to rest again. If the pastry is being prepared in the evening to be baked the following day, fold twice in the evening and leave two foldings for the day of baking. To rest the pastry overnight, keep it in a polythene bag.

There follow some recipes using this pastry. For baking it the oven should be hot until the pastry turns light golden (400°F, gas 5–6, is usually enough for 5–10 minutes) and then it can be turned down. If the oven is not hot enough, the butter in the pastry merely melts and flows out.

If there are trimmings, lay them one on top of the other and roll them out until they join firmly. They can be used for *pogácsas* and cheese pastries.

Two of the lightest and most popular sweets after a rich Sunday dinner make use of two thin layers of this pastry with a cream filling between them. They amply repay all the folding and rolling!

Krémes – Cream Pastries

To make about 24, use 250g (8 oz.) butter and 250g (8 oz.) flour (that is, halving the basic quantities given above).

For the cream

6 eggs
120g flour (4 oz.)
6 dl milk (just over 1 pint)
250g sugar (8 oz.)
1 vanilla pod

Beat the egg whites with two thirds of the sugar over steam until the mixture is stiff. Set it aside.

Bring two thirds of the milk to the boil with the vanilla.

Cream the egg yolks with the remaining sugar and then add the remaining milk (cold) and the flour. In a thin stream pour in the hot milk (after removing the vanilla pod) and by the side of the heat stir continuously until it becomes so thick that the mixture comes away from the bottom of the pan. Remove it from the heat and while it is still hot gradually fold in the egg whites. Pour into a cold bowl.

Roll out the dough until it is paper thin and cut two sheets from it which will fit your baking sheets. Bake each sheet of pastry in a hot oven until golden. Pour the cream onto one sheet while it is still warm and smooth it over with a wet knife. Cut the other sheet of pastry into 24 equal rectangles or squares and place them on top of the cream. Following the lines of the cuts on top, slice into pieces right through with a wet knife. When completely cold (but still as fresh as possible) sprinkle with icing sugar and serve on a flat plate.

Franciakrémes – French Cream Pastries

Prepare and bake two sheets of pastry as for the ordinary creams above, and also prepare a cream using half the quantities given above.

Spread the cream over the bottom pastry sheet and allow it to become completely cold. Then on top of that cream spread another layer of equal depth – this should be a layer of whipped fresh cream (you will need about 4 dl – ¾ pint).

Cover the top pastry sheet with fondant made from 200g (7 oz.) sugar and brush the fondant with a little strong black coffee to make it light brown. Cut up the pastry layer which is to go on top and then continue as for ordinary *krémes*.

Búrkifli – Walnut Kiflis

Basic puff pastry from 250g (8 oz.) flour and 250g (8 oz.) butter.

Filling

Beat two egg whites and 150g (5 oz.) sugar to a stiff cream. Mix in 150g (5 oz.) ground walnuts, 2 tablespoons breadcrumbs and the grated rind of 1 lemon.

Roll out the pastry thinly, but not so thinly as for *krémes* – it should be just about ⅛-inch thick. Cut the pastry into long strips about 2½–3 inches wide. Down the centre of each strip pipe out the creamy walnut filling.

Roll up each long strip into a long cylinder and divide the cylinders into 4-inch lengths. Bend each of these lengths carefully into horse-shoe form.

With the joins underneath place the horseshoes on a greased baking sheet, brush the tops with beaten egg and sprinkle on some roughly chopped walnuts.

Bake the *kiflis* in a moderate oven, 380°F, gas 5, for 12–15 minutes.

Sajtkrémes tekercs – Cheese-Cream Rolls

One of the most familiar and welcome sights in Hungarian restaurants is the *sajtkrémes tekercs*, or cheese-cream roll. They are placed on the tables ready for you to nibble at while you are waiting for your order, or the waiter, to appear.

Prepare the basic puff pastry using 100g (4 oz.) flour and 100g (4 oz.) butter or margarine. This will give enough pastry for 8–10 rolls.

Roll out the pastry finally until it is very thin, making one side about 60 cm (24 inches) long. Cut the sheet into strips 1 inch by 4 inches and roll up each strip round a cylindrical mould not more than an inch in diameter (wood will do perfectly – I wrap them round the handle of a few long wooden spoons) so that there is an overlap of about ¼ inch. Set these out on the baking sheet with the joins underneath. Brush the tops with beaten egg and bake in a fairly hot oven until golden brown. While they are still hot remove the moulds by holding the whole roll in one palm and pulling out the moulds gently with the other hand. Once they have cooled, pipe in cheese cream (*see* p. 180) from both ends and dip each end in grated cheese.

It is sometimes possible to find this same kind of roll filled with whipped cream mixed with chopped fruit, but it is the cheese rolls which really are a part of everyday life.

Half butter doughs

Some interesting recipes are based on a variation of the buttery dough in the preceding recipes. This variation makes use of yeast, and the proportion of butter to flour is considerably smaller – usually about one half. In Hungary this sort of mixture is known as a 'half butter dough'.

Basic Dough

½ kg plain flour (1 lb.)
20g yeast (¾ oz.)
2 dl milk (⅜ pint)
1 egg and 1 yolk
350g butter or margarine (10½–11 oz.)
50g sugar (1½ oz.)
salt

With a knife work the butter together with 100g (3 oz.) of the flour. Shape the combined mixture into a brick form and set it aside in a cool place.

Make the milk barely lukewarm and dissolve the yeast in it. Leave it to start working for 20–30 minutes.

Cream the egg and the egg yolk with the sugar and mix, along with the yeast mixture, into the sifted flour, adding a pinch of salt.

Work it all thoroughly together to make a smooth soft dough. Set it aside in a warm place to rise for about 1 hour and then let it cool down in a cold place for about 20 minutes.

Turn out the dough onto a floured board, place the butter-and-flour 'brick' in the middle and go through precisely the same folding process as described in the basic puff pastry recipe given earlier (*see* p. 170).

Once the dough is placed in the baking tins, following the requirements of each individual recipe, allow it to rest at room temperature for about 15 minutes before baking it.

Vajaskifli – Croissants

This recipe describes how to make one of the finest of the bread products available from every baker in Hungary – *croissants* are delicious for breakfast with fresh unsalted butter and coffee.

Prepare the basic dough as given above and roll it out thinly. Cut it into triangles with a 6–7 inch base and 2½–3 inches from the base to the point opposite it. Starting from the base, roll up the triangles, curl these rolls into crescent form and place them on a greased baking sheet about 1½ inches from each other. Brush the tops with milk which has a little sugar dissolved in it, leave to rest for 15 minutes, then bake the *kiflis* in a fairly hot oven until they are well browned (about 25 minutes at 380°F, gas 5).

Túrós táska – Curd Pockets

Prepare the basic dough as described earlier and for the filling use the same curd filling given in the *rétes* pastry section (*see* p. 160).

Roll the dough out to a rectangle no more than ⅜ inch in thickness. Divide it into 4-inch squares. Place some of the curd filling in the centre of each square. Brush the corners of the pastry with egg, gently stretch them a little and fold them up over the filling. Press the ends well together and leave the 'pockets' in a warm place to rise for at least 15 minutes. Bake in a hot oven (about 400°F, gas 6) for about 25 minutes, but reduce the heat to moderate if the curd pockets brown too quickly.

Diós csiga – Walnut Snails

Prepare the basic folded yeast dough as above.

Filling

200g ground walnuts (7 oz.)
200g castor sugar (7 oz.)
1 egg for brushing

Mix together the walnuts and sugar. Roll out the pastry until it is about ⅜-inch thick, making a rectangle about 16 inches in width. Brush with a dampened pastry brush and sprinkle on the walnut filling evenly. Roll up the dough and then from this roll slice off rounds about ½-inch thick.

Set the rounds out on a greased baking tray about 3 inches away from each other. Brush the tops with beaten egg and allow them to rise in a warm place for 10–15 minutes. Bake golden in a moderate oven – it must not be too hot for this recipe or the walnuts will burn.

Lard Dough and Pogácsas

Hájas pogácsa – Lard Pogácsas

For some folded doughs the butter of the basic recipe is replaced by lard. In Hungary the lard used for baking is absolutely pure, carefully preserved from the pig-killing ceremony.

The Hungarian word *pogácsa* is usually translated into English as *scone*. Although *pogácsas* are indeed about the same size as scones, and although some varieties of *pogácsa* (e.g. the Butter *Pogácsa* described below) might resemble a scone in general appearance, the translation is not a good one because the method and ingredients used to prepare most *pogácsas* are entirely different from those for scones. In the basic *pogácsa* method, which becomes clear from the first recipe below, you will recognize a relationship which is closer to flaky or rough-puff pastry than to scones. This is followed by a variation using 'crackling' which is by far the best of the Hungarian savouries. The section ends with four recipes for savouries, the first three of which belong to the family of small savouries first introduced on page 166 with Beer Kiflis.

½ kg plain flour (1 lb.)
1 tbs. sour cream
½ tsp. sugar
20g yeast (¾ oz.)
¼ kg lard (8 oz.)
50–60g dripping (1½–2 oz.)
½ tsp. salt
1 egg yolk
beaten egg

Start the yeast working in 6 tablespoons lukewarm water with the sugar.

Make a pastry dough from the flour, dripping, sour cream, salt and egg yolk.

Add the yeast mixture to the dough together with as much lukewarm water as is necessary to make a fairly soft dough. Work it well together with a wooden spoon and leave it to rest for 30 minutes.

Meanwhile break up the lard and beat it until it is thoroughly creamy.

Roll out the dough very thinly, spread one third of the lard over it, roll it up and then press it out a little with a rolling pin. Fold twice – from the right inwards and from the left inwards – and leave it in a cool place for 15 minutes. Repeat this process twice more – roll it out, spread it with one more part of the lard, roll it up and leave it to rest. After the last resting, roll out the dough to finger thickness, cut it with a small fluted round into *pogácsas*, make a fine criss-cross pattern on the top and brush the tops with beaten egg. When brushing, take care that the egg does not spill down the sides. If it does the dough will not be so free to rise. Bake in a hot oven (400°F, gas 6) until golden – about 20 minutes.

Töpörtyűs pogácsa – Crackling Pogácsas

300g plain flour (10 oz.)
100g pure bacon dripping (3½ oz.)
2 egg yolks
90g *töpörtyű* – pork fat fried or grilled until golden and absolutely crisp (3 oz.)
10g yeast (½ oz.)
sour cream
1 tsp. salt
beaten egg

Chop the fried pork fat very finely.

Start the yeast working in about 4–6 tablespoons of sour cream, leaving it for at least 15 minutes in a warm place.

Mix the flour with the bacon dripping, crumbled fried fat, egg yolks and salt. Some of the finest bakers I know also like to add a good sprinkling of freshly ground black pepper. Pour in the rising yeast mixture and work well together to give a smooth dough. Roll it out three times and fold it three times as described for the preceding recipes, leaving it to rest in between. Finally roll it out to about 1-inch thickness. Cut a fine criss-cross pattern over the whole sheet of dough and then with a very small cutter cut out little rounds. Place the *pogácsas* on a lightly greased baking sheet, not too near each other, brush each carefully with beaten egg and bake them in a very hot oven for 5 minutes and then reduce the heat for 20–25 minutes.

These crackling *pogácsas* are particularly scrumptious when eaten hot.

An alternative and popular method is to make the pastry dough without including the fried fat crumbs, which are instead sprinkled onto the dough when it is first rolled out.

Tejfölös pogácsa – Sour Cream Pogácsas

½ kg flour (1 lb.)
30g yeast (1 oz.)
salt – about ½ tsp.
6 tbs. lukewarm milk
¼ kg margarine (8 oz.)
12 tbs. sour cream
2 egg yolks
1 teaspoon sugar

Start the yeast in a little lukewarm milk with 1 teaspoon sugar.

Rub the margarine into the flour, add the salt, bind with the egg yolks, the yeast mixture, the sour cream and the lukewarm milk to make a medium dough. Work it well and then leave it for half an hour to rise.

Roll out the dough and fold it up twice and then repeat this process twice more, allowing 20 minutes rest after each folding.

Finally roll out to finger thickness, cut a criss-cross pattern on top and cut out small rounds. Set these out on a baking sheet and allow them to rest again for 10 minutes, otherwise the *pogácsas* may fall over during baking. Bake in a hot oven (400°F, gas 6) for about 20 minutes.

Instead of being used to make *pogácsas*, this mixture is sometimes shaped into fingers.

Burgonyapogácsa – Potato Pogácsas

¼ kg cold mashed potatoes (8 oz.)
¼ kg flour (8 oz.)
1 level tsp. salt
¼ kg butter or margarine (8 oz.)
1 egg
egg to brush

Rub the butter into the flour and potatoes, add the salt and bind with the beaten egg. Roll this dough out, fold it up and then repeat the rolling and folding once more. Leave the dough to rest for 3–4 hours.

Finally roll out the dough to finger thickness, brush it with a little egg and cut out very small rounds. Bake the *pogácsas* for 10–15 minutes in a moderate oven (350°F, gas 4).

Potato *pogácsas* are among the finest for eating hot.

Vajas pogácsa – Butter Pogácsas

¼ kg butter (8 oz.)
2 egg yolks
½ tsp. vinegar
300g flour (10 oz.)
about 12 tbs. sour cream
salt and sugar
beaten egg

Prepare a dough from 50g (1½ oz.) butter, 250g (8 oz.) flour, the egg yolks, sour cream and a pinch of salt and sugar. Work the ingredients together thoroughly and then rest the dough for half an hour.

Meanwhile combine the remaining flour and butter and form this mixture into a rectangular brick shape. Place it on the rolled out dough. Fold up and roll out three times as described earlier in the basic puff pastry recipe (*see* p. 170) – resting the dough 1 hour after the first folding, but 20 minutes will be enough after the other two.

Finally roll out the dough to half-inch thickness and with a small fluted round cut *pogácsas* from the sheet of dough. Brush the tops with beaten egg, taking care not to let it drip over onto the sides. Bake the *pogácsas* in a hot oven (400°F, gas 6) for 15 minutes and then finish them off with 10–15 minutes in a moderate oven (350°F, gas 4).

Sonkás Kifli – Ham Kiflis

Prepare the same dough as in the preceding recipe.

Roll out the dough finally until it is very thin and cut it into triangles. Place a little finely minced ham towards the broad base of the triangles, brush the opposite tip of the triangles with beaten egg, roll them up, starting from the base and then gently curve the resulting rolls into crescents. Set them out on a baking sheet with the tip of the triangle underneath to ensure that the *kiflis* do not unfold. Brush the tops with a little beaten egg and bake in a moderate oven for 10–15 minutes.

These ham *kiflis* are often enhanced by a simple cheese cream. The dough is cut into cup-sized rounds, filled with ham as described above and folded over just once – that is, not rolled up. The cheese cream is then piped onto the join in the pastry.

Cheese Cream

For the cheese cream cook 12 tablespoons of milk and a scant 2 teaspoons of flour to a thick sauce. Remove it from the heat and beat in two egg yolks singly. In a bowl beat 100g (3½ oz.) butter or margarine until it is creamy, and once the sauce has cooled down, work it into the butter with 100g (3–4 oz.) grated cheese. Beat the mixture well until it is smooth and creamy.

Mixed Doughs

Meggyes lepény – Sour Cherry Pie

200g flour (7 oz.)
4 eggs
750g morello cherries (1½ lbs.)
200g butter (7 oz.)
150g sugar (5 oz.)
100g sugar for sprinkling (3 oz.)

Cream the butter with half the sugar and add the egg yolks one by one. Beat the whites stiff with the other half of the sugar. Once the mixture is glossy fold it into the yolks. Finally fold in the sifted flour very carefully. Pour the mixture into a tin lined with greaseproof paper.

Stone the sour cherries, sprinkle with the 100g (3 oz.) sugar, press the juice out a little and set the cherries on top of the mixture. Bake until golden in a moderate oven (360°F, gas 4–5). When the pie is ready leave it for a few minutes before cutting it into squares. Sprinkle some sugar over the squares – this cake can be eaten hot or cold.

Isler – Ischler Biscuits

200g flour (7 oz.)
150g butter (5 oz.)
1 tbs. rum
100g ground almonds or walnuts (3½ oz.)
50g sugar (1¾ oz.)
grated rind of ½–1 lemon

Work all the ingredients together thoroughly with a knife and once you have formed a smooth dough, leave it to rest for half an hour. Then roll it out to ¼-inch thickness and cut out biscuit rounds. Bake the biscuits until they are light golden in a warm to moderate oven (350°F, gas 4).

When the biscuits are cool, stick them together in pairs – for this use about 250g (7–8 oz.) jam. *Isler* are sometimes coated on one or both sides with an icing made from 250g (8 oz.) sugar and 30g (1 oz.) cocoa, but they are just as delicious without.

The two recipes for Hazelnut Pies which follow are both quite standard recipes in Hungary – I find the second one more attractive and interesting, but it is valuable to decide which you prefer by trying each of them out rather than by reading the recipes. There is another Hazelnut Pie on page 192 among the recipes which use the rubbing-in method.

Hazelnut Cake

70g butter (2½ oz.)
¼ kg sugar (8 oz.)
200g flour (7 oz.)
12 tbs. milk
2 eggs
100g hazelnuts (3½ oz.)
1 tsp. baking powder

Cream the butter and sugar thoroughly and add the egg yolks singly with half the milk. Beat the egg whites stiff and add them to the yolk mixture.

Roast the nuts in the oven or in a dry frying-pan – if you choose the latter method move them around more or less continuously to prevent them from being burnt. Grind the nuts and then fold them into the mixture with the sifted flour and baking powder. Thin with the rest of the milk.

Bake the cake in a moderate oven (360°F, gas 4–5) for 25–30 minutes. Once it is cold, slice in two horizontally and spread with jam. Sprinkle vanilla sugar on top.

Hazelnut Pie

200g flour (7 oz.)
1 egg yolk
about 5 tbs. sour cream
130g margarine (4½ oz.)
50g vanilla sugar (1¾ oz.)
pinch of salt

Rub the margarine into the flour, mix in the sugar and a pinch of salt and then add the egg yolk and the sour cream to make a pastry dough.

Divide the dough into two pieces. Roll out each piece and with one sheet line a shallow baking tin, spread the filling on it and from the other rolled out sheet of pastry cut long strips to make a criss-cross pattern on top of the filling.

Bake the pie in a moderate oven (360°F, gas 4–5) for 20–25 minutes.

Filling

130g (4½ oz.) roasted and ground hazelnuts
100g castor sugar (3½ oz.)
4 egg whites
20g cocoa (½ oz.)

To make the filling, mix the dry ingredients and fold in the stiffly beaten egg whites.

Piskótacsók – Sponge Kisses

Of small cakes and biscuits for nibbling at there is a great variety, and the commonest is probably the *Piskótacsók* described below. These little cakes in all sorts of shapes, are usually sold by weight and all mixed up together so that individual names tend to be lost sight of.

5 eggs	200g flour (6½ oz.)
¼ kg castor sugar (8 oz.)	1 tsp. strong vanilla sugar

Beat the eggs with the castor sugar to a thick cream over hot water. Once the mixture is really thick remove it from the heat and continue to beat it until it has become lukewarm. Then mix in the vanilla sugar and fold in the sifted flour.

Line a baking sheet with greaseproof paper and set out walnut-sized blobs of the mixture on it. Sift a little vanilla castor sugar onto the top of each. Bake in a moderate oven until golden and while they are still warm remove them from the paper. Cover the bottom of each with a chocolate glaze. If they have not risen well and look rather flat, stick them together in twos by spreading jam on the bottoms. If this mixture is not light enough, it is usually because it has been overcooked at the beginning whilst beating the eggs and sugar over hot water or because the proportion of flour was not sufficiently precise.

The next two recipes are for whisked sponge mixtures. The first takes its name from the unusual procedure in preparing it – the little knobs of sponge are left all night 'to dry' before being baked. The second is based on egg whites and proves an economical way of using up whites which have been left over.

Estike – Night Cakes

280g castor sugar (9½ oz.)	4 eggs
250g flour (8½ oz.)	

Whisk the eggs and the sugar together for no less than 40 minutes – the assistance of an electric mixer is an obvious advantage here, but it is still wise to whisk by hand for at least 10 minutes after using the machine; the action of the hand is different and makes for greater bulk and lightness. Add the sifted flour and continue to fold and mix for a further 20 minutes. Place teaspoons of the mixture on a greased and floured baking sheet and leave them in a warm place to dry overnight. A single sultana is usually pushed in from the top of each after the knobs of mixture are set out. The tops become dry during the long resting and they should then be baked in a good moderate oven for 8–10 minutes.

If the *estike* are successful, the mixture rises and a sugary crust forms on the top like an icing.

***Fehér piskóta* – White Sponge**

To 1 egg white use 20g (⅔ oz.) sugar, 30g (1 oz.) flour, 15g (½ oz.) butter.

Beat the egg whites until they are stiff. Add the sugar and beat again until the mixture is glossy. Fold in the sifted flour and finally the melted butter.

Pour the mixture into a greased and floured long shallow tin, or a fluted, 'biscuit-loaf' tin, and bake it in a slow oven. Once it has cooled, cut it into slices horizontally and fill it with any cream desired, pouring the same cream over the outside as well.

Four or five egg whites are a good quantity on which to base this recipe. The sponge is quite chewy and I like to make it in a very large tin so that it comes out about ¼-inch thick. It is best to add the cream (I use a butter cream flavoured with a little cocoa and coffee and a lot of ground, roasted hazelnuts) about 12 hours before you want to serve the sponge. This gives the cream time to soften the sponge slightly.

Fruit Breads

The more solid English cakes such as Madeira, Dundee or the traditional Christmas cakes are entirely unknown in Hungary. The recipes which follow are probably those which come nearest to what we in this country are used to thinking of as cake. The fact that the titles indicate 'bread' points in some small way to the reaction of Hungarians to such preparations – they are not quite cakes.

These breads are usually baked in a small rectangular loaf tin.

Kossuth-kenyér – Kossuth Bread

3 eggs
20g cocoa (¾ oz.)
140g flour (4½ oz.)
lemon rind
120g sugar (4 oz.)
60g finely chopped almonds or walnuts (2 oz.)
cinnamon

Beat the egg yolks with the sugar to a fluffy cream. Add the cocoa, the nuts, a pinch of cinnamon and a little grated lemon rind.

Beat the egg whites stiff and fold them into the mixture.

Finally add the sifted flour.

Bake in a moderate to slow oven (320–350°F, gas 3–4) for 40–45 minutes.

Diákkenyér – Student's Bread

7 egg whites
160g flour (5½ oz.)
50g sultanas (1½ oz.)
80g margarine (2¾ oz.)
180g castor sugar (6 oz.)
60g walnuts (2 oz.)
grated rind of 1 lemon

Beat the egg whites until they are very stiff. Add the sugar spoonful by spoonful, then the broken walnuts, the sultanas and the lemon rind. Fold in the sifted flour and finally add the melted margarine very carefully – it should not be more than lukewarm, just barely melted.

Grease and flour a long rounded (or biscuit-loaf) tin, pour in the mixture and bake for about 50 minutes in a moderate or slow oven (320–350°F, gas 3–4).

Püspökkenyér – Bishop's Bread

6 eggs
¼ kg flour (8 oz.)
90g finely chopped quince conserve (3 oz.)
¼ kg sugar (8 oz.)
100g sultanas (3½ oz.)
150g chopped almonds or walnuts (5 oz.)

Whisk the eggs and the sugar with an electric mixer for at least 3 minutes.

Add the sifted flour and mix for just a few minutes.

Lastly add the chopped fruit and nuts – freshly chopped apple is a tolerable substitute, if you can find no quince.

Line a baking tin (usually a long rectangular one for this recipe) and bake in a moderate oven for 40–45 minutes.

Here the sultanas are often replaced to great effect by chopped preserved sour cherries. The mixture is more quickly prepared if the egg whites are stiffly beaten and then folded in separately. Half quantities are also perfectly feasible with this recipe.

Crumbed Doughs

The next group of recipes are those using the rubbing-in method, working the flour and shortening together first and then adding the sugar and other ingredients, which vary from recipe to recipe. The basic recipe uses 100g (3½ oz.) sugar, 200g (7 oz.) butter and 300g (10½ oz.) flour, with 1 egg. In the interests of economy part of the butter is sometimes replaced with milk or sour milk, in which case a little baking powder is also used. In some of the best recipes in this section yeast is used as a raising agent and I have grouped these recipes first.

To prevent the dough from splitting during baking:

1. it must not be too soft – in other words, be sparing with the milk;
2. there must not be too much sugar in the filling;
3. do not let the dough *over*-rise in the warmth; and
4. the oven must be hot – at least 400°F, gas 7, for the first 10 minutes.

Mákos patkó – Poppy Seed Horsehoes

$\frac{1}{2}$ kg flour (1 lb.)
2 eggs
20g yeast ($\frac{3}{4}$ oz.)
pinch of salt
$\frac{1}{4}$ kg butter (8 oz.)
50g castor sugar ($1\frac{1}{2}$ oz.)
$1\frac{1}{2}$ dl milk ($\frac{1}{4}$–$\frac{3}{8}$ pint)
white of egg

Start the yeast working with a little sugar in about 4 tablespoons of the milk.

Rub the flour and the fat together, mix in the two well beaten eggs, the yeast mixture and the sugar. Add the pinch of salt with just enough of the remaining milk to give a fairly firm dough. Work it together quickly and then rest it for 2 hours.

Divide the dough into two larger or four smaller lumps. Roll each out to an oval shape about $\frac{3}{8}$ inch in thickness. Leaving an inch round the edge of each oval quite free, spread on the filling (see below) and roll up each piece. Then shape each of the rolls into horseshoe form, with the joins underneath. Place the horseshoes on a lightly greased baking sheet, brush them with beaten egg and leave them to rise in a warm place for about 1 hour.

Once the horseshoes have risen brush them with white of egg and leave them in a *cool* place for half an hour – this helps to marble the surface of the dough. Before baking the horseshoes, pierce the sides here and there with a fork. Bake them in a hot oven for 25–30 minutes, and avoid opening the oven door during the baking. Start with the oven at 420°F, gas 7, and lower the heat to 380°F, gas 5, after 10 minutes.

Filling

300g ground poppy seeds (10 oz.)
4 dl milk ($\frac{3}{4}$ pint)
60g semolina (2 oz.)
200g sugar (7 oz.)
lemon rind

Mix the poppy seeds with the semolina. Bring the milk to the boil and pour in the poppy-seed mixture. Add the sugar (and a few sultanas are a not uncommon addition which should be included at this stage if you want to include them at all). Mix very well, cool the mixture and work in a little grated lemon rind. When the filling is quite cold spread it over the dough as described above.

Walnut Horseshoes

An alternative filling is made from a walnut mixture. To make these walnut horseshoes, prepare the dough as above and for the filling use the following ingredients:

300g ground walnuts (10½ oz.)
100g fine breadcrumbs (3½ oz.)
90g sultanas (3 oz.)
200g sugar (7 oz.)
lemon rind

With about ¾-pint water make a thick syrup from the sugar. Pour in the ground walnuts and mix well together. Remove the mixture from the heat and mix in the breadcrumbs, a little grated lemon rind and the sultanas.

Pozsonyi kifli

To make *Pozsonyi kiflis* use the same ingredients as for walnut horseshoes but divide the dough into 30 little balls, roll each out into an oval shape. Spread on the filling, leaving the edges free. Roll them up and turn in the ends to give the shape in the illustration. Leave to rise for 20–30 minutes then bake as for the preceding two recipes but for slightly less time (15–20 minutes).

Kígyórétes – Snake Pastry

½ kg flour (1 lb.)
1 egg and 1 egg yolk
20g yeast (¾ oz.)
¼ kg butter (8 oz.)
2 tbs. sugar
a little lukewarm milk

Start the yeast working with a little sugar in 5 tablespoons lukewarm milk, leaving it in the warmth for 5–10 minutes.

Beat the butter until it is creamy, beat in the sugar, the egg and egg yolk, the yeast mixture, a pinch of salt and finally mix in the flour.

Turn the dough onto a floured board, knead it lightly until it is smooth and elastic, and leave it in a warm place to rise a little.

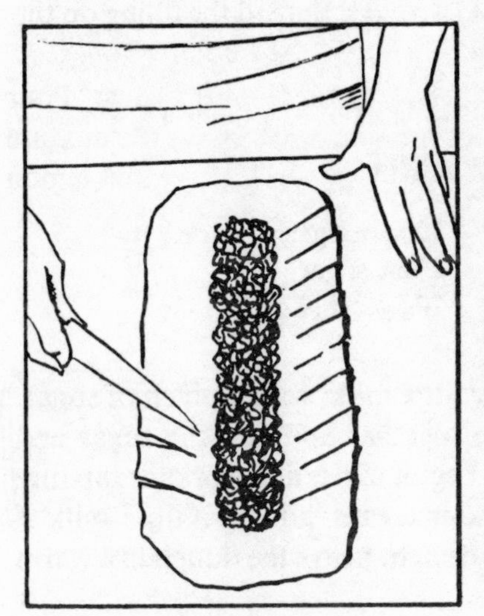

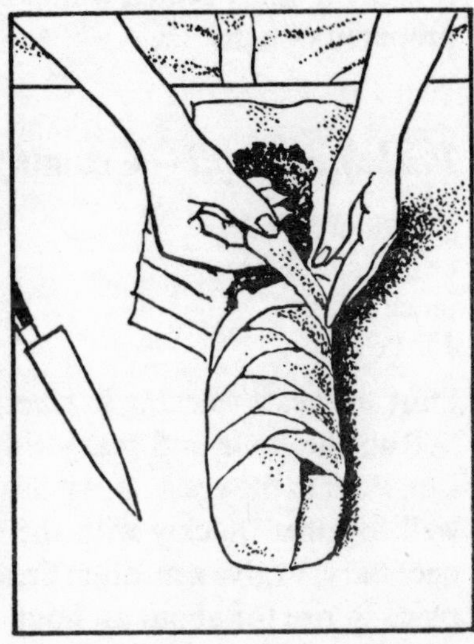

Divide the risen dough into four pieces. Roll each piece out to a rectangle about 16 inches long and 10 inches wide. Make cuts about 3 inches in length into the two long sides of each sheet. Sprinkle the middle with a little semolina (or fine breadcrumbs) and spread on the filling. Now fold the protruding strips up over the filling, plaiting them into each other on top. Brush the 'snake' with beaten egg and leave to rest for 20–30 minutes. Bake in a hot oven (420°F, gas 7), for 30–35 minutes, reducing the heat (380°F, gas 5) after the first ten minutes to prevent burning. Cut diagonally, sprinkle on some icing sugar and serve fresh. Use the apple filling for two of the braids and the curd filling for the other two.

Apple Filling

Stew 2 large apples (peeled and cored) with 100g (3 oz.) sugar until all the liquid evaporates. Flavour with a little lemon juice and cinnamon. Leave the mixture to become cold and then spread it on the dough.

Curd Filling

Press ½ kg (1 lb.) curds through a sieve to make them smooth and mix in 2 egg yolks, 30g (1 oz.) melted butter, 3 tablespoons sugar, and if the mixture is too wet add 1 tablespoon semolina. Finally fold in the stiffly beaten whites of two eggs. Spread the filling on the prepared dough.

Porhanyós kifli – Crumbly Kiflis

½ kg flour (1 lb.)
6 tbs. sour cream
pinch of salt
a little milk
200g margarine (7 oz.)
1 tbs. sugar
20g yeast (¾ oz.)

Start the yeast working in a very little milk, with a pinch of sugar.

Rub the flour and margarine together and add the sugar and salt. Pour in the yeast once it has begun to rise and work the mixture well together quickly with the sour cream, adding a little milk if necessary, to give a medium firm dough. Leave the dough in a warm place to rise for about an hour.

Roll the risen dough out to about ⅜-inch thickness. Cut out rounds, spread them with jam, chestnut *purée* or ground poppy seeds mixed with sugar. Roll up the rounds and shape them into slight crescents. Leave to rest for 10 minutes and bake them for 10–15 minutes in a hot oven (400°F, gas 6) and turn them in vanilla castor sugar while they are still hot.

Tejfölkifli – Sour Cream Kiflis

3 teacups flour
1 teacup good thick sour cream
¼ kg jam (8 oz.)
1 teacup butter or slightly less fat
30g yeast (1 oz.)
salt
milk

Start the yeast in a tablespoon of milk.

Rub the shortening into the flour and work into a dough with the yeast, sour cream and a pinch of salt. Set the dough aside in a warm place to rise for about an hour. Roll the risen dough out to ⅜-inch thickness – there is no folding for this recipe. Cut out circles with a large cutter, place some jam in the middle of each round, fold them over and bend them carefully into a slightly crescent shape. Let them rise again for about 10 minutes on the baking sheet.

Bake the *kiflis* until golden in a fairly hot oven (400°F, gas 6). When they are ready and still fairly hot, sprinkle them with vanilla granulated sugar.

Vizen kelt kifli – Kiflis Raised in Water

These kiflis, made in roughly the same way as *brioches*, are baked specially for weddings in the Nagykunság area of Hungary.

½ kg flour (1 lb.)
2 dl sour cream (⅜ pint)
2 egg yolks
pinch of salt
200g sugar for sprinkling (7 oz.)
20g yeast (¾ oz.)
100g butter (3½ oz.)
6 tbs. milk
lemon rind

Start the yeast working in a little lukewarm milk with a good pinch of sugar.

Rub the butter into the flour, add the salt and mix to a smooth dough with the egg yolks, the sour cream, the yeast and a little lemon rind.

Sprinkle a large cloth with flour and tie up the dough in it loosely, leaving enough room for the dough to expand. Hang the bundle on the handle of a wooden spoon so that the cloth and its contents hang down into a large pan full of water and leave it until the dough comes to the surface of the water – about 1 hour.

Sprinkle the baking board with granulated sugar, turn out the dough and cut little lumps from it. Turn these about in the sugar and then roll them into fingers 3–4 inches long and bend them into crescent shape. Set the *kiflis* out on a greased baking sheet, leaving plenty of room between them. Let them rest in a warm place for half an hour and bake them until they are golden brown in a fairly hot oven (400°F, gas 6). They will need 10–12 minutes.

Sajtos rúd – Cheese Fingers

Like many of the recipes in this book, this excellent one comes from Marika Kostyál. She deserves special mention because she introduced me to most of the best dishes in traditional Hungarian cooking, and her cheese savouries are particularly good. They were in demand at any time, but along with the curd pie described earlier, they were favourites for picnics, and no journey of any length at all could be embarked upon without a copious supply of them.

½ kg flour (1 lb.)	¼ kg margarine (8 oz.)
150g smoked cheese (5 oz.)	3 small teaspoonfuls salt
50g yeast (1½ oz.)	6 tbs. sour cream (or yoghurt)

Put the yeast in about 6 tablespoons warm milk. Add to this a spoonful from the flour and a teaspoon of sugar. Set this aside in a warm place for 15 minutes to start the yeast working.

Rub the margarine into the flour and salt.

When the yeast mixture has risen, add it to the crumbed mixture and then add half of the cheese (grated) and the sour cream. Work it all together and then leave to prove for at least an hour, in a warm place and under a damp cloth.

Roll out the dough, brush it with beaten egg and sprinkle the rest of the cheese over it.

Cut into fingers and bake for 20–30 minutes in a moderate oven (380°F, gas 5).

Mogyoróbéles – Hazelnut Pie

350g flour (11½ oz.)	140g butter (4½ oz.)
50g sugar (1½ oz.)	2 eggs
10g yeast (¼ oz.)	milk

Start the yeast working in 1 tablespoon lukewarm milk with a pinch of sugar. Rub the butter into the flour. Add the sugar, the beaten eggs and the yeast. Work the mixture together quickly and divide it in two, making one piece somewhat larger than the other. Roll out the larger of the two thinly and line a shallow baking tin with it, covering the sides as well. Put it aside to rise a little while you make the filling.

For the filling use

6 eggs
150g ground, roasted hazelnuts (5 oz.)
¼ kg sugar (8 oz.)
lemon rind
100g jam (3–4 oz.)

Beat the egg yolks to a thick cream with the sugar and the lemon rind. Add the hazelnuts and fold in the stiffly beaten egg whites.

Spread the jam over the bottom lining of dough, pour in the filling and cover with the other sheet of dough. Bake in a moderate oven (375°F, gas 5) for 20–30 minutes. Turn out the pie very carefully and sprinkle the slices with sugar.

Some recipes using the crumbing method are prepared without yeast. Here, for example, is yet another Cherry Pie, which is nevertheless different in detail from those which have preceded it in the book. This is followed by a recipe which differs from the basic methods in that it includes potato in the dough.

Cseresznyés lepény – Cherry Slices

300g flour (10 oz.)
90g castor sugar (3 oz.)
2 egg yolks
pinch of salt
1–2 tbs. rum
150g butter (5 oz.)
2 dl sour cream (⅜ pint)
a good pinch of baking soda
lemon rind
beaten egg, sugar

Filling

1 kg cherries (2 lbs.)
60g breadcrumbs (2 oz.)
ground cinnamon
100g walnuts (3–4 oz.)
120g granulated sugar (4 oz.)

Rub the butter into the flour and then add the sugar, salt and a little grated lemon rind. Bind to a smooth dough with the two egg yolks and the sour cream, first mixing the baking soda into the sour cream. Finally add the rum. Leave the dough to rest and then divide it in two and roll each piece out thinly.

Put one sheet of the pastry dough into a lightly greased baking tin and semi-bake it in a fairly quick oven – it will need about 5–10 minutes.

For the filling combine the ground walnuts, the sugar and the breadcrumbs and a little cinnamon, and then sprinkle half this mixture on the partly baked pastry. Spread the stoned cherries over this, sprinkle the remainder of the walnut mixture over the cherries and top with the other sheet of pastry dough.

Brush the top with 1 beaten egg, pierce here and there with a fork and bake the pie for about 20 minutes in a moderate oven (380°F, gas 5). When it is ready sprinkle with sugar.

This pie tastes even finer if one third of the cherries is replaced by sour cherries (morellos), but if you do use sour cherries add a very little more sugar as well.

Burgonyás linzer – Potato Cake

300g flour (10 oz.)
1 egg yolk
100g margarine ($3\frac{1}{2}$ oz.)
100g ground hazelnuts ($3\frac{1}{2}$ oz.)
200g cold mashed potatoes (7 oz.)
1 small tsp. baking soda
100g sugar ($3\frac{1}{2}$ oz.)
jam, beaten egg

Rub the margarine into the flour. Add the mashed potatoes, the sugar, the hazelnuts and the baking soda. Bind the mixture quickly with the egg yolk until smooth.

Take two thirds of the dough, roll it out and place it in a greased baking-tin. Spread this sheet of dough with a rather tart jam. Roll out the remaining dough and cut it into strips (with a fluted cutter if possible) to make a criss-cross pattern over the jam. Brush the strips with beaten egg and bake in a moderate oven (380°F, gas 5) for 25–30 minutes.

Mézesek – Honey Cakes

There is an old honey-cake tradition in Hungary, and connected to it is the wonderful tradition of honey-cake moulds, which display an astonishing variety of pattern.

Honey is plentiful in Hungary, so the baking of these cakes is easy to contemplate and their popularity is enhanced by their being nourishing and easily digestible, not to mention that they keep well. A touch of individuality is added by the honey which is most readily available in Hungary – it comes from the blossoms of the acacia trees and it has a fine discreet sweetness which enhances the flavour and fragrance of the honey.

When you are baking honey cakes it is a good idea to prepare the mixture in the evening and leave it overnight before baking the cakes – the dough becomes much lighter with resting. They should generally be baked in a good moderate oven but beware of over-browning as a certain degree of bitterness can ensue.

Mézespogácsa – Honey Pogácsas

¼ kg honey (½ lb.)
90g butter or margarine (3 oz.)
1 egg and 2 yolks
½ kg flour (1 lb.)
90g sugar (3 oz.)
1 level tsp. baking soda

Warm the honey just enough to melt the butter in it, remove the pan from the heat and add the egg and yolks, the sugar and finally the flour sifted with the baking soda. Work the ingredients into a smooth dough and flavour to taste with a little grated lemon rind, ground cinnamon or ground cloves.

Roll out the dough to about ⅜-inch thickness and cut out very small rounds. Set these out on a greased baking sheet, brush the tops carefully with a little egg yolk mixed with some sour cream, and decorate with half an almond. Bake for 6–8 minutes.

Mézes kalács – Honey Bread

½ kg honey (1 lb.)
60g sugar (2 oz.)
1 tsp. baking soda
a little grated lemon rind
2 eggs and 2 yolks
½ kg flour (1 lb.)
good pinch cinnamon
chopped walnuts

Warm the honey gently until it is easy to stir, mix in the eggs and the yolks, the cinnamon and the lemon rind. Beat the mixture until it is light and foamy. Then beat in the sugar.

Sift the flour with the baking soda and fold it in gradually (half the flour may be brown or strong bread flour – in Hungary they use rye flour for this). Work the dough thoroughly and pour it into a greased and floured shallow tin. Sprinkle chopped walnuts on top and bake in a moderate oven (350°F, gas 4) for about 30–35 minutes.

Olcsó mézes kenyér – Cheap Honey Bread

1 cup honey
1 scant cup milk
1 cup sugar
1 egg
a little cinnamon, clove and lemon rind
as much flour as the other ingredients absorb to give a medium soft dough
80–90g margarine (2½–3 oz.)
1 level tsp. baking soda
60g walnuts (2 oz.)

Cream the margarine thoroughly with the sugar. Add the egg, and the honey, spices and lemon rind and mix thoroughly. Thin the mixture with the milk and gradually add the flour with the baking soda to give a medium dough. Beat it well with a wooden spoon, pour it into a greased and floured tin and decorate the top with chopped walnuts. Bake in a moderate oven (350°F, gas 4) for about 40 minutes.

Török mézes lepény – Turkish Honey Pie

150g sugar (5 oz.)
1 egg
1 tsp. baking soda
2 tbs. honey
2 tbs. milk
450g flour (15 oz.)

Beat the sugar, honey, egg, milk and baking soda over hot water for about 15 minutes until the mixture is light and foamy. While it is still warm work in the sifted flour and divide the mixture into four. Roll out each piece to the same size and shape and bake until just beginning to brown. Then stick the four pieces of cake together with the following cream.

Cook 6 tablespoons semolina to a thick *purée* with ½ litre (1 scant pint) milk and half a vanilla pod, and then allow it to cool. Remove vanilla pod.

Cream 200g (7 oz.) butter with 200g (7 oz.) castor sugar and little by little fold in the semolina *purée*, working the mixture very thoroughly together. Spread a third of this cream over the bottom layer, put another on top, and continue to make layers, finishing with a cake layer. Sprinkle sugar on top. Leave this 'pie' until the following day before cutting it – by then it will have softened a little.

Kaukázusi mézes torta – Caucasian Honey Torta

½ kg flour (1 lb.)
50g butter (1½ oz.)
2 tbs. milk
1 level tsp. baking soda
1 egg and 1 yolk
150g castor sugar (5 oz.)
3 tbs. honey

Beat the egg and the yolk. Then mix all the ingredients together except the flour and cook them gently in a saucapan for 2–3 minutes. Pour the hot mixture onto the flour, work to a dough and divide the dough into four. Roll each part out and bake them separately on greased and floured sheets for 10 minutes in a hot oven and then for 5–7 minutes in a slow oven.

To make the cream for the filling roast 2 tablespoons sugar and then cook it to a smooth mixture with 4 dl (¾ pint) milk.

Mix 2 egg yolks, 2–3 tablespoons milk, 2 tablespoons sugar and 2 tablespoons flour until smooth and gradually add the caramel mixture. Stirring constantly, cook until the two mixtures are well combined and then fold in the two stiffly beaten egg whites.

Cream 150g (5 oz.) butter with the same quantity of sugar until the cream is really fluffy and add the caramel *purée* gradually. Spread the bottom layer of the honey cake with half of this cream, the next one with blackcurrant jam, the third one with the remainder of the cream and the top with more jam.

Cover the top layer of jam with this cocoa mixture. Put 80g (2½ oz.) castor sugar and 80g (2½ oz.) margarine, 30g (1 oz.) cocoa, 1 tablespoon milk, ½ teaspoon flour in a saucepan and heat it gently, bringing it just to the boil. Spread the mixture on top of the cake.

This *torta* should be left for at least one day before it is cut.

Torták – Gâteaux

The Hungarian *torta* (*gâteau*, layered cake with sundry creams and fillings) is a rich affair – usually a fairly dry sponge filled with creams of walnuts, lemon, strawberries or chestnut *purée*. The decoration on top can be gaudily gay with fruit or whirls of cream, or quite discreet like the famous *Dobostorta*.

Since to describe and give recipes for all the individual *tortas* currently popular in Hungary would require a separate book in itself, I have included here, first of all, the generally used basic sponge mixtures; these are then followed by examples of creams which are well known fillings in the Hungarian layered cakes, and finally there are a few recipes for particular *tortas*. A list and brief description of the *tortas* you will find in any Hungarian *cukrászda* (pastry-shop) is also included.

First of all, then, here is the recipe for the basic cake mixture.

6 eggs
6 tbs. sugar
6 tbs. flour

First heat the oven to moderate (380°F, gas 5) and line the tin with paper – either a large rectangular tin measuring 10 inches × 6 inches or a round cake tin with a diameter of 9 inches.

Separate the eggs and beat the whites absolutely stiff. Beat in the sugar spoonful by spoonful, continuing to beat until the mixture is firm and glossy. Add the yolks one by one and beat for 4–5 minutes. Finally sift in the flour gradually, no longer beating but folding it in lightly with a wooden spoon. Pour into the prepared tin immediately. Bake the sponge mixture in a moderate oven – if you are using a shallow tin it will only take about 12–15 minutes, but if you are using a more vertical cake tin then reduce the heat a little after the first 15–20 minutes if necessary, and bake for 40–50 minutes altogether. Take care not to open the oven door in the first 10 minutes as the mixture collapses easily. Test eventually with a needle into the centre and if it comes out quite dry the sponge is ready.

The texture of the baked mixture should be springy. The oven should not be too hot to begin with or the sugar will tend to form a firm crust on the outside and this may prevent the middle from becoming evenly cooked. Cover with paper if the sponge browns too much too soon.

When you have removed the sponge from the oven, leave it to dry out for a few minutes, then cut round the sides of the tin with a thin sharp knife, turn out the sponge gently onto a floured board and ease off the paper lining. Set the sponge on a baking tray to cool and only then cut it.

The recipe given above is the traditional way of preparing the basic sponge mixture for Hungarian *tortas*. However, eggs are not cheap and Hungarian housewives have always had the following slightly less extravagant recipe to hand, in which the eggs are eked out by using some water. This mixture needs to be blended very thoroughly but if you have no electric mixer and you find half an hour of arm gymnastics more than a little daunting, then help things on their way with a good pinch of baking soda.

4 eggs
200g flour (7 oz.)
(pinch of baking soda)
8 level tbs. sugar
8 tbs. water

Beat the egg yolks to a cream with 6 tablespoons of the sugar and 4 tablespoons of the water – beat continuously for 25–30 minutes.

Beat the egg whites with the remaining 4 tablespoons water until they are very stiff and then beat on with the remaining 2 tablespoons sugar.

Sift the flour, together with the baking soda if you use it, and add half of it to the yolk mixture. Fold in half the egg white mixture, then the remaining flour and finally, very lightly, the rest of the beaten whites.

Have a tin prepared and bake the sponge as in the preceding recipe.

Another variation of the basic sponge recipe is the sour-cream base which follows.

3 eggs
3 dl sour cream (good ½ pint)
1 tsp. baking powder
8 level tbs. castor sugar
300g flour (10 oz.)
lemon rind

Beat the eggs with the sugar to a creamy foam. Add the sour cream spoonful by spoonful, mixing it in well. Flavour with a little grated lemon rind. Finally sift in the flour with the baking powder little by little and mix for about 5 minutes. Pour the mixture into a greased and floured tin and bake it in a moderate oven for about 30 minutes.

Creams for the Gâteaux

Milk and Butter Cream

7 level tbs. castor sugar	6 tbs. fresh cream
150g butter (5 oz.)	1 tbs. strong vanilla sugar

Melt the castor sugar and vanilla sugar in the cream in a warm place. Add to the butter and whisk the mixture to a thick cream.

To this basic cream flavourings such as chocolate, cocoa powder, ground walnuts or ground hazelnuts are added.

Egg and Butter Cream

7 level tbs. sugar	3 egg whites
1 tbs. vanilla sugar	200g butter (7 oz.)
flavourings	

Cook 5 tablespoons of the sugar to a syrup thick enough to form a ball when a little is dropped into water. Beat the egg whites stiff, adding the remaining sugar and the vanilla sugar. Pour in the hot syrup in a thin stream and continue to beat hard until the mixture has become no more than lukewarm. Cream the butter well and work in the other mixture gradually. Flavour.

This cream can be used for the outside of a *torta* as well, with cocoa, chocolate gratings, ground walnuts, sweet crumbs or crushed wafers sprinkled on the top.

Chocolate Cream

Sift 1 heaped teaspoon cocoa powder mixed with vanilla sugar into the cream.

Coffee Cream

1. Use very strong black coffee instead of water to make the syrup.

2. Prepare the cream as above and then flavour it with 2 tablespoons strong black coffee and 1 tablespoon extremely finely ground coffee beans.

Walnut or Hazelnut Cream

Into the prepared cream stir 100g (4 oz.) finely ground walnuts or hazelnuts and add 1 tablespoon rum.

Lemon or Orange Cream

For this cream omit the vanilla. Into the finished cream work the grated rind of 2 lemons or 1 orange, adding a few drops of juice as well.

Potato Cream

¼ kg boiled potatoes (8 oz.)
100g butter (3½ oz.)
50g margarine (1½ oz.)
2 tbs. rum
¼ kg sugar (8 oz.)
60g walnuts (2 oz.)
1 tbs. vanilla sugar

Mash the boiled potatoes and press them through a sieve twice. Mix in the sugar and vanilla sugar.

Beat the butter and margarine to a thick cream and whisk together with the potatoes until light and fluffy. Mix in the ground walnuts and the rum.

To fill the *torta* with this cream, first spread each layer with raspberry jam and then with a liberal layer of the cream.

This cream is also useful for covering the outside of layer cakes. It is an easily digestible and relatively cheap cream; it approaches the more unusual chestnut cream in flavour.

Chestnut Cream

¾ kg chestnuts (about 1½ lbs.)
150g castor sugar (5 oz.)
200g butter (7 oz.)

Cook the chestnuts until soft, rinse them in cold water and shell them. You will need about 300g (10–11 oz.) chestnuts once they are shelled. Mince the chestnuts and then press two thirds of the pulp through a fine sieve.

Cream the butter and sugar until light and fluffy, add the chestnut *purée* and mix well. If it seems too stiff, stir in 1–2 tablespoons fresh cream or milk. 1 tablespoon rum is an excellent, but not essential, addition.

Cover the *torta* with this cream and grate the remaining third of the chestnut pulp over the top. Set the cake in a refrigerator before serving.

Tinned chestnut *purée* is readily available in delicatessens – and the excellent Clement Faugier *purée* is stocked by some Sainsbury stores.

Chocolate Glaze

Grate 100g (3½ oz.) cooking chocolate, melt it and add 6 tablespoons water with 80g (2½ oz.) castor sugar. Cook the mixture gently, stirring constantly, until it is so thick that it will not break apart when a little is dropped onto a cold plate. Then melt in 10g (¼ oz.) butter and pour the glaze onto the cake – it can be used as a filling or as a top covering. Smooth over the icing with a knife.

Before giving the descriptions of the best known Hungarian *tortas*, it is worth including a few very basic recipes which are somewhat anonymous but which give the cook an opportunity to escape from traditional recipes and vary the basic *torta* as imagination suggests.

Fehér torta – White Torta

7 eggs
200g flour (7 oz.)
200g sugar (7 oz.)

For the cream

3 dl milk (good ½ pint)
7 level tbs. sugar
half a vanilla pod
3 level tsp. strong bread flour
150g butter (5 oz.)

Prepare and bake the sponge as described above. Once it has cooled, slice it into three and fill it with the cream.

To make the cream, bring two thirds of the milk to the boil with the sugar and the vanilla. Mix the flour with the remaining milk, add it to the hot vanilla milk and cook slowly until the mixture becomes very thick, stirring all the time. Remove the pan from the heat and continue to stir until the cream has cooled down. Take out the vanilla pod.

Beat the butter until it is light and creamy and then gradually work it together with the cooled vanilla mixture. Fill the *torta* with this and cover the outside with it as well.

For decoration roast 80g (2½ oz.) sugar until it is just light golden. Remove it from the heat and mix in 50g (1½ oz.) chopped walnuts. Turn out onto a dampened board, flatten the mixture out a bit and leave it till it is quite cold. Then crumb it down and sprinkle it liberally over the top and sides of the *torta.*

The above cream is varied to produce a Brown Torta by replacing one third of the milk with very strong black coffee – not coffee essence, but freshly made coffee from freshly ground beans.

Babtorta – Bean Torta

4 eggs
¼ vanilla pod
½ litre beans (scant pint)
¼ kg castor sugar (8 oz.)
90g ground walnuts (3 oz.)
100g jam, preferably blackcurrant (3–4 oz.) or cream
grated lemon rind

Cream the egg yolks with the sugar and vanilla (ground) until light and fluffy and then add the walnuts.

Boil the beans one day in advance and press them through a sieve, leaving them to drain overnight.

Add the beans to the egg and sugar cream, with a little grated lemon rind if desired. Finally fold in the very stiffly beaten egg whites.

Pour the mixture into a cake tin lined with paper and bake it in a moderate oven for 35–40 minutes. While it is still fairly warm cut it and fill with the jam or with cream.

The top of this bean *torta* should be given a lemon glaze, for which mix 300g (10 oz.) very fine castor sugar, the juice of two lemons, 1 tablespoon water and 1 teaspoon rum until you have a very smooth mixture – it will take up to 25 minutes!

Egytojásos torta – One-Egg Torta

½ kg flour (1 lb.)
80g sugar (2½ oz.)
1 egg
1 level tsp. baking soda
100g butter (3 oz.)
180g honey (6 oz.)
6 tbs. milk

Rub the butter into the flour, add the sugar and mix in the egg, honey and milk. Work to a smooth dough and finally add the baking soda. Divide the mixture into 6 equal portions, roll each out into a square and bake them separately in a moderate oven until golden.

Filling

½ litre milk (scant 1 pint)
300g sugar (10 oz.)
1 tbs. strong vanilla sugar
100g flour (3½ oz.)
200g butter (7 oz.)

Roast the sugar until it is light golden and mix it to a smooth paste with 3 tablespoons water and half the milk.

Combine the flour with the rest of the milk, pour this onto the caramel and cook the mixture gently until it is thick. Allow it to cool, stirring it all the time, until it is just lukewarm and then add the butter in knobs, with the vanilla sugar, and continue to mix until it is smooth and quite cold.

Even off the edges of the layers of cake and fill with the cream, leaving plenty of cream for the top as well. Because of the honey in it, this *torta* is best left for a day to rest before cutting.

Pastry-Shop Tortas

These are some of the *tortas* you will find in any Hungarian pastry-shop but of course every individual baker has his own special recipes to add to the well known ones, which makes for a riot of chocolate balls and slices, red and yellow glazes, creams and marzipan delicacies.

Dobostorta – Drum Torta

Probably the most famous Hungarian *torta*. There are up to 6 slim layers of sponge with a thin chocolate butter cream between them, but *Dobostorta* achieves its unique character by the almost transparent layer of medium brown caramel which forms the top – it should be firm but not hard and has a very attractive glossy glow.

Stefániatorta

This is prepared in the same way as the *Dobostorta* but the caramel glaze is replaced by a chocolate cream which is then sprinkled with grated chocolate or sweet crumbs.

Citromtorta – Lemon Torta

The grated rind of half a lemon is included as flavouring when the sponge is being made. The sponge is cut into three and a light lemon cream is used as the filling.

Csokoládétorta – Chocolate Torta

The sponge for this *torta* includes ground almonds or hazelnuts and some cocoa; the filling used is the same chocolate cream as for the *Dobostorta* and the top and sides are then covered with a chocolate fondant icing.

Diótorta – Walnut Torta

This is a rich *torta* with ground walnuts in both the sponge and in the cream. This cream is further enhanced by the addition of some rum. A similar *torta* is prepared using hazelnuts instead of walnuts.

Puncstorta – Punch Torta

A subtly flavoured cake which is made up of blocks of different colour and given a pink fondant icing.

Oroszkrémtorta – Russian Cream Torta

The cream for this *torta* is a little unusual in Hungarian cooking – it includes 5 eggs, 150g (5 oz.) sugar, 120g (4 oz.) sultanas soaked in rum, 120g (4 oz.) fruit with sugar if necessary, 2½ dl (½ pint) milk, 30g (1 oz.) gelatine, ½-litre (1 pint) fresh cream and half a vanilla pod. The ingredients are mixed together beginning with a thick cream formed by cooking the eggs, sugar and milk together, using the vanilla for flavouring.

The Cold Table

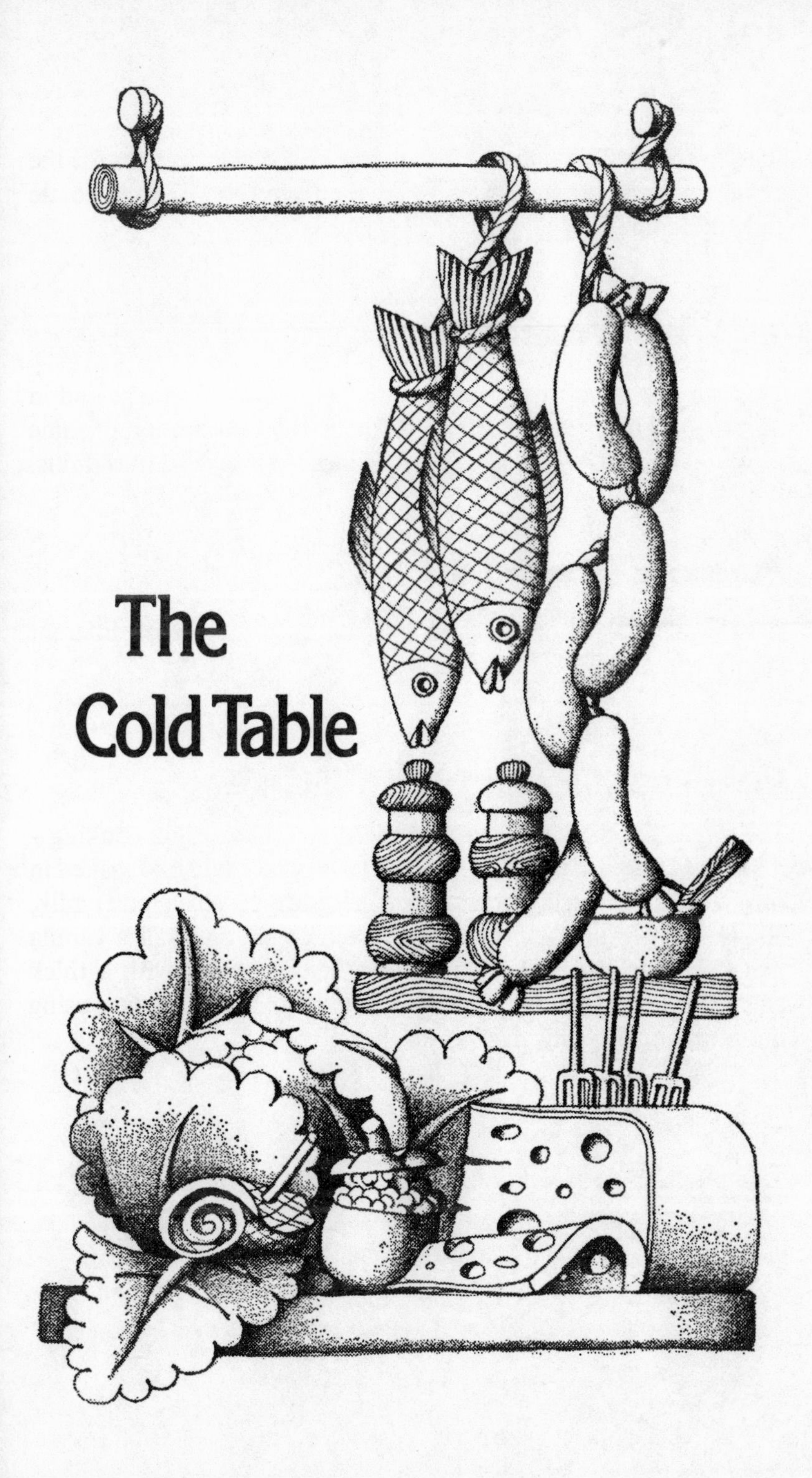

Dishes for the cold table are viewed rather differently from most other food: whereas many Hungarian housewives would be too proud to buy, say, packeted shop *pasta* or *rétes*, preferring the satisfaction of making their own, it would be rare indeed to find any housewife who would go to the trouble of preparing the standard dishes which usually grace a cold table.

The cold table foods which you can buy are generally excellent in quality, so people frequently take advantage of this convenience and take home a ready-made batch of Casino Eggs, or rolls of ham filled with a nippy horseradish sauce, or a finely flavoured mushroom salad, all of which provide a quick and tasty supper for the family.

Of course the centre-piece of any Hungarian cold table is bound to be *téliszalámi* (literally, winter salami), which is undoubtedly one of the finest salamis in the world: it is to be found in many shops in this country and although it tends to equal the best steak in price, I have no hesitation in assuring any reader who has not yet tasted this delicacy that it equals the best steak in every aspect of quality as well.

On a more everyday level there are other excellent salamis and an inexhaustible variety of sausages, the best of which to my taste are *turistaszalámi* (tourist salami) and *gyulai kolbász* (sausages from Gyula), but if you visit Hungary, you should be adventurous in sampling these products, which you will find displayed at food shop counters – I feel certain you will consider your effort amply repaid.

It is with these salamis and sausages that the Alföld wines are so good. Two I would recommend particularly are *Csongrádi zöldszilváni* and the wine from *Gyöngyösvisonta.*

Among other dishes of the Hungarian cold table which require no actual recipe are radishes, sweet peppers cut into strips, pigs' tongues, and fish in oil.

Hungarian cheeses have been unjustifiably neglected or overlooked by our delicatessens and international food shops. Apart from excellently prepared Emmental and Trappista cheeses, which are not originally Hungarian, Hungary does have some cheeses of her own to offer. *Óvári* cheese is a typical example – a yellowish cheese which arrives in the shops in discs weighing between 3 and 5 kilograms. It is slightly springy and easy to cut, and although it does not crumble too easily, it seems to melt away in the mouth. It has lots of very tiny holes all through it – these are not produced by the maturing process but remain from the time when the cheese is first pressed.

There are curd cheeses and cream cheeses and one of the most interesting of the cheeses prepared from sheep's milk is the delicious *Paranyica* 'ribbon-cheese' which has a delightful character all its own – the cheese is made into long, flat 'ribbons' a couple of inches wide and less than half an inch thick, rolled up, bound by two thin 'strings' which themselves are formed from the cheese, and the whole bundle is then smoked over a period of several days. Each *Paranyica* cheese weighs between 10 and 16 ounces.

The third Hungarian cheese I would like to see on sale in Britain is the simple but unique cheese from Göcsej; it is firmer than Camembert but remains almost creamy, and its smooth texture and light flavour defy description – a connoisseur's cheese.

Liver pastes

Goose liver is not generally made into a *pâté* in Hungary but roasted in its own abundant fat without the addition of any seasoning whatsoever. It is also prepared 'in the Hungarian style' – braised with onion, tomato and sweet peppers and seasoned with salt and paprika powder. For making pastes Hungarians use calves' or pigs' liver. The first of the two recipes given here produces a fairly firm paste whereas the second is a soft cream, good for spreading on bread or savoury biscuits. With these liver pastes Hungarians like to drink a dry wine such as the *Pécsi furmint* or *Pécsi cirfandli.*

Májpastétom – Liver Paste

350g calves' or pigs' liver (12 oz.)
60g fat (2 oz.)
3 eggs
6 tbs. sour cream
¼ kg shoulder of pork (8 oz.)
1 onion
2 rolls soaked in milk
salt, freshly ground black pepper and lemon rind

Fry the finely chopped onion in the fat and braise the liver and meat in it adding just a minimum of water. Once the meat is tender put it through a fine mincer twice, together with the rolls, which should first be squeezed free of any surplus milk. Add the egg yolks and sour cream and season with salt, pepper and a little grated lemon rind. Finally fold in the stiffly beaten egg whites.

Grease a longish tin or mould and spread out the mixture in it. Stand the tin in water, cover the top, and steam for 1 hour. Turn out the paste while it is still hot and serve it cold – whole or sliced. Accompany with hard boiled eggs and pickles.

Kenőmájas – Liver Paste for spreading

400g pigs' liver (13 oz.)
100g butter (3 oz.)
1–2 tbs. sour cream
100g smoked bacon (4 oz.)
60g fat (2 oz.)
50g onion (2 oz.)
salt, pepper, lemon rind

Clean the liver, cut it into thin strips and fry these with the onion and bacon in the fat – add a very little water to prevent over-browning. Cool and put through a mincer twice.

Cream the butter and combine it with the sour cream. Add the minced liver and season with salt, pepper and a little grated lemon rind. Set the paste out on a plate, leave it in the refrigerator to become thoroughly cold and the paste is ready.

Nyúlpastétom – Rabbit Paste

The neck, ribs, shoulders, liver, heart and lungs of 1 rabbit
1 roll soaked in milk
1 tbs. sour cream
200g smoked bacon (4 oz.)
60g fat (2 oz.)
2 eggs
1 medium onion
spices to taste

Marinate the rabbit pieces in a spicy marinade for about 24 hours. Then cook the rabbit in the marinade until the meat is tender. Drain it well and brown it with the onion and bacon in the fat. Remove the bones, mince the meat twice together with the roll (which should be soaked in milk and then squeezed free of any surplus liquid). Add the eggs and sour cream, season to taste and work well together; put the paste into a decorative mould (a long or round fluted tin), stand it in water and bake it in a moderate oven for about an hour – until a testing needle comes out quite clean.

Húspastétom – Meat Paste

¼ kg veal or boiling beef (8 oz.)
1 carrot
50g fat (2 oz.)
50g smoked bacon (2 oz.)
50g butter (2 oz.)
¼ kg pork (8 oz.)
1 small onion
1 small parsley root (or parsnip)
2 eggs (hard boiled)
1 tbs. fresh cream
salt, pepper, mustard

Braise the cubed meat and the sliced vegetables with the onion and bacon in the fat. Put them through a fine mincer twice with the two hard-boiled eggs; beat the butter to a thick cream and add it to the meat. Season with salt, pepper and a vinegar mustard, and then add the cream. Mix well to a smooth paste.

This paste is equally good for spreading on bread or for slicing.

Kaszinótojás – Casino Eggs

Next comes a recipe for stuffed eggs: Casino Eggs are probably the first thing that would come to a Hungarian mind if you mentioned the cold table. They are always available in the shops at various prices, depending on the quality of the stuffing, but even the cheapest is usually delicious.

4 eggs
mustard
12 tbs. sour cream
sardine paste

Boil the eggs until they are hard, open them at one side and remove the yolks with a narrow knife. Break down half the yolks to a pulp and mix to taste with sour cream, a vinegar mustard, sardines crushed to a paste with a minimum of butter, salt and a pinch of sugar. Refill the egg whites with the mixture.

Prepare a thick vegetable salad from diced cooked carrot, peas, and potato with mayonnaise and form a base with this on a flat serving dish. Set the stuffed eggs on this with the opening downwards. Prepare a tartare sauce from the remaining cream and the remaining egg yolks and pour this over the eggs and salad. Decorate with rounds of lemon, diced aspic and chopped parsley.

Körözött liptói

Liptói is a sandwich spread which has a strong air of country cooking about it – it takes its name from the one-time County of Liptó and its piquant flavour is something virtually all Hungarians celebrate.

120g sheep's curds (4 oz.)
1 tbs. fresh cream
salt
caraway seeds
60g butter (2 oz.)
at least 1 tsp. paprika powder
grated onion

Beat the butter to a fluffy cream with the curds and the cream. Measure the flavourings according to taste and mix them in well. Pile on a plate, smooth over the surface with a knife, and with the handle of a spoon press patterns into the surface.

If the curds are from cow's milk, use sour cream instead of fresh – sheep's curds are much sharper and do not need the help of sour cream for flavour, but rather the help of fresh cream for texture.

Sajtkrém – Cheese Cream

60g firm cheese (2 oz.)
60g margarine (2 oz.)
6 tbs. sour cream
60g softer, creamy smoked cheese (2 oz.)

Beat the margarine to a cream, combine with the sour cream and then the grated cheeses. Flavour to taste with paprika, caraway seed, or finely chopped raw onion. The addition of 1 tablespoon mashed boiled potato makes for a considerable improvement in texture.

Tojáskrém – Egg Cream

4 hard-boiled eggs
100g butter (3–4 oz.)
half a lemon
100g onion (3–4 oz.)
salt and paprika powder

Break down the eggs and beat them well with the butter. Add the finely chopped onion and flavour with salt and paprika. Spread on bread and sprinkle with lemon juice. This is a simple favourite for eating with beer.

Halikra-saláta – Roe Salad

Clean and wash the roe of a perch or carp thoroughly and sprinkle it with a pinch of salt. Put it on a plate above a pan of boiling water and stir the roe about until it turns red. Remove it from the heat.

Soak a roll in water, squeeze out the surplus liquid, crumble the roll and add it to the roe. Add about 9 tablespoons good oil drop by drop, alternating with lemon juice – the quantity will depend on the size of the roe. Beat well for about half an hour until the mixture becomes frothy and then flavour with a little grated onion. Refrigerate for a few hours before serving.

This mixture is good for sandwiches, with lemon rounds and parsley, but it is also a useful salad for accompanying spicy meat or vegetable dishes.

Babsaláta – Bean Salad

200g big white or red beans (7 oz.)
1 onion
lemon juice (or vinegar)
¼ kg tomatoes (8 oz.)
¼ kg sweet peppers (8 oz.)
6 tbs. good oil
salt
dill

Cut the onion into rings and fry them lightly in the oil. Add the sliced peppers and fry them gently (without salt) until they soften. Do this without the lid on the pan. Peel the tomatoes and add them to the mixture – if they are very juicy, use only the fleshy part and keep the rest for soup.

Have the beans already soaked overnight and boil them gently until they are soft, but take all possible care that they do not break. Mix them in very carefully to the peppers and tomatoes, flavour with a few drops lemon juice or vinegar and salt and refrigerate. Serve this salad as a course on its own, decorated with fresh chopped dill.

Babmajonéz – Bean Mayonnaise

½ kg white beans (1 lb.)
half a lemon
paprika
11–12 tbs. oil
1 onion
salt

Cook the beans until they soften, drain them (the liquid is a good basis for a soup) and break them down by pressing them through a sieve. Add the oil spoonful by spoonful to the bean *purée* and then add the chopped onion. Flavour with the paprika, salt and the juice and grated rind of the half-lemon. Beat the mixture until it is light and fluffy. Pile up on a serving plate, sprinkle with chopped parsley and surround with round slices of a light sausage and cucumber.

Töltött paradicsom – Stuffed Tomatoes

4 large tomatoes
100g grated horseradish (3 oz.)
half a lemon
lettuce leaves
2 apples
salt and sugar

Slice the tops off the tomatoes, remove the seeds and invert the tomatoes so that the juice will run out. Sprinkle the insides with salt.

Grate the apples roughly and the horseradish finely. Mix them together and flavour with salt, a little sugar and lemon juice. Fill the tomatoes with the mixture, dot the top with mayonnaise and surround with roughly cut strips of lettuce.

Töksaláta – Marrow Salad

1 kg young marrow (2 lbs.)
6 tbs. yoghurt (or soured milk thickened with 1 tbs. sour cream)
3 tbs. oil
juice of 1 lemon
salt
dill (or parsley)

Skin and clean the inside of the marrow. Slice (or plane) it into thin strips. Salt the strips and leave them for half an hour. Press out the juice gently and fry the marrow in oil, with the lid on the pan, until it becomes soft and glassy. Do not stir the pieces during this braising – shake the pan a little from time to time.

Beat the yoghurt with the lemon juice until very smooth, pour it over the cooled marrow and decorate with chopped dill or parsley.

Mustármártás – Mustard Sauce

Mix 1 tablespoon ready-made mustard with 6 tablespoons sour cream. Thin with about 6 tablespoons water and flavour with salt, a little vinegar and a good pinch of sugar. This is an excellent sauce for cold roast meats or for garnishing salad dishes.

Ecetes torma – Vinegar Horseradish

Clean ¼ kg (8 oz.) horseradish and grate it very finely. Mix it with 6 tablespoons boiling water and a little salt and vinegar. Press out all the liquid (this helps to remove some of the strength of the horseradish) and mix in 6 tablespoons good beef stock. Add a good pinch of sugar and serve with hot or cold boiled meats.

A variation which gives a slightly different emphasis is to soak the horseradish and press it dry as above and then mix in 6 tablespoons fresh cream (or sour cream), flavouring with a little vinegar, sugar and salt.

Almás tormakrém – Apple Horseradish Sauce

150g horseradish (5 oz.)
2–3 apples
beef stock
6 tbs. sour cream
salt, vinegar, sugar

Clean the horseradish and grate it very finely. Put it in a very hot oven for a couple of minutes to remove some of its fierceness. Mix well with the grated apple and the sour cream. Add the salt and the sugar; beat the mixture until it becomes a firm cream. If you want instead to make a sauce from the cream, thin it down with a little beef stock and flavour as desired with vinegar, adjusting the salt seasoning. It is a good sauce for cold meats and hot boiled meat.

One of the most enticing variations is to mix the grated horseradish with grated beetroot, using a few caraway seeds for flavouring.

Preserves

CHERRIES
TOMATOES
ORANGES
ROSE SYRUP
PLUMS
MIXED
CUCUMBERS

Like the cold table, preserves are a part of the Hungarian cuisine on which, in my experience, the average housewife does not lay much emphasis. There are, however, few homes where one would not find a large jar of ridge cucumbers in vinegar, plums in vinegar with cinnamon, or *lecsó* put away for use as flavouring during the months when peppers and tomatoes are not readily, or cheaply, available in the markets.

The quality of the tinned foods, bottled vegetables and fruits, and jams which can be bought in the shops in Hungary is high, everything from *Székelykáposzta* and liver *pâté* to apricot jam and jars of cherries vying for your attention at very reasonable prices. The purity of the product is more highly prized by the factories than over-emphasis of attractive appearance and this tends to make Hungarian preserved foods retain the fullness of their flavour when fresh.

In home preserving there is one method of sterilization which is worth mentioning. It is called dry steaming and alongside other methods it is widely used in Hungary today. The essential point in dry steaming is that the hot preserve is placed in hot jars and then kept continuously at a good temperature and allowed to cool only very slowly.

Spread a thick blanket on a table or on the floor, place paper on top and then set out the preserve jars closely beside one another – the preserves having been put into the jars very hot and immediately firmly covered and bound. Cover over the jars with cloths and cushions and then fold up the edges of the blanket so that no cool air will reach the jars. Another way of going about this is to place the jars in large baskets lined well with straw and a blanket. Leave the jars parcelled up like this for a whole day and night – there will be very gradual cooling only and this makes the sterilization more effective.

Ecetes szilva – Plums in Vinegar

Plums preserved in a thin vinegar syrup form a sparkling accompaniment to the finest roast meats and even surpass apricots preserved in a similar way.

Place 2 kg (4¼ lbs.) plums (unstoned) in a broad basin.

Bring 400g (13 oz.) sugar and 4 dl (¾ pint) water to the boil with 6 tablespoons wine vinegar, a little cinnamon and grated lemon rind, and pour the syrup over the plums. Leave until cold.

Take out the plums and place them in large jars. Bring the syrup to the boil again and pour over the plums in the jars. Set the jars in a pan of water which comes three quarters of the way up the jars, bring the water very slowly to bubbling point and keep it at that temperature for 6–8 minutes.

Orange Preserve

1 kg oranges (2 lbs.)
1 kg sugar (2 lbs.)

Use blood oranges if they are available. With a clean and firm nail-brush brush the orange skins all round; pierce the skins here and there with a fork and this will help to remove the bitterness of the inner skin. Place the oranges whole in a large jar and soak them in enough water to cover them for 4 days, changing the water each day.

Make a thick syrup with the sugar and 2½ dl (½ pint) water and add the sliced and seeded oranges. Cook them gently in the syrup until the liquid is very thick – about 30–40 minutes. Pour the oranges and syrup into wide-brimmed jars, cover and tie them firmly and give them the dry steaming process as described above. Open only two months later, by which time the mixture will have begun to become like a jelly.

Orange Rind Preserve

1 kg orange rinds (2 lbs.)
800g sugar (1½ lbs.)
1 lemon

The best oranges for this preserve are the thick skinned Jaffas. Peel off the orange rinds in strips half an inch wide. Curl up each strip into a coil like a snail's shell and bind them with thread. Soak the coils in cold water in a cool place for 5–6 days, changing the water daily.

Then bring the orange rind curls to the boil in enough water to cover them (about 2 pints) and simmer them until they soften. Remove the rinds from the water, drain them well and weigh them. Add their weight in sugar to the pan of liquid and boil to a thick syrup, adding the juice of 1 lemon. Remove the threads from the strips of rind and add them to the syrup. Boil for 20 minutes. Leave the pan overnight and bring it to the boil again. Bottle the orange rinds and cover and tie them at once.

This preserve is very useful for fillings in layered cakes or pastries or for decoration.

Sour Cherry Preserve

This preserve requires no cooking at all and is in itself perfect as a dessert, as well as being good for pies and cake fillings.

4 kg stoned sour cherries (8 lbs.)
2 kg sugar (4 lbs.)
6 tbs. rum
10g powdered aspirin (¼ oz.)

Mix the sour cherries with the sugar in a deep basin. Keep them there for 3 days, mixing them about each day, meanwhile adding the aspirin.

Wash out jars with hot water, dry them thoroughly and fill them with the fruit. Put 2 tablespoons rum on top of each jar. Tie down the tops and store the jars in a cool, dry place.

Raw plums, halved and stoned, can be preserved in a similar way, using about 1 part sugar to 3 parts plums, but don't forget the rum.

Narancsszörp – Orange Syrup

Peel the oranges thinly. Soak the rind for 1–2 months in alcohol, using 12 tablespoons alcohol to the rind of 5 medium oranges.

Prepare a thick syrup from ½ litre (1 pint) of water and 1 kg (2 lbs.)

sugar. Boil it for 5 minutes, skim off the foamy top and cool the syrup. Add the alcohol orange mixture, all of it or part of it depending on how sweet you want the syrup to be.

Rózsaszörp **– Rose Syrup**

Bring 300g (10 oz.) scented red rose petals gently to the boil with about 4 pints water. Simmer until the water becomes red and the petals pale or white. Strain off the liquid, taking care not to press the petals. Measure the liquid and take 1 cup sugar for every cup of juice, bring them to the boil together and boil for 20 minutes. Pour into prepared bottles and cork them when the syrup is cold.

Vegetables

For vegetable preserves described in the following recipes it is best to use jars which hold no more than enough for you to use at one time – the preserves will not generally keep reliably well once the jars have been opened.

Pepper Preserve

This preserve is useful if you want to have peppers for stuffing when they are not in season and when they are very expensive if available at all.

Remove the tops, inner veins and seeds from the peppers and throw them into boiling water for a couple of minutes, so that they will soften slightly. Drain them well and place them in jars, fitting them into one another like saucers. Fill the remaining space in the jars with freshly boiled and mashed (or sieved) tomatoes. Season with a little salt. Cover and tie the jars while the contents are still very hot and then give them the dry steaming treatment.

Lecsó Preserve

This preserve is made during the summer in most Hungarian households when tomatoes and sweet peppers are at their best. The other ingredients for *lecsó* itself (*see* page 104 for the recipe) are available throughout the year, so having the peppers and tomatoes carefully preserved as described in the recipe which follows, ensures that you can enjoy the dish in winter as well.

Take 4 kg (8 lbs.) sweet peppers (green or red) to 2 kg (4 lbs.) large ripe tomatoes.

Clean the peppers, removing the seeds and inner veins, and cut them into slices. Peel the tomatoes and quarter them. Heat the tomatoes in a wide pan and when they come to the boil add the peppers. Bring just to the boil again and pour immediately into jars. Tie the jars down while the contents are still hot and dry steam overnight.

Sorrel Preserve

For each 1 kg (2 lbs.) of sorrel leaves, take 60g (2 oz.) fat.

Braise the sorrel in the fat, with the lid on the pan, until it softens. Put it into jars as hot as possible, pour a thin layer of oil on top of each jar, cover and tie immediately, and dry steam until completely cold.

When the preserved sorrel is being used later (for example in soup) there is no need to use more fat for it.

Paprikalekvár – Pepper Jam

For this recipe use the round flattish *paradicsompaprika* – they are generally available in Britain in the late summer and autumn.

Clean out the insides and inner veins of the peppers and put the flesh through a mincer. Mix each pound of peppers with 100g (3½ oz.) salt, put the mixture into jars, cover and tie.

This preserve is useful to have around for flavouring dishes throughout the year – remember, however, that this preserve is already fairly salty and so you will probably have to adjust the quantity of salt asked for in any recipe to which you add this preserve for flavouring.

Dill leaves and tarragon can also be successfully stored in this way. The leaves should be left whole. Put them in jars with alternate layers of salt, using one part salt by weight to five parts dill leaves. Before using the leaves later, you should rinse them lightly under running water.

Vizes uborka – Cucumbers in Water

Wash some ridge cucumbers. Put a layer of fresh green dill in the bottom of a large jar, such as a sweet jar, stand the cucumbers on end on the dill with plenty of horseradish sliced lengthwise in between them. On top place some unripe grapes or gooseberries.

To 1 litre (1¾ pints) water use 30g (1 oz.) salt, bring it to the boil, cool it and pour it over the cucumbers. Screw down the top of the jar and leave in a warm but shady place for 4–5 days until the liquid in the jar is quite clear. Once opened, this preserve will keep in a cold place for 2–3 weeks.

Ecetes uborka – Cucumbers in Vinegar

Use freshly picked ridge cucumbers 3–4 inches in length, wash them well in running water, and place them in jars. The flavourings customary in Hungary are dill, horseradish, ginger, sour-cherry leaves, peppers.

To 1 litre (1¾ pints) water use 3–4 dl (½–¾ pint) vinegar, 20g (¾ oz.) salt and 40g (1¼ oz.) sugar. Bring this solution to the boil, cool it and pour it over the cucumbers. If the taste is too vinegary when you open them, stand the cucumbers for a couple of days in salt water.

Tomato-Peppers in Vinegar

Choose faultless late September peppers, wash them well in running water. The best kind are the rather flat peppers known in Hungary as 'tomato-peppers' but any sweet red peppers will do. Cut the stems off short but otherwise leave the peppers intact. Place them in large jars. To 1 litre (1¾ pints) water, use 4–5 dl (¾–1 pint) vinegar, 30g (1 oz.) salt and 30g (1 oz.) sugar. Bring this solution to the boil, cool it and pour it over the peppers. To prevent the peppers from floating to the top place two small sticks crosswise in the neck of the jar and see that the liquid comes above these. On top pour a half-inch layer of good oil. Once the contents of the jars are cold, put on the lids. This preserve keeps well even after it has been opened.

Similar treatment is given to green tomatoes and small, not quite ripe melons.

Mixed Salad Preserves

In fairly equal proportions use ridge cucumbers, white cabbage, green tomatoes, green and red peppers and a quarter proportion of onion.

Shred the cabbage finely, slice the other vegetables into rounds and mix in 30g (1 oz.) salt to every 1 kg (2 lbs.) vegetables. Leave the vegetables to stand for a few hours.

Place the vegetables in jars but do not press them down as they will soften too easily. Mix 1 part vinegar with 2 parts water, using enough to fill the jars.

Tárkonyecet – Tarragon Vinegar

Transylvania shares tarragon with France as its favourite herb, and likewise the vinegar prepared from it.

Take 200–250g (7–8 oz.) fresh tarragon leaves, wash them well and hang them up to dry. Place them in a large jar, pressing them well down, and pour on 3 tablespoons pure alcohol.

Set aside for half an hour and then pour on 2 litres (3½ pints) vinegar. Close the lid tightly. The vinegar can be used after it has rested for a few days.

Wines and Other Drinks

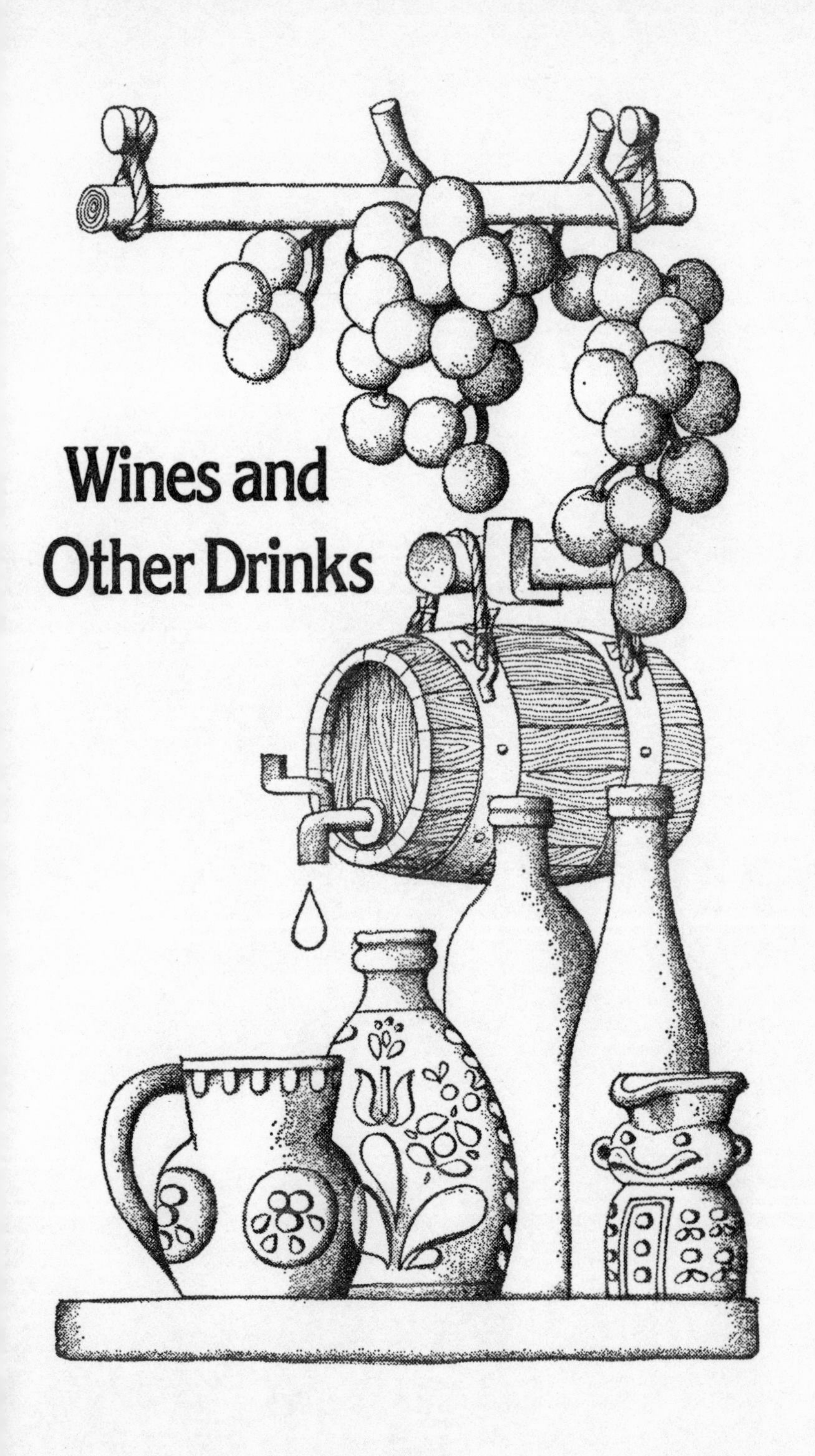

Although Hungary's vine-growing *area* is tiny in comparison with that of the leading wine producing countries, this is not altogether a disadvantage as Hungary tends as a result to concentrate on constantly improving quality.

There is an honesty about Hungarian wines and their production which dispenses with superfluous mumbo-jumbo and the wines are subjected to rigorous examination and testing based on a highly sophisticated appreciation of the elements involved. No privately produced wine finds its way onto the market, and the standards of wines with recognized and recognizable names are reliable. This is not to say that no wine at all is produced by individual wine-growers; if you visit Hungary you may be fortunate enough to sample some such wine and it may please you more than any of the famous wines produced on the state-owned vineyards.

Research has shown that the vine grew in Hungary in ancient times and has established that there was deliberate and conscious cultivation of the plant before the Hungarians occupied the area in the eleventh century. A little later it must indeed have taken quite a quantity of wine for King Mátyás to have wine flow from the fountains in the courtyard of his palace at Visegrád. But gone now are the Buda wines and who would believe that a hundred to a hundred and fifty years ago Csepel Island sprouted vines where it now presents a maze of iron and steel works?

Hungarian wines are distinguished from each other by naming them according to the variety of grape used and further the name of the vineyard or region which produced it. So that, for example, *Tokaji hárslevelű* denotes wine from the *Hárslevelű* grape grown in the Tokaj region. As far as classification by region is concerned, a wine that bears the Tokaj, Badacsony, Villány or Eger name can claim to be of special quality. These regions have a clear edge in reputation over other *areas* but not necessarily over certain individual wines from other regions – for example the Kékfrankos wine from Sopron. One famous name which no longer appears on the list of wine regions at all is *Debrő*: this name now comes under the Mátraalja region but its most distinguished wine, *Debrői hárslevelű*, has lost nothing of its quality for all that and certainly ranks as one of the finest and one of the first for anyone not familiar with Hungarian wines to acquaint himself with.

Hungary is officially divided into fourteen wine regions and although it would be impossible here to give an exhaustive description of each wine produced by each region, I should like nevertheless to go into some detail to show just what an enormous variety of good wine Hungary does put on the market, on which we in Britain are at the moment largely missing out.

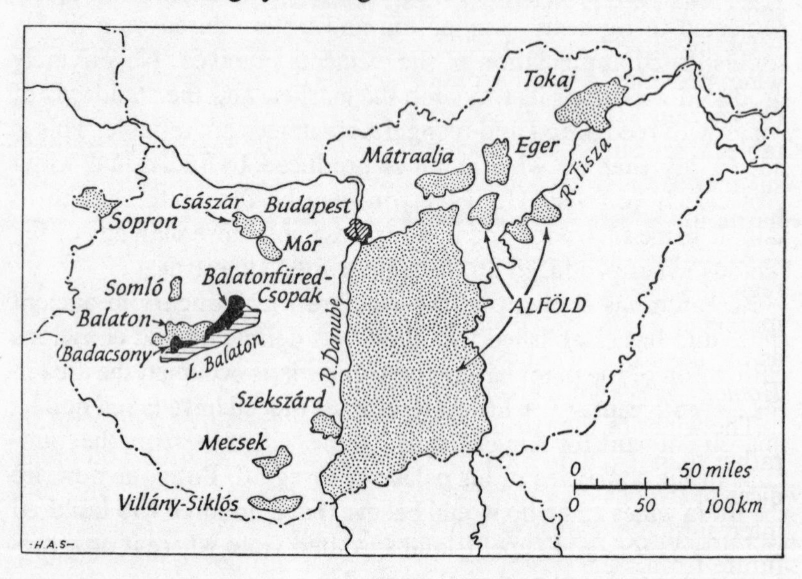

1. *The Alföld Region*

This is the largest of the wine regions in Hungary, taking up about two thirds of the whole of Hungary's wine producing area. Most of the wines from the Great Plain are table wines. The more hilly regions tend to sneer even today at the endless flat Alföld with the confusing result that where wine is produced in the Plain, the word *hegy* (hill, mountain) has sometimes been added to the name of the place with a sort of innocent guile. The Alföld could, if it chose, no doubt sneer in its own way: the region produces several times the amount of wine that the hilly and more renowned regions do. A further important point to its advantage is that phylloxera, which has shattered Hungary's wine production twice in living memory, cannot live in the Alföld's sand, which has a large quartz content.

The main distinguishing mark of the Alföld wines is that the character of the various grapes dominates, rather than the character of any particular area. Wine from the same kind of grape is much softer in the Great Plain than in the uplands of the country. The chief red wine grape here is the *Kadarka*. In the Great Plain this grape produces a wine which is full of body and considerably fiery. Although the *Kadarka* speciality of the area, the *vörös aszú* wine, is not available commercially, a visitor may occasionally be offered some: the offer is at all costs to be taken up!

Of the white wine grapes, *Ezerjó* probably leads in quality and its wine provides a fair proportion for the export market. The *Olaszrizling* (Italian Riesling) grape produces a fine full-bodied table wine, but in some years it can contain 2–3 per cent invert sugar and its alcohol content rises to 12–13 per cent, giving a golden, harmonious wine of some quality.

Kövidinka is an unfussy grape which is grown throughout the region. It gives a table wine which does not often arrive on the market as a wine in its own right and under its own name, but rather as the basis of the wines known as *Asztali fehér* (table white) and *Homoki fehér* (white from the sands).

The wines of the Alföld region can look forward to their future rather than dwell on their past. The misunderstandings and prejudices of the past against any wines produced on such flat and 'uninteresting' land are now being set aside and much is expected in the future from wine producers in the region using the most modern approaches and methods.

2. *The Badacsony*

This region takes its name from a hill with a very distinctive outline on the north-western shore of Lake Balaton. Experts hold the region to be the true pearl among the several excellent wine producing areas around the Balaton. The Badacsony Hill itself rises up as if to rule over the region with its massive basalt solidity.

Most of the grapes grown in this region are of the *Olaszrizling* variety. In the Badacsony the wine produced from this grape is such a delight to the eye as to give anyone the immediate desire to taste it. Its colour hovers between gold and green, it has an almost mignonette-like aroma, and gentle acidity. Here there is also a worthwhile *rizling* which is sometimes made from over-ripe grapes, and when it is available for sale, it bears the name *Badacsonyi szemelt rizling* to distinguish it from the ordinary *rizling* of the region. To some Hungarians this *Szemelt rizling* of the Badacsony is a better wine than the renowned *Tokaji aszú* – but discussions on such points scarcely ever reach the stage of an argument, because someone will quickly step in with the popular peasant adage, 'Some like the priest, some his wife'. It is quite common in Hungary to hear that when you drink Badacsony wine, even if it goes to your head it will at most make you smile and never make you quarrel.

The other notable grape grown in the Badacsony, and indeed only there, is the Hungarian *Kéknyelű* (literally, 'blue stem'). It does not easily win the confidence of growers as it has a slight tendency to remain infertile, but when it is grown successfully, its quality is acknowledged to be all the finer. The *Kéknyelű* grape always produces a dry wine. The perfect harmony of the *Badacsonyi kéknyelű* makes it an elegant wine certainly worthy of recognition beyond the limits of its homeland.

Undoubtedly the best known wine from this region is the *Szürkebarát* (literally, 'grey friend'). This grape which came originally from France (where it is known as the *Pinot gris*) is considered to have far surpassed in Hungary the quality it achieved in France. It is a rich, round, almost oily wine with a high glycerine content, and the harmony between the glycerine and the alcohol makes this wine quite exquisite. Of all the wines of Hungary, *Szürkebarát* from the Badacsony is my own special favourite: I would like to see it exported more generously than the ubiquitous, and in my opinion over-emphasized, Bull's Blood.

Zöld szilváni is another excellent, but less familiar, grape grown in this region – it is reputed to be originally a Transylvanian grape. Of the wine made from it in the Badacsony area it is the bouquet that sets people hunting for comparisons, the aroma of cloves, aniseed, vanilla, and even hay being frequently mentioned. It is sometimes summed up as being like a basic foundation for a heavy, round, full-bodied, natural dessert wine.

In this region of Hungary there are almost too many good things for the visitor to choose from, but they do have to be sampled rather than read about for, as any Hungarian will tell you, when it comes to describing and praising these Badacsony wines, words are grey and dry.

3. The most striking feature of the *Balatonfüred–Csopak region* is its ground: its base rock is slate, which is covered by limestone, sandstone and the top soil is a reddish sand.

The region is a continuation of the Badacsony region on the north bank of the Balaton. Here, too, *Olaszrizling* is the most commonly grown grape and in this part of Hungary it produces the palest, greenish wine which has a somewhat spicy flavour.

The two main areas, Füred and Csopak, do, however, offer wines quite recognizably different in character. This difference is mainly to be found in the acid content. The Füred wines are soft and smooth whereas the Csopak wines are sharper and drier.

Furmint is the other main grape grown in the region. The *Furmint* wines here have a fairly high acid content but they still succeed in being harmonious.

Much of the muscat wine available in Hungary comes from Akali, which belongs to this region. The two leading grapes are *Muscat lunel* and *Muscat ottonel.*

4. The vineyards surrounding the Balaton which do not belong to the more acclaimed regions just described are grouped together into one region, the *Balaton region.* Its wines are thought to be of less value than those of the Badacsony and the Balatonfüred – Csopak regions, and they are listed as being good, full-bodied table wines.

About three quarters of the region's wine comes from the *Olaszrizling* grape. It has an alcohol content of at least 12 per cent and the experts usually classify it as dry wine.

5. *Eger*

The historical town of Eger is the centre of this region of legendary wines which also includes no less than eleven other wine producing communities. The gently sloping hills, volcanic in origin, offer favourable soil and situation for vine growing.

The region is famous first and foremost for its red wines. *Kadarka*, brought in originally by the Serbs, is the most commonly grown grape, but *Kékfrankos*, *Médoc noir* and *Oporto* are all grown in significant quantities. The best known of the white varieties is *Leányka*.

This is the region of Hungary's Bull's Blood, which is known throughout the wine-drinking world. Oral tradition traces the wine back to the siege of Eger in the middle of the sixteenth century, when the heroic Captain István Dobó had wine brought by the women to the men defending the town – so that the noble drink would give them strength.

When the Serbs first introduced the *Kadarka* grape, the Eger people, who had hitherto produced only white wine, called it simply 'the black grape'. They soon learned, however, to distinguish between different black grapes. The Serbs held what they called the 'flat-footed black grape' in the highest esteem and although they believed it to be an independent plant, it was merely a variety of *Kadarka* which took its name from the shape of the leaf. Other varieties were the 'cross-leaved', the 'springy' and the 'noble' *Kadarka* – all of which have formed the basis of Bull's Blood to this day. Other components, such as the *Médoc noir* and *Oporto* grapes, were added later. Although each variety of grape makes its own quite recognizable contribution to Bull's Blood, it is through the softness of *Oporto* and *Cabernet franc* that it achieves its inimitable velvet smoothness. Add to this its deep dark colour, its fiery bouquet and its full flavour and you have one of the world's great wines. It is however often chosen for superficial reasons which have more to do with habit and sentiment than good judgement; this wine must be matched with care.

Wines other than Bull's Blood are also made in this region from the *Médoc Noir* grape. In its homeland this grape is known under the name *Cot rouge*.

Leányka is another grape taken to be of Transylvanian origin. To my taste *Egri leányka* is one of several Hungarian wines whose praises cannot be too highly sung, particularly outside their homeland where they are almost entirely unknown. *Egri leányka* is a quality wine more sweet than dry, with no trace of heaviness.

A special point of interest in this region is the Eger cellars. Cut into the hillsides, these picturesque cellars will tempt you to peep in at the doorway and there is scarcely a day in the year, whatever the season, when you will not find the cellarmaster there, who will almost always be happy to show you round and even give you a taste. Professionally, the cellars are highly valued because after the Tokaj region it is here that the fungus Cladosporium (*Rhacodium*) is found in considerable quantities The fungus enhances the flavour of the wine.

6. *The Mátraalja region*

This region, the second largest in Hungary, is formed by the vineyards on the south-facing slopes of the Mátra mountain range. Although the Mátra vineyards get a rich share of annual sunshine, it has to be remembered that they are in the north of Hungary and on relatively high ground, so they get a greater share of spring and autumn frosts than the rest of the country.

Place names which you will find in the names of the region's wines are, among others, Gyöngyös, the centre of the region, Debrő and Domoszló. The grapes which produce the best wines in the area are *Hárslevelű* (literally 'linden leaf'), *Leányka*, *Olaszrizling* and *Muskotály*.

The Mátraalja wines are mostly classed as being among the better table wines, but the best known wine of the region, *Debrői hárslevelű*, is yet another outstanding Hungarian dessert wine – and this particular one can, I am told, be found from time to time in this country. It ought to be much more widely and readily available.

7. *The Mecsek*

The Mecsek Hills are well known in the south of Hungary, not very far from the Yugoslav border, and here the conditions of soil and climate are particularly favourable. This wine region is centred round the historically important town of Pécs. The Mecsek wines are predominantly white and the most important grapes are *Furmint*, *Olaszrizling* and *Cirfandli*, the last two of which provide the specialities of the area.

The *Olaszrizling* wines here retain some of the characteristics of the grape itself and combine them with pronounced regional characteristics. *Pécsi olaszrizling* is considered a harmonious, dry, quality wine.

The Mecsek offers an interesting variety of table wines and more highly prized wines. Wines produced here from the *Cirfandli* grape, for example, are famous throughout Hungary for their bouquet, which does indeed remind one of a varied bunch of fragrant wild flowers.

8. *Mór*

The wide area from the Bakony to the Vértes Hills grows almost exclusively one particular kind of grape: the *Ezerjó* (literally 'a thousand goods'), and the most characteristic wine of this region is *Móri ezerjó.*

In good years this wine can reach the standard of a good natural dessert wine. It is then referred to by the slightly exalted name of *Móri aszú.* The most characteristic feature of *Móri ezerjó* is its acid content which gives it a decidedly hard quality. It might be described as a wine with plenty of backbone; its alcohol content and its sugar content are perfectly appropriate, and it is a finely balanced, full bodied wine. If one were to take exception to any of its features it would have to be that it is lacking in bouquet. A glass of *Móri ezerjó* is, however, enough to make you realize why this region is known as the 'home of manly wines', unrivalled in its own way. It is not always easy to match, but Hungarians suggest it should be drunk with goose liver braised in the Hungarian style with tomatoes and sweet peppers. They also hold it to be a good wine to go with ham.

9. *The Bársonyos–Császár Region*

The Bársonyos and Császár wines were at one time famous throughout Europe, but phylloxera cut the vines to a tenth of their original number – which left very limited scope for this region, which is in any case small. Although some vines did survive, the wines had nevertheless lost something of their quality. They more or less disappeared from the public's mind. But the possibilities remained and in 1959 the area was declared officially a new wine region.

The Bársonyos–Császár wines are characterized by their light greenish colour and their pleasant tartness. Hungarians call these wines 'fresh wines' and today it is accepted that such wines are to the taste of a wider public than those which have a high alcohol content.

10. *The Somló Region*

The Somló region is the smallest of Hungary's official wine regions, consisting of the vineyards of Somlóvásárhely and three neighbouring districts on the slopes of the symmetrical hill, the Somló-hegy. The leading grape is *Furmint* and the Somló wines are already of good quality in spite of the gradual process of reconstruction necessary after the vineyards were destroyed by phylloxera.

When the Turks occupied Hungary, Somló, its castle and its vineyards, changed hands constantly – but the reputation of the wine itself remained undiminished. This reputation was summed up in the saying *Vinum Somloviticum est lac senum, pueris venenum* (The wine of Somló is milk to the old, poison to the young), the latter part referring to the consequences of a combination of the fire of youth and this powerful wine. It is supposed to have been the cause of 'unrestrained unruliness' among the nuns of Somlóvásárhely, against which special rules had to be introduced. The wine, however, proved stronger than the rules and in the end it was felt necessary to close the convent!

As far as I can discover, it was in Somló that heat treatment was first applied to wine so that it would endure transport. A long piece of white-hot spring-steel was inserted into the barrel of wine, the process was repeated five or six times, with the same end in view as the pasteurization of our own day. It would seem the treatment was to some degree effective, because throughout the country Somló wine was known and recognized as a medicine against all ills.

Somló wines once competed with the wines of Tokaj, and indeed there was considerable similarity in the kinds of grapes grown and in the methods of making the actual wine. Today, however, as a result of phylloxera, the reputation of the Somló wines has diminished. The new vineyards now being developed in the region use mainly *Furmint* and *Tramini* grapes; the old traditional methods are being revived and it is hoped the old volcanic Somló-hegy will again put the fire back into the wines of the region.

11. *The Sopron Region*

Sopron, one of Hungary's most beautiful towns, stands far to the west of the country, near the border with Austria. It has always been a 'border town' and all parties who have fought in that part of Europe for territory have always tried their best to keep the people of Sopron on their side. And it is a town which has always been at the centre of the wine trade.

The Sopron wine region is not very large in area, however, consisting of Sopron itself and five other neighbouring districts. It is mainly red wine that is produced here.

Soproni kékfrankos counts as one of the finest and most famous Hungarian wines. It is rich and pleasing in colour, but if it is allowed to mature it achieves excellence in flavour and a spicy bouquet as well.

Among the white wines of the region the *Leányka* is well known in Hungary because this grape usually produces a slightly sweet wine, whereas around Sopron the *Leányka* wine is dry.

Perhaps the main point about the Sopron wines, a comforting one for visitors, is that if you do visit the area – which has a life very different from the more publicized life of the open Great Plain but which is none the less just as characteristically Hungarian – whatever wine you are offered, you may be sure it will be good.

12. *The Szekszárd Region*

This region is known as the true home of the *Kadarka* grape. There is no end to the written references to the excellence of Szekszárd wine. It can, I suppose, be no small recommendation that Schubert is held to have written the 'Trout' quintet through being inspired by this wine. There is talk of its medicinal powers, its flavour, its fire and its aroma, and Liszt recommended it to the King of Holland. *Szekszárdi kadarka* has a fine ruby colour and its flavour is described as being 'discreetly rough'.

13. *The Villány–Siklós Region*

This region is Hungary's most southern and its warmest wine producing region. Around Villány it is the red wine grapes *Kadarka*, *Oporto* and *Kékfrankos* which predominate, while the Siklós area lays more emphasis on the white varieties, *Olaszrizling* and *Hárslevelű*.

In good years the *Kadarka* grape produces a ruby coloured wine but in less good years its colour is too light. It is a slightly hard wine with a relatively high acid content, and its alcohol content varies between 12 per cent and 13·5 per cent, which is perhaps undesirably high in a red wine. But to these unfavourable remarks it must be added that wine experts in Hungary unanimously agree that Villány wine will in the future become among red wines what *Tokaji aszú* is among white wines. Old traditions and modern developments are both regarded with respect in Hungary and there is a great awareness of the possibilities of the future which may result in a growing international respect for wine production in Hungary.

14. *The Tokaj–Hegyalja Region*

I have left this region to the end of this quick journey through the wines of Hungary for more or less the same reason as at wine tastings in Hungary it is always the Tokaj wine which comes at the end; there is no better wine which can be offered after it.

Historians remind us, however, that the Tokaj wines were not always so esteemed as they are today. King Béla IV of Hungary had Italians brought into the area after the Mongol War in the thirteenth century, and it is to those Italian settlers that the import of the *Bakator* and *Furmint* grapes is attributed (these being known in Italy as *Bacca d'oro* and *Camoformino* respectively). The firm establishment of the vines brought in by the Italians marked the first steps towards the recognition of the Tokaj wines. By the middle of the eighteenth century Tokaj wine was famous – Louis XV of France exclaimed, 'This is the king of wines and the wine of kings.' Voltaire praised it, too, while Maria Theresa instructed the University of Vienna to examine whether there really were specks of gold in the Tokaj grapes, for it had already been rumoured that 'real gold' dripped from some bunches of these grapes.

Ground conditions, climate, situation, the vines used – all combine to make Tokaj wines of truly outstanding quality.

The chief grapes grown in the region are three in number: *Furmint* (which constitutes around two thirds of the total), *Hárslevelű*, and *Sárga Muskotály* (*Muscat lunel*). Of these only *Furmint* is generally put on the market as an independent wine, although *Hárslevelű* does very occasionally appear in this way, too:

it is different combinations of all three which are used to produce the more famous Tokaj wines.

Four classes of quality are applied to the wines of all the other regions, but in Tokaj there are no less than eight different qualities. The Tokaj table wines come from the less favoured vineyards or from the less favourable years. Quality as such begins to appear with the *Tokaji furmint* and the *Tokaji hárslevelű* wines. These are usually harmonious wines with plenty of body, with an alcohol content of 13–13·5 per cent, their acids are not sharp and there is already a rich flavour to them.

One of the two famous names used for the more exceptional wines of the Tokaj region is *szamorodni.* The word itself stems from Polish and long ago the meaning of the word – 'born by itself' or 'fallen by itself' – was used to indicate that the dried up grapes were not in any way selected, but were put into the press 'just as they came'. From must prepared in this way it is possible to produce either dry or sweet wine, depending on the sugar content.

Dry *szamorodni* has a classic quality and achieves its full individuality only through long storing, but this very long storing can also hold disadvantages for the wine, so the production of first rate *szamorodni* is considered a highly challenging task. Its colour tends to be yellowish brown. The extravagance in bouquet of the Tokaj wines reaches a culmination in dry *szamorodni*: there is even something of the aroma of fresh breadcrust in it.

Sweet *szamorodni* is a more full bodied wine than the dry and it is richer in flavour.

Tokaji aszú is recognized beyond Hungary's borders as being one of the most distinguished of natural dessert wines. There have been innumerable attempts to imitate it, to discover its secret. All of these attempts have failed simply because there is no secret. Anyone can go along to the Tokaj cellars, and the cellar masters will take no end of delight in explaining the methods and processes employed. Every detail of the whole process is directed at preserving the particular qualities which have been provided by nature itself. One factor does nevertheless deserve elaboration. In the preparation of the *aszú* an important part is played by *Botrytis cinerea*, the fungus of 'noble rot'. As with any fungus, this one too needs a particular degree of warmth and a particular level of dampness.

The former is provided by the very even sunshine of the long Hungarian autumn and the latter by the vapour rising from the two sizeable rivers which pass through and join together in the area, the Bodrog and the Tisza. The fungus causes the grape skins to become thinner and crack, after which the grapes' water content largely evaporates and so the original 20–24 per cent sugar content becomes condensed to 50–70 per cent. The *Botrytis cinerea* which has settled on the surface also gives rise to unique flavour and aroma.

Precisely because the production of this wine depends on so many natural factors, it is not always uniformly successful. Late vintage is an important prerequisite – in Tokaj this comes at the very end of October or even into November if possible. The overripe grapes are individually picked and stored separately from the other grapes in special baths until the first, honey-like liquid oozes out from them – that is, with no actual pressing except their own weight on each other: this is the *Tokaj Essence* – closely guarded in Hungary as a great treasure.

The *Tokaji aszú* wine itself, as it is marketed, is a combination of 'basic' wine and the dried grapes, after they have delivered themselves of the must by their own weight in this way. The pulp which remains is called the *aszú tészta* (*aszú* dough). The basic wine draws the sugar out of the grapes or dough, together with the unique flavour and aroma. On each bottle you can read the word *puttony*, together with a number which precedes it. The *puttony* is the measure used for the dried grapes and if you see, for example, '3 puttony' on the bottle this means that three puttonys of these special grapes were used to each measure of basic wine. The unit for measuring the basic wine is known as a *gönci hordó* (Gönc barrel), which holds approximately 136 litres. An official list of the contents (the data refer to minima) of the *aszú* wine can be seen in the table on page 244.

I have never seen *2* or *6 puttonyos aszú* (*puttonyos*, incidentally, is merely an adjective formed from the noun *puttony*) on sale in the shops in Hungary. The general feeling seems to be that 3 is good but you might as well buy 4 while you are about it, if it is available. *5 puttonyos aszú* is not easy to find, and when it is, it is naturally more expensive but worth it.

Wine	Alcohol % by volume	Total extract	sugar-free extract	inverted sugar
		in grams per litre of wine		
2 puttonyos aszú		55	25	30
3 puttonyos aszú	At least	90	30	60
4 puttonyos aszú	13 per cent	125	35	90
5 puttonyos aszú	rising to	160	40	120
6 puttonyos aszú	18·5 per	195	45	150
Essence	cent	250	50	200

I have not even mentioned the more than twenty Hungarian sparkling wines, most of which are made in Pécs (those bear the name *Pannónia* in their title), or in Budafok, which is just outside Budapest (the sparkling wines made up there include *Hungária* or *Törley* in their titles). They are excellent in all their variety.

Drinks

Apart from wines there are in Hungary other drinks which range from the faintest tea and sparkling mineral waters to the most powerful *barackpálinka*, the apricot brandy which you must drink whenever offered it by downing the whole glassful at one go – it took an old lady in the country to persuade me that a burning effect on the throat is only produced if you sip at your *pálinka* and that it is better to get it all down in one gulp!

You can now find first class *barackpálinka* from Kecskemét in Britain. In addition to this apricot brandy, plum brandy (*szilvapálinka*) is also much favoured, and cherry brandy (*cseresznyepálinka*) is regarded as being somewhat finer – although I must emphasize that Hungarian cherry brandy has nothing to do with the sweet cherry brandy liqueurs we are used to in western Europe.

Hungary is very rich in natural mineral waters and there is always plenty of variety to choose from if you prefer not to drink wine with a meal.

The method of preparing coffee in Hungary resembles that of Italy, although the best coffee I have ever tasted came from a farmer in Sarkad who insisted it was all due to the roasting, which he carried out himself. If you can at all find natural, unroasted coffee beans, try it out. You can get special pans for the roasting but an ordinary frying-pan will do just as well. Put in the beans dry and roast them over a medium or stronger heat – they pop and bang and sometimes leap; let them become very brown but not black. Turn them about more or less constantly. When you remove them from the heat pour them into a porcelain jar and cover them immediately. Leave them covered until they are quite cold. Then keep them until required in a box that can be closed tightly.

As for tea in Hungary, the basic approach is to count *half a teaspoon of tea* per person. That might not suit British tastes even with sugar and lemon, but there is an endless range of other potions to tempt one in the form of 'teas' made from dried rose hips, dried sour-cherry leaves, jasmine, lime leaves, aniseed and even caraway seed.

The recipes I give below are for drinks which are all favourites in Hungary, some for the summer, some for the cold weather, and some for special occasions at any time of the year. First there is a Tea Cocktail for which you will need:

20g tea (¾ oz.)
2 egg yolks
1 litre water (good 1¾ pints)
100g sugar (3½ oz.)

Put the tea in a teapot or pan, boil the water, pour it over the tea and infuse it for 5 minutes. Strain off the liquid.

Beat the egg yolks to a white cream with the sugar. Add half the hot tea and over the smallest possible heat cook the mixture carefully until it is thick. Then add the remainder of the tea, mix it well and serve in glasses, chilled.

Csája

1 tbs. tea
1 litre water (1¾ pints)
150g sugar (5 oz.)
¼ vanilla pod
6 tbs. rum
lemon

Roast 2 tablespoons of the sugar until it is light golden, pour in the water and the rest of the sugar. Bring the mixture to the boil with the vanilla and pour it on to the tea. Let it infuse for 2–3 minutes. Add the rum and strain off into cups. Place a slice of lemon in each cup.

Forralt bor

There is no Hungarian winter without *forralt bor* – wine heated with spices – but there is of course no need to wait for a cold spell to make this special treat.

½ litre wine (1 pint)
100g sugar (3½–4 oz.)
a large pinch of cinnamon
½ litre water (1 pint)
1 clove
juice and rind of half a lemon

Mix all the ingredients together except the lemon juice and set them aside for about half an hour. Then bring them just to the boil, remove the pan from the heat immediately and pour in the lemon juice. Strain off into tumblers and serve as hot as possible.

Forralt bor is at its best when equal amounts of red and white wine are used, rather than just one or the other.

A richer variation is to prepare the hot wine as above. Meanwhile mix 2 egg yolks to a light cream with 1 tablespoon sugar and 1 tablespoon water. Pour in the hot wine very gradually, taking care not to let the egg curdle. Strain off as above into tumblers.

Csipkebogyóbor – Rose Hip Wine

2 kg rose hips (4 lbs.)
2 kg sugar (4 lbs.)
1¼ litres water (2¼ pints)

Clean the rose hips thoroughly, wash them and place them in a large sweet jar, or a pan.

Melt the sugar in the water, heating it slowly, and bring it just to the boil. Allow it to cool and when it is warm pour it over the rose hips. Cover the jar or pan with a fine cloth and keep it covered at room temperature until fermentation begins and bubbling stops – about 3–4 weeks. Then strain off the liquid into bottles, cork them well and keep them in a cool larder or cellar – the longer the better.

Almabor – Apple Wine

1 kg apples (2 lbs.)
1 kg sugar (2 lbs.)
5 litres water (scant 9 pints)

Clean away all imperfect parts from the apples and grate them roughly. Place them in a large glass or porcelain jar.

Dissolve the sugar in the water and pour it over the apples. Cover them with a cloth and keep them at room temperature for 9–10 days for the main fermentation process to take place. Then strain off the liquid through clean muslin. Return the liquid to the jar and keep it for 3–4 weeks until the liquid clears completely and matures. Bottle it and cork it. If the wine is colourless a little sugar is roasted and added.

The same method is used to make simple wines from sour cherries, plums, and from mixtures of different kinds of fruit.

Bólé is the name given to a range of drinks made from fresh fruit, light wine and spirits for immediate use. The idea is for the liquids to take on the taste of the fruit and for the fruit juices to mix with the alcoholic drinks. Before serving, cold soda water is added (or even light champagne). Serve *bólé* in a large basin-shaped glass or porcelain bowl.

Perhaps the most common of these drinks in Hungary is the *bólé* which uses peaches as a basis. Peel 1 kg (2 lbs.) peaches and slice them thinly. Cover them with 200g (7 oz.) castor sugar and leave them for an hour so that the juices will come out of the peaches. Add 1 jar or tin of preserved apricots, about ½ kg (1 lb.) in weight, the juice of 1 lemon and then pour on 1 litre (scant 2 pints) white wine, the same quantity of sweet red wine, and 6–9 tablespoons brandy. Mix the *bólé* about and keep it on ice for 2 hours. Just before serving, add two small bottles of chilled soda water.

To make a strawberry *bólé*, wash and drain 1 kg (2 lbs.) strawberries. Place them in a deep wide bowl and sprinkle ¼ kg (8 oz.) castor sugar over them. Add the juice of 1 lemon and leave on ice for 2 hours. Pour on 1 litre (2 pints) white wine and the same of red wine. Add 1 or 2 small bottles of soda water before serving.

Something more unusual is this very fresh drink made from cucumber. Peel a large cucumber and cut it into very thin slices. Set these out in a deep bowl and sprinkle 100g (3½ oz.) castor sugar and the grated rind of 1 lemon over these slices. Set the bowl aside for half an hour. Then pour on 1 bottle white wine and keep the *bólé* on ice until required. Before serving strain off the liquid and add 1–2 bottles of chilled soda water.

Index

of English Recipe Titles

Index

of Hungarian Recipe Titles